Mastering Amiga Beginners

Phil South

Bruce Smith Books

Mastering Amiga Beginners

© Phil South
ISBN: 1-873308-03-5
First Edition: First printing October 1991
Second printing September 1992

Typesetting: Bruce Smith Books Ltd
Editor: Mark Webb
Series Cover Design: Ross Alderson
Bruce Smith Books is an imprint of Bruce Smith Books Limited.

Disclaimer: While every effort has been made to ensure that the information in this publication (and any programs and software associated with it) is correct and accurate, the Publisher cannot accept liability for any consequential loss or damage, however caused, arising as a result of using the information printed herein.

Published by Bruce Smith Books Limited,
PO Box 382, St. Albans, Herts, AL2 3JD.
Telephone: (0923) 894355. Fax: (0923) 894366.

Registered No. 2695164.
Registered office: 51 Quarry Street, Guildford, Surrey.

Printed and bound in the UK by Ashford Colour Press, Gosport, Hants.

The Author

Phil South is a freelance writer and journalist, who started writing for a living in 1984, when he realised he couldn't actually stand working for anyone but himself. He says his popular columns in computer and other magazines are much harder to write than they are to read. Apart from being a writer he's also a heavy duty film buff, and owns a huge collection of ex-rental and sell-through videos. In his spare time he runs the White Goods Support Group, helping people to rid themselves of the insatiable desire to add more automatic washers, driers, cleaners and toaster ovens to their homes.

Phil lives in Somerset with his wife Stacey, a mouse called Ralph, and a dishwasher. (Oops!)

Contents

Dedication

To Mickey, for giving me my interest in music and graphics, Sheila for teaching me to try anything. But above all to my wife Stacey for all her support with the book and my work in general, despite being five months pregnant and not feeling very well either.

Thanks to Bruce Smith for asking me to do this book in the first place, and long overdue thanks to Kevin Cox, for giving me my first break way back, and making sure I got to where I am now. Where exactly that is I'm not sure yet, but I'll get back to you on that.

Contents

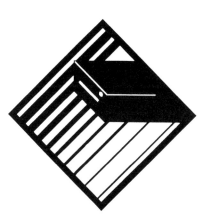

Preface

So many different people ask me so many different questions about the Amiga. I can't count the amount of queries I must have had over the years in my capacity as columnist on the many Amiga magazines I've worked for. Probably enough to choke a bison. Anyway, in most cases the answers to people's problems seem simple and straightforward. But I forget sometimes that I've been working with the Amiga since it came out, and so have a lot of experience to fall back on in time of need. Also I know a lot of people at various dealers and software houses who I can call if I have a problem. Yuri Large at Alternative Image in Leicester for example. Now there's someone who loves getting calls from me, usually beginning with "How are you?" and ending with "While I've got you on the blower, mate, there's this problem..."

But for the beginner who's seen an Amiga working and thought "WOW, I must have this" and bought one, life is not so simple. I thought the time had come to write down some of this stuff that I know, to help to squash any simple problems people might be having and give a basic grounding for people that are struggling with their first state-of-the-art computer.

More people who never had a computer before are getting them now, so a book like this is needed right now, especially on the Amiga. Folk can see how nice the graphics are, and they hear the sound and flip out. But when they finally get the thing home they discover, as you probably have, that there's more to a modern computer than just switching it on. And the Amiga, for all its ease of use, is actually a very complex piece of electronics, and requires a bit of effort if you want to get the best out of it.

So that's why you need this book. It's a way of getting all the basic knowledge you need in one volume, without having to struggle through piles of magazines or books to get at the one tiny piece of information you need. A common complaint from my readers and friends is that most manuals and books assume you know the information already, and the only way to navigate through the *docs* to some package or other is if you already know where to find the answer you seek. This is obviously not the way things should be.

The Amiga can be a very simple thing to use, using just a point and click method to run most programs. And indeed this is the case most of the time. But for those times when things go wrong or the computer does something you didn't expect, here is your standard reference work.

Some of the contents of this book are slightly technical, some of it is just part of Amiga folklore and of interest in passing. But all of it is essential if you want to enjoy your machine to the full.

Finally just a bit of technical detail. The book was written on an Amiga 500, recased in a prototype of the Checkmate Digital A1500 box, with 3 megs of memory and a 20 meg hard disk drive fitted internally.

The software used was a combination of Gold Disk's Transcript (an oldie but goodie) and Microsoft Word 3 running on a Readysoft A-Max II Apple Macintosh Emulator. The files were converted to Mac format using the A-Max, and posted to Bruce Smith who did all the typesetting on his Mac. The pictures were copied onto MS DOS disks using CrossDOS by Consultron, and sent to Bruce, who converted them to Mac picture files using Adobe Photoshop.

New Edition

Although this is a new edition of the Mastering Amiga Beginners book, Workbench 1.3 and Workbench 2.0 are both covered. The reason for this is that 1.3 is still used on the majority of machines and therefore deserves our attention. Upgrade kits are available however and, come the next edition, I'm sure this situation will have changed.

Phil South, Somerset, September 1992

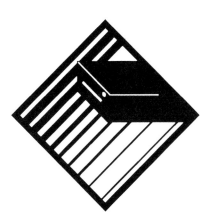

1:
Introducing
The
Amiga

Welcome to the exciting world of Amiga. In its scope, the Amiga is the first computer ever to come close to the kind of quality of sound and graphics you see on TV or at the movies. It puts in your hands, or rather on your table, the kind of computing power which just a few years ago was beyond even the most expensive large computers.

The computer is just a calculating machine beneath the case, a machine with the ability to perform the same task over and over again in a variety of different ways. This calculation process can be something simple, like totting up your accounts, or it can be quite frighteningly complex, like calculating the light rays around a theoretical object, as in those amazing computer generated cartoons by the likes of Pixar Inc you see on TV.

In order to get the computer to do something, you have to program it, and you can do this is two ways, either program it yourself, or run a program that someone else has written. The program is loaded from disk, and then it is started.

Although the commands you give to any computer are similar, the construction and design of computers are so different that you can't run a program from one computer in another. It's like giving a book in Japanese to a German and asking them to read it. So you can't just take an Amiga disk and run it in an IBM. But all programs for an Amiga will run in all Amigas. If a friend buys a disk with a game on it, for example, when he gets bored with it, you can run it on your machine. It might be an idea to ask him if he's finished with it first, though.

What You Have

The Commodore Amiga is a computer based on the powerful Motorola 68000 micro chip which is also used in other popular home computers.But what separates the Amiga from these other computers is that it not only has the power of the 68000, but it also uses three custom chips (ie, specially built) which take the strain of most of the advanced functions such as audio and video.

The graphics of the Amiga are stunning by any standards, featuring a full 32 colour resolution of 320 x 256 pixels (or dots on the screen), and high resolution displays of up to 640 x 512 pixels, plus a technique called *Overscan* to stretch the picture to the very edge of the screen. This is particularly good for video applications.

The sound is amazing too, as the Amiga has four independent audio channels, and a digital synthesiser with which you can (with proper software) synthesise any sound you like. More important than this though to the musically inclined, is the sound *sampling* capability, similar to that found in many modern digital musical instruments. Also, there is a built-in speech synthesiser, able to mimic human speech using basic building blocks called *phonemes*. You can also get the Amiga to speak text directly.

The Amiga can be a friend in business, leisure and education, with its rapidly expanding range of software. For business there are spreadsheets, databases and wordprocessors. For leisure there are stunning arcade quality games, adventures and more creative pursuits like computer graphics, music and MIDI. In education, the Amy can be used to study computer science, programming or even to run BBC educational computer programs, using a BBC Emulator, although this is rather limited in scope.

Lastly, the Amiga is a *multi-tasking* computer, meaning that it can do more than one thing at once. More than one program can be run at one time, provided you have enough memory, and as long as the programs don't take up the same resources, each program acts as if it had the machine to itself.

As with any computer and, as I said before, in order to make your Amiga do things you have to run a program, either one you've bought or one you've written yourself. On the Amiga, running a program is easy. You do this in one of two ways: either you *double-click* on the icon on the Workbench, or you type the name of the program at the CLI prompt. We'll come to what these two things mean in a minute.

The Theory of Disk Drives

A disk drive is a unit into which you can slot a floppy disk, in the case of the Amiga a 3.5" style disk. The disk has a protective metal slider on it, and under this you can see the surface of the disk. The magnetic material that the disk is coated with is not unlike that of a conventional cassette tape, except a much higher density of oxide particles is used.

The data from your computer is stored on the disk, not as sound, but as digital magnetic impressions in the fabric of the disk. Once a piece of data is stored on the disk, it is on there for good, unless you overwrite it with something else or erase it. You can't erase something by saving to the disk, as the files you store on the disk make room for each other. Unless you accidentally overwrite a file with the same name as the one you are saving. Most programs guard against this and ask you to confirm your action, but be on your guard.

To help you visualise this, imagine a series of files going into a little filing cabinet. Each file goes into a folder in each of the drawers. If you want to get rid of a file, you just take it out of the drawer and tear it up. A file can't be merged with another file unless you take it out and staple it to the other one. All the files stay separate, until you run out of space to put files. Then you have to take all the files you don't want any more out of the filing cabinet and destroy (or relocate) them, making room for more files.

So lets apply this to a disk. The disk is the filing cabinet. You can put programs into it by saving them, and take a copy of them out to use by loading them. When you load the programs up, you are using a copy, so the original file you saved to the disk stays on the disk. You can get rid of the files by deleting them. If you run out of space on the disk you can delete files to make room, or you can get another disk and start afresh, setting the other disk aside with all its files intact. The programs and data on a disk are called *files.*

Graphical User Interfaces

All the typing you used to have to do with conventional computers got people down, and for most people typing in commands was the source of the confusion they experienced when using computers. It seemed to ordinary folk that in order to use a computer you had to understand all the complex commands, and type them in correctly or you'd break the computer. Computer types were not ordinary people in those days, you understand. They were obviously gifted professionals, who had devoted their life to the calling, and had passed some esoteric exam in a Tibetan monastery in order to have the secret knowledge of computing.

Obviously this kind of paranoia only served to make the people who knew about computers feel like they were in some way special. And so the knowledge was guarded from normal people, so that the guys with the stripy shirts and all the pens in their top pockets could keep their jobs, and nobody would know that they in fact were no more or less intelligent than mere mortals.

Clearly this situation had to change if the power of computers was to go anywhere or do anything for the majority of people. Computers are too interesting and too useful to be left in the hands of a bunch of self-important geeks. So one day in Xerox's Palo Alto Research Centre, a bright spark came up with the idea of a computer which could be used by anyone, merely by pointing at what he wanted to do in order to do it. The computer would work in exactly the same way it ever had, but the method of using the computer, the interface, was made up of graphics rather than text.

A disk would appear on the screen when you put a disk into the drive as a little picture of a disk. These pictures were named *icons*. By using a mouse to control a pointer on the screen, you would click on icons to make the computer do things. A simple idea in itself, but like all simple ideas, it had the capacity to change life as we know it forever when applied in certain ways to computers.

Once the disk icon was on the screen, you clicked on it, and from the disk on the screen was generated a *window*, a frame containing the contents of the disk. In the window, the programs on the disk, and the files the programs create, were seen as different types of icon, each a little picture giving an idea of what the program does, and underneath the icon a name, the *filename* of the program. This is what you would type to run the program if the program were on a conventional computer. In fact all you did on the new computer was point at the icon and click the mouse button twice in quick succession to make the program load and run in the same move.

This change in the way we think about computers has totally altered the face of the computer industry. With computers so easy to use, they could sell them to anybody. After the success of the Apple Macintosh, all hell broke loose. Everybody wanted a Graphical User Interface (GUI) and by Jove they got them in abundance.

Finally the Amiga

The Amiga 1000 came out in 1985, and the system software was still on disk, the *Kickstart* disk. You had to insert this disk before you could insert the *Workbench* to start the computer. In the later versions, the 500 and the 2000, the Kickstart is on a chip, and the only software you need to get your machine started is the

Workbench or other bootable disk. The Amiga 3000 was released in 1990, and is a top of the range machine. This model has Kickstart on a chip also, but this time it's Kickstart 2. The Workbench used on the Amiga 3000 is also version 2, and we'll look at this later. This was followed by the Amiga 500 Plus which is basically a 500 with Kickstart and Workbench 2, and more recently the A600 and A600HD – a new generation of Workbench 2 specific Amigas.

Booting up

So, the computer you have in your possession, as I spelled out very clearly at the beginning of this chapter, is a very powerful bit of kit, and there are two ways to get it to do what you want: The Workbench and the *Command Line Interface*, or CLI. When you switch your computer on, it is blank like a sheet of paper, until you insert a disk. This can be a game or an application program like a wordprocessor, or it can be one of the disks that comes with your computer, called the Workbench disk.

When you turn the computer on, you will see a hand holding a disk, telling you to insert the Workbench disk. At this prompt you can either insert the Workbench as prompted or you can put in any other disk which will start or *boot* the computer. So if you want to load a game that you've bought, all you need to do is insert it at this prompt and it will self start (or *self boot* as we say) the computer.

What's the Workbench?

The Workbench is the *WIMP* (Windows, Icons, Mouse, Pointer) interface of the Amiga, and it auto loads into the Amiga when you insert the Workbench disk. When the disk has finished loading you will be presented with the Workbench screen. Across the top of the Workbench screen is a title bar, marked Workbench, in case you missed the point. Also you see the disk icon, the little picture of a disk, and underneath it the name of the disk which, in the first instance, will probably be Workbench 1.3 or something like that. Double-clicking (clicking twice on the left button on the mouse with the pointer over the icon) produces a window on the screen with all the contents of the disk.

A Word about Mouse Buttons

At this point it might be of use to tell you about the mouse buttons. At all times, unless otherwise stated, the left button is used for selections, pointing to things and clicking on icons and the other gadgets on the screen. The right button is used for menus. If you press and hold the right button on the mouse, you reveal any menus which are currently available on the Menu Bar at the top of the screen. The right button is held down until the menu item is selected with the pointer (shown by a dark bar over the menu item) by moving the pointer to the top bar and pulling it up and down the pop down menus. When you get to the menu item you want, you let go of the button. The menu item you selected is then executed.

So to recap, if you want to click on an icon or *gadget* use the left button, the *selection button*. If you want to choose a menu item, then use the right button or *menu button*.

What Are Gadgets?

I mentioned *gadgets* there a couple of times, and this is another important piece of Amiga jargon. A gadget is a sort of button on an Amiga screen which, when pressed, performs some function or other. This is all a part of Workbench being a WIMP interface, where you can just point and shoot at what you want to do. The word *gadgets* is used to describe on-screen buttons on the Workbench. There are several which crop up again and again on just about every Amiga program which uses the Workbench interface.

Starting at the top left of a window, you have the *close gadget*. It is a little square with a dot in the middle. Click on this and the window will vanish It has been closed by your clicking the close gadget.

On the right-hand side at the top, you will generally find a pair of gadgets made from interlinked squares. These are called the *back and front gadgets*. As the Amiga windows can overlay one another, you can sometimes obscure a window that you need to get at. By clicking the back and front gadgets you can push a window to the back of the screen, revealing windows underneath it, or pull it forward, laying it on the top of all the other windows.

Imagine the windows as sheets of paper on a desktop. Using the back and front gadgets, you can shuffle the papers on the desk and see each one in turn. Windows all have gadgets, but Amiga screens also have front and back gadgets, and this allows you to see if you have any other programs running behind the Workbench, or *multi-tasking* as they call it. You can either click the front and back gadgets to shuffle through the screens, or you can even grab the title bar at the top of the screen (sometimes called the Menu Bar) and pull it down. You do this by putting the pointer on the bar and holding down the left or selection button. Then as you pull the mouse down, the whole screen will slide down like a roller blind! In most cases there will be nothing to see behind the Workbench, just a black screen, but later on when you're more adept at using the Amiga you can have a few programs running together at the same time. (We'll use the abbreviation WB for Workbench sometimes.)

Finally, we have the re-sizing gadget, which always sits on the bottom right-hand corner of the window. Grab this with the pointer by pressing the left button and holding it down and you can drag the size of the window around, re-sizing it to fit the available space on the screen.

(Note: On Workbench 2, the gadgets have been altered in appearance and sometimes in operation, but this will be covered in more detail in the chapter on Workbench 2!)

Bootable Disks

The Workbench is already on a lot of the disks you will use, so it's not necessary to boot (a computer term meaning starting the computer) by using the WB disk every time you use your computer. In most cases the program you are using will have its own Workbench installed on the disk, so all you have to do is put it in the drive at the Insert Workbench prompt. Although the Workbench you find on a program disk may be a different colour and have a different shaped pointer, it is still the same thing which is on your master Workbench disk. The colours of the Workbench and the shape of the pointers are options that you can change to suit your own taste. I'll cover customising when we get down to talking about the Preferences program in more detail.

Okay that's one way to interact with computer, the GUI way, but how about the more conventional text input method. To do this we need to use the CLI or Command Line Interface.

Command Line Interface

The CLI is a more traditional method of telling your computer what to do, and the way that you can really get to grips with the internals of the machine. Of course being a computer which uses a graphic interface you don't have to use this method, but with the Amiga, as always, you have the option to work with it in any way you like. If you like typing in commands, then please yourself.

Although using the computer in the CLI is harder than using the Workbench, it's not that hard. All you have to do is get a book, like this one and others in the *Mastering Amiga* series, which teach you which commands to type in at the slightly baffling:

    1 >

prompt. The commands you type in are AmigaDOS commands, and they tell the computer to do all kinds of housekeeping jobs. You can get a directory of a disk to see what's on it by typing:

```
dir
```

And then the computer will display a directory of the disk. Or you can activate a program by typing its name. Take this directory for example:

```
Work (dir)

Play (dir)

     asteroids

     spacemonkeys
```

If you wanted to play the asteroids game you'd have to type:

```
asteroids
```

and then press the big L shaped key with the bent arrow on it. This executes the command you typed.

(Note: This big key is called the Carriage Return, a hangover from the old typewriter days when teletypes had typewriter style keyboards and paper rolls.)

The most frequently used AmigaDOS commands will be explained in full in the chapter on AmigaDOS.

Computer Languages

Most of the time you will be running the commercially produced programs that you buy, and with the Amiga that process can last you a long while before you run out of things to do. The option after you get fed up with purchased software, is to write your own. Before you try creating your own programs I would caution you to try and find a program that does what you want *first* to save yourself the effort of re-inventing the wheel.

AmigaBASIC

If you want to program your computer to do things, you have to use a computer language. There are many ways you can write your own programs, most notably as far as you are concerned with the AmigaBASIC interpreter program you got with your machine and which is on the Extras disk which is supplied with your Amiga. You load the BASIC interpreter from disk and it creates an environment in which you can write lists of commands that execute a line at a time, one after the other. BASIC stands for Beginners All-purpose Symbolic Instruction Code, and it is one of the most widely-used programming languages.

Other Languages

Other approaches to programming the computer are by learning C, another computer language, or by programming directly in machine code. The difference between speaking to the computer using a BASIC or C interpreter program and speaking to it in machine code can be seen like this:

To speak to a Frenchman you can do one of two things, 1) use an interpreter or 2) learn to speak French like a native. BASIC can be seen as a sort of interpreter between you and the computer, a program which speaks both English (sort of) and machine code, and can tell the computer what it is you are trying to do. This is the same way as a human interpreter is a person who knows both English and French and can tell a Frenchman what you are talking about. Of course if you learn to speak French then you don't need an interpreter, but you spend a few months of your life learning the lingo.

So the basic (that word again) rule is this: the more time you spend learning a language to program in, the more power you have at your disposal. But the amount of time you can devote to the computer may limit what you have time to learn. (It's a sort of law of increasing returns, really!)

Beginners are happiest with BASIC because the commands are basically English words and not just numbers or mnemonics like in machine code or C.

When you outgrow BASIC then C is better, and will give you more control over the machine. And finally when you become a mega programmer you can graduate to machine code. You don't *have* to go this route, but to be honest it's best to stay with BASIC as a first step, as you can do almost anything in BASIC with the minimum of effort. (There is also the option to compile BASIC programs into machine code to make them faster, using a program like Hisoft BASIC.)

The Disks

The disks that come with the Amiga are as follows: Workbench 1.3 (or in some cases now WB 2) and Extras. The Extras disk contains AmigaBASIC (actually this has been dropped in recent Amiga packs partly because there are many third party BASICs available), some utilities, printer drivers for the most commonly-used printers (one of which must be moved to your Workbench disk to drive your printer) and some files which didn't fit on the regular Workbench disk extra hardware that we'll ignore for now. For your information, and just to show you that they are there these are both listed below. Don't be worried if it all looks a bit off putting –

they are listed just to get you used to them. They will be explained in due course and by the end of this book they will be as familiar as as your favourite TV programme.

The Workbench listing shows you the AmigaDOS commands in their C directory, and these are the commands you can type at the CLI or Shell prompt. For more details about their use, see Chapter 4 on AmigaDOS and Appendix B on AmigaDOS commands.

A Typical Workbench Directory Listing

```
Trashcan (dir)

c (dir)
        AddBuffers          Ask
        Assign              Avail
        Binddrivers         Break
        CD                  ChangeTaskPri
        Copy                Date
        Delete              Dir
        DiskChange          DiskDoctor
        Echo                Ed
        Edit                Else
        EndCLI              EndI
        EndSkip             Eval
        Execute             Failat
        Fault               FF
        FileNote            GetEnv
        IconX               If
        Info                Install
        Join                Lab
        List                LoadWB
        Lock                Makedir
        Mount               NewCLI
        NewShell            Path
        Prompt              Protect
        Quit                Relabel
        RemRAD              Rename
        Resident            Run
```

```
        Search              SetClock

        SetDate             SetEnv

        SetPatch            Skip

        Sort                Stack

        Status              Type

        Version             Wait

        Which               Why

Prefs (dir)

        info                CopyPrefs

        CopyPrefs.info      Pointer.info

        Preferences         Preferences.info

        Printer.info        Serial.info

System (dir)

        info                CLI

        CLI.info            Diskcopy

        DiskCopy.info       FastMemFirst

        FastMemFirst.info   FixFonts

        FixFonts.info       Format

        Format.info         InitPrinter

        InitPrinter.info    MergeMem

        MergeMem.info       NoFastMem

        NoFastMem.info      SetMap

        SetMap.info

l (dir)

        Aux-Handler         Disk-Validator

        FastFileSystem      Newcon-Handler

        Pipe-Handler        Port-Handler

        Ram-Handler         Shell-Seg

        Speak-Handler

devs (dir)

        keymaps (dir)

        gb                  usa1

        printers (dir)

        .generic

        clipboards (dir)
```

```
        clipboard.device  MountList
        narrator.device   parallel.device
        printer.device    ramdrive.device
        serial.device     system-configuration
s (dir)
        CLI-Startup       DPAT
        PCD               Shell-Startup
        SPAT              Startup-Sequence
        Startup-Sequence.HD           StartupII
t (dir)
fonts (dir)
        ruby (dir)
                          12              15
                           8
        opal (dir)
                          12              9
        sapphire (dir)
                          14              19
        diamond (dir)
                          12              20
        garnet (dir)
                          16              9
        emerald (dir)
                          17              20
        topaz (dir)
                          11
        diamond.font      emerald.font
        garnet.font       opal.font
        ruby.font         sapphire.font
        topaz.font
libs (dir)
        diskfont.library  icon.library
        info.library
        mathieeedoubbas.library
```

```
       mathieeedoubtrans.library        mathtrans.library
       translator.library              version.library
    Empty (dir)
  Utilities (dir)
       info                             Calculator
       Calculator.info                  Clock
       Clock.info                       ClockPtr
       ClockPtr.info                    CMD
       Cmd.info                         GraphicDump
       GraphicDump.info                 InstallPrinter
       InstallPrinter.info              More
       More.info                        Notepad
       Notepad.info                     PrintFiles
       PrintFiles.info                  Say
       Say.info
  Expansion (dir)
    .info                               Disk.info
       Empty.info                       Expansion.info
       Prefs.info                       Shell
       Shell.info                       System.info
       Utilities.info
```

A Typical Extras Disk Listing

```
  Trashcan (dir)
  FD1.3 (dir)
       BASIC FD files here!             BASIC FD files
       .info
       clist_lib.fd                     console_lib.fd
       diskfont_lib.fd                  dos_lib.fd
       exec_lib.fd                      expansion_lib.fd
       graphics_lib.fd                  icon_lib.fd
       intuition_lib.fd                 layers_lib.fd
       mathffp_lib.fd              mathieeedoubbas_lib.fd
       mathieeedoubtrans_lib.fd         mathtrans_lib.fd
       potgo_lib.fd                     romboot_lib.fd
```

```
            timer_lib.fd              translator_lib.fd
            devs (dir)
            keymaps (dir)
            cdn                       ch1
            ch2                       d
            dk                        e
            f                         gb
            i                         is
            n                         s
            usa0                      usa2
            printers (dir)
            Alphacom_Alphapro_101     Brother_HR-15XL
            CalComp_ColorMaster       CalComp_ColorMaster2
            Canon_PJ-1080A            CBM_MPS1000
            Diablo_630                Diablo_Advantage_D25
            Diablo_C-150              EpsonQ
            EpsonXOld                 EpsonX[CBM_MPS-1250]
            Howtek_Pixelmaster        HP_DeskJet
            HP_LaserJet               HP_PaintJet
            HP_ThinkJet               ImagewriterII
            Nec_Pinwriter             Okidata_293I
            Okidata_92                Okimate_20
            Quadram_QuadJet           Qume_LetterPro_20
            Toshiba_P351C             Toshiba_P351SX
            Xerox_4020
    Tools (dir)
            .info                     Fed
            Fed.info                  FreeMap
            FreeMap.info              IconEd
            IconEd.info               IconMerge
            IconMerge.info            KeyToy2000
            KeyToy2000.info           MEmacs
            MEmacs.info               Palette
            Palette.info              PerfMon
```

```
        PerfMon.info
  BasicDemos (dir)
        .info                        AboutBmaps
        AboutBmaps.info              ball
        ball.info                    BitPlanes
        BitPlanes.info               ConvertFD
        ConvertFD.info               Demo
        Demo.info                    dos.bmap
        dos.bmap.info                exec.bmap
        exec.bmap.info               graphics.bmap
        graphics.bmap.info           Library
        Library.info                 LIST-ME
        LIST-ME.info                 LoadACBM
        LoadACBM.info                LoadILBM-SaveACBM
        LoadILBM-SaveACBM.info       Music
        Music.info                   ObjEdit
        ObjEdit.info                 Picture
        Picture.info                 Picture2
        Picture2.info                SaveILBM
        SaveILBM.info                Screen
        Screen.info                  ScreenPrint
        ScreenPrint.info             Speech
        Speech.info                  Terminal
        Terminal.info
  fonts (dir)
        Courier (dir)
                                     11        13
                                     15        18
                                     24
        Helvetica (dir)
                                     11        13
                                     15        18
                                     24        9
        Times (dir)
                                     11        13
```

```
                    15              18
                    24
          Courier.font         Helvetica.font
          Times.font
PCUtil (dir)
          .info                PCCopy
          PCCopy.info          PCFormat]
          PCFormat.info        Read Me
          Read Me.info         ToPCCopy
          ToPCCopy.info        .info
          AmigaBASIC
          AmigaBASIC.info      BasicDemos.info
          Devs.info            Disk.info
          FD1.3.info           Fonts.info
          PCUtil.info          Tools.info
          Trashcan.info        Utilities.info
```

Versions

Computer software is continually being updated and new versions of existing products released at a regular rate. Luckily, the fundamental nature of their operation generally remains the same. So, if you have a version of software that is more recent than the one described in this book (indicated by a larger number), Don't Panic! The nature and format of this book is such that – in most cases – that the content will remain relevant.

Summary

So to recap this chapter. The Amiga is a powerful 68000 based multitasking computer. It uses a graphical user interface, called the Workbench, and a more traditional interface called the CLI. The Workbench can be used either from the master Workbench disk, or from a version of the Workbench installed on a bootable disk. The mouse has two buttons on it, the left one for selecting things, and the right one for activating and choosing items from menus. AmigaBASIC is the easiest language to learn to program in, followed by C and then machine code, which is powerful but hard to learn. Simple really.

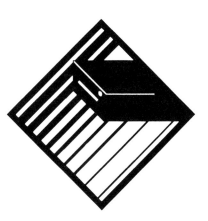

2:
Workbench

In the last chapter I mentioned that there were two methods of getting the Amiga to do what you want it to do, and they are the Workbench and the CLI or Shell. This chapter is about how to start and use the Workbench, which is the graphical user interface or GUI of the Amiga. Using this method of interacting with the computer, you can examine disks and run programs using a simple point and click method, which is very easy to use. Using the mouse supplied with your computer you can move the pointer (a small arrow) around the screen and point to the icons on that screen. If you point at an icon and click the left button the icon will be selected. If you point at an icon and click twice in quick succession (or double click as we say in Amigaland), the icon will be activated. If the icon is a disk icon, in other words the graphical representation of a disk on screen, then double-clicking will open the disk and show the contents of that disk. If the icon is a program on the disk, then double-clicking will run that program.

Starting the Workbench

To get the Workbench on your screen all you have to do is insert a disk with a Workbench on it (what we call a *bootable* disk) at the *Insert Workbench* prompt. A bootable disk can be any disk that has the Workbench on it, from the master Workbench disk which comes with your computer, to a program which you buy. Some programs have the Workbench installed on them, but only if they have enough space left once the program has been put on the disk.

When you insert a Workbench disk the computer starts the Workbench and gives you control of the computer. You are presented with the Workbench screen (see Figure 2.1) consisting of a title bar on the top of the screen and a disk icon down the right-hand side. In Figure 2.1 we've removed the disk icon, which varies with different versions of Workbench.

Figure 2.1. The Workbench screen.

On the title bar you will see the words Workbench Release and a number followed by the words Free Memory. The number before the words Free Memory is the amount of RAM (memory) you have in your computer. On the right-hand side of the title bar you have the back and front gadgets, that is to say the two little buttons in the right-hand corner of the screen made from interlinked squares. These are for use when multitasking a number of programs allowing you to step back and forward through the screens. Screens can also be pulled down by grabbing the title bar using the pointer and the left button. (see Figure 2.2 opposite) Point at the title bar, hold down the left button of the mouse and the screen will pull down like a roller blind, revealing the screen behind the current screen. In most cases, unless you are running two programs, this will be blank. Double-clicking on the disk icon on the right-hand side of the screen brings up a window on the main body of the Workbench screen. This window is a graphical representation of the programs and file folders, called drawers, on the disk (see Figure 2.3 opposite).

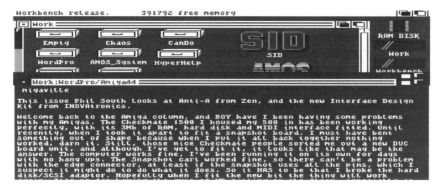

Figure 2.2. The GUI in its full glory.

If your Workbench disk is Workbench 1.3 then opening the Workbench disk will present you with a window in which are the following drawers (little icons that look like drawers in a desk) and programs: Utilities, System, Expansion, Empty, Shell, Prefs and Trashcan. To open a drawer, clearly depicting a drawer in which things can be kept, all you have to do is double click on the icon. To activate a program like Shell, Clock or Preferences, all you do is double click on the icon and the program will run.

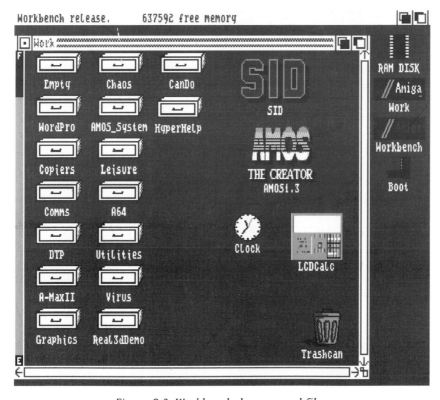

Figure 2.3. Workbench drawers and files.

(Note: The Shell is the newest interface for AmigaDOS released with Workbench version 1.3. This is a better and more convenient version than the old CLI interface you can find in the System drawer, and Shell should always be used in preference to the plain boring old CLI. I'll cover using the Shell in Chapter 4, AmigaDOS.)

The Menus

The three menus on the Menu Bar/title bar of the Workbench are called Workbench, Disk and Special (please refer to Chapter 3 if you own Workbench 2, as this is different in that system). The Workbench menu allows you to open and close windows or selected icons using a menu command rather than the point and click method. It also allows you to duplicate disks simply by clicking on the disk in question and selecting the Duplicate menu item (see Figure 2.4).

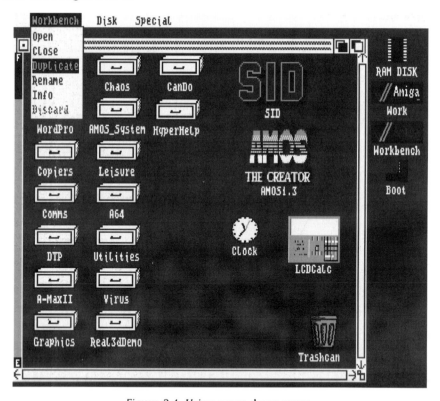

Figure 2.4. Using a pop-down menu.

This is handy if you only have the one disk drive ie the internal disk drive normally mounted on your Amiga. (A different method is to copy items to the Ram Disk, but we'll come to that in a moment.) Another menu selection on the Workbench menu is Rename. This allows you to rename an icon, either disk or program or drawer icon, to something else. All you need to do is select the icon you wish to change the name of, then select Rename from the Workbench menu and a small text requester will appear in the centre of the screen. Delete the name in the requester, this being the current name, and replace it with the new name and press Return. You are prompted to do this from the Menu Bar which displays the message "Enter the new name, Press Return when done."

Info and Types

A further selection from the Workbench menu is the Info item. Info brings up a window of information about the icon you have selected giving you the name, type and status of that icon (see Figure 2.5). These are complicated matters which need a little explanation.

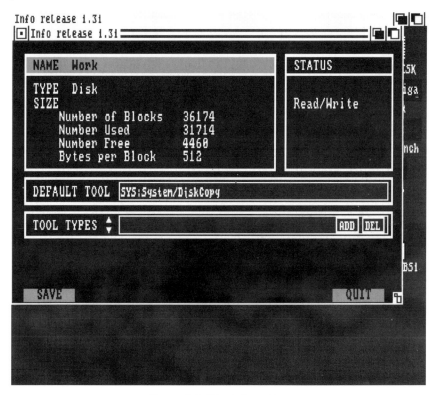

Figure 2.5. The Info option.

All icons on the Workbench have what we call a *Type*. The types of icons on the Workbench fall into a few specific categories. For example if you select the Workbench disk icon and select the Info menu item you will see that the type of the icon is disk, that is to say it is a disk icon. Other pieces of information in the Info box will tell you the size and the amount of free space on the disk.

If you select a drawer icon like Expansion or Utilities the Info window will come up and show you that the type of icon is a drawer icon meaning that it is not a program or a disk but in fact a sub directory into which you can place programs. Drawers are useful for keeping the Workbench clear. If you have a lot of icons on screen, you can put them into drawers to keep the place looking tidy.

Another type of icon, for example the Clock icon, when selected with Info says that it is a tool. A tool type indicates that the icon is in fact a program which the Amiga can use, for example double-clicking on the Clock icon will bring up a clock which matches the internal clock on the Amiga. The time will be given on an analogue clock face giving you an idea of the time, or at least the time according to your Amiga. The time can be set from the Preferences program but we'll go into that in the chapter on Preferences.

Most of the icons on the Workbench fall into the category of Drawer, Disk or Tool but another type of icon can exist on the Workbench and this is the type called Project. A Project type indicates that the icon in question is the product of a particular program, for example a document from a wordprocessor or other type of program.

Project icons cannot be booted generally from the Workbench unless, inside the default tool section of the Info window, you have the name of the program that the Project is used with. In the case of a wordprocessing document, for example, the default tool requester in the Info window will display the name of the Word Processor which the file was created by. This is done automatically when you save a document using a program, but the default tool can be changed by you if you click the mouse in the slot after the words Default Tool in the Info window, but we'll cover that sort of stuff in a minute.

The final type of icon you get on a Workbench screen is the Trashcan icon. Trashcans vary in shape on different releases of the Workbench, and in fact you can create your own with Trashcan editors but the function of the Trashcan is the same. If you double click on the Trashcan a small window will open up giving you the impression that the Trashcan is some kind of drawer icon, which in fact it is. However, the difference between a normal drawer icon and the Trashcan icon is that if you put documents into the Trashcan then select the Trashcan with the left button you can dispose of the documents by going up to the disk menu at the top of the screen, and by using the right button to select Empty Trash. All the documents, programs and drawers that are in the TrashCan will be wiped. This is one way of getting rid of files and programs that you don't need any more, although another way is to use the Discard menu selection on the Workbench menu, which I'll talk about in a minute.

So there are many different types of icon, and you can easily see which type an icon is by selecting Info from the Menu Bar on the Workbench. This will be much more important to you later, but file it away for now until we come to Chapter 9 about Making Icons. Another thing which Info is good for is to find out what the *default tool type* is for any icon. This means that if a program was saved by a certain program, the name of this program is stored in the icon. If you click on the icon, the Amiga looks for the program with which the file was created, which is only sensible. If you click on a picture file created with Deluxe Paint III, for example, the Amiga will load Deluxe Paint automatically...if you have it in any of your drives that is. So you can click on an icon, and the program will load automatically to allow you to examine the file. To find out what program you need to have loaded, just look at the Info screen of that file, and the program needed will be shown at the *default tool* line. You can change this to another tool, but I wouldn't recommend this until you really know what you are doing. So that's Info, and a very useful little program it is too.

Right, back to the menus. I spoke about the Discard menu item before, right? Well, the Discard menu item is for getting rid of things from your Workbench. For example an icon (and therefore the program attached to it) can be removed to make space on your Workbench. To do this, start by selecting the icon using the left (or selection) button. Then move up to the title bar and press the right (or menu) button, and select Discard from the Workbench menu. Simply click on the right button and hold it down revealing the menu selection: Workbench, Disk, Special. Move the pointer up to the word Workbench and a pop down menu will reveal itself with the menu selections: Open, Close, Duplicate, Rename, Info and Discard. Select Discard and the icon will disappear.

On the disk menu the only other menu selection is Initialize. This is the way that you create disks in the Amiga format for use in the Amiga using the Workbench. (There is a way of initialising disks in the CLI, but I'll cover this in the chapter on AmigaDOS.) In order to Initialize a blank disk all you have to do is put the disk in a drive, select the disk using the left mouse button when the pointer is over the disk icon, and select Initialize from the disk menu at the top of the screen using the right button. When a disk is not selected with the left mouse button, the Initialize menu item will be *ghosted* and will not be selectable. When you select a disk for initialisation a small window comes up at the top of the screen asking you whether it is alright to initialise this particular disk. If you wish to initialise the disk then you can press Continue, or if the menu selection was an accident you can press Cancel to get out of it.

The final menu at the top of the screen on the Workbench is the Special menu selection. Special menu items are Clean Up, Redraw, Last Error, Snapshot, and Version. Clean Up organises messy windows. Open a disk icon by double clicking. Now click once on the disk to highlight it, and select Clean Up from the Special menu. The icons will all be shifted into neat rows. The only other menu item you may use from this menu is Snapshot. If you highlight an icon in a window, or a disk, and select this menu item, the position of the icon or disk will be stored on the disk. So for example if you wanted a disk to appear not on the right-hand side but in the middle of the screen, you can snapshot it there, and the next time you boot the disk it will appear where you left it. If you don't snapshot the position of something, then the window and icons will go to their default settings.

The other menu items on the Special menu are pretty useless. Version gives you the version number of your Workbench disk, although why you'd want to know that I don't know. Redraw does just that, redraws the screen in case any glitches crop up. This happens rarely and usually when it does Redraw isn't the answer, a complete re-boot is usually in order! Last Error lets you see a clue to why something didn't work, and this clue is printed in the Menu Bar. Most errors on the Amiga are accompanied by an error number, and you will find a list of them in Appendix D.

Using Windows

A window is an opened icon, which can either be a disk or a program. Programs generally open a whole new screen over the top of the Workbench and open a window in that.

To use windows, you have to click on the window in question to activate it. Then you can click on any of the icons in the window and use the program it represents.

Windows are not just static objects, they layer up on the Workbench screen and can be moved around and resized. The stripy bar on the top of a window is called the *drag bar*. If you point to this with the pointer and hold down the left button, you can move the window around the screen and, by moving the mouse, position it in any place you like by merely letting go of the mouse button. Windows can also be resized by dragging the *resizing* gadget at the bottom right of the window. Just point to the gadget, hold down the left mouse button and drag the window to resize it to how big you want it to be (see Figures 2.6 and 2.7).

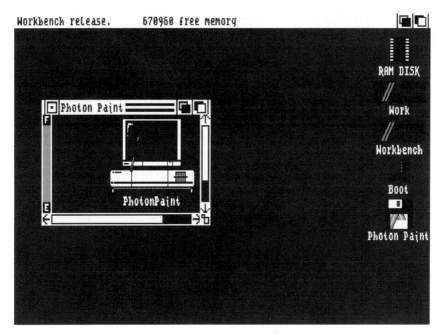

Figure 2.6. Photon Paint window – before.

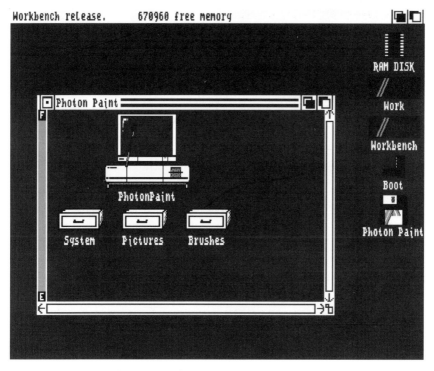

Figure 2.7. Photon Paint window – after.

Another way of dealing with a number of windows on a screen is with the back and front gadgets. These are located on the top right of the window, and just as the screen has them, so does a window. And they work in the same way, except that they shuffle the windows within a screen rather than shuffling the screens themselves.

If you have a pair of windows (as in Figure 2.8a) and you want to see what it in the window below without closing the window on top, simply point to the back gadget (the gadget showing a black square over a white one) and click the left mouse button (Figure 2.8 b). The window will disappear and reappear behind the other window. In reverse, if you want to bring a window to the front, then you click on the front gadget (the one with a white square over a black one) and the window will pop to the front.

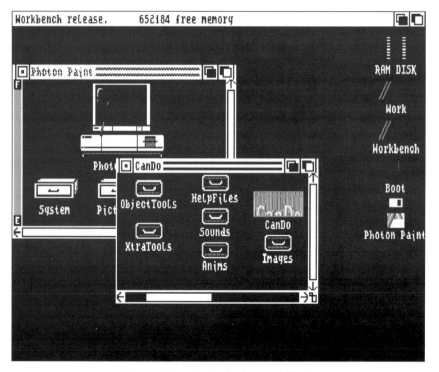

Figure 2.8a. CanDo before and front.

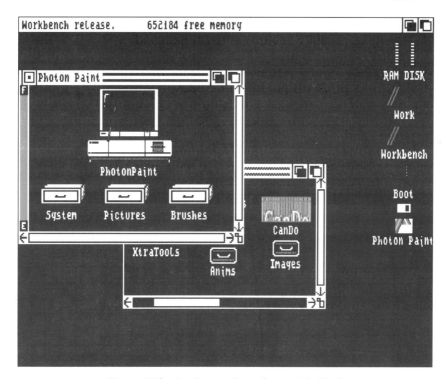

Figure 2.8b. CanDo window after and behind.

Finally, the close box is there for you to close the window. The close gadget is located at the top left corner of every program or Workbench window, allowing you to close down the window or program in operation. This removes the window if you're not using it, and makes space on the screen and room in your memory.

Expansion Drawer

On the Workbench there is an empty drawer called Expansion, and some of you might be curious as to what it does. In fact this is a special drawer for drivers of external devices such as hard disks etc. The only problem is that so many manufacturers used the devs directory to store their drivers for hard disks that this idea has dried up rather, except for users of the PC Bridgeboard on the 2000/1500 or the 3000. In most cases there is no need to keep this drawer active on your Workbench. If you do ever find a use for it, all you have to do is drag the icons for the drivers into the Expansion drawer. So, not much of a mystery after all.

The mysteries of Expansion are as nothing compared to the mysteries of the Utilities drawer, and this is in fact so complex I've devoted a whole chapter to it, Chapter 7 in fact.

A Word about Bootable Disks

Ironically the only way to make your own bootable Workbench disks is using the Shell. See Chapter 4 for an explanation of what you need to do.

Summary

This chapter dealt with the Workbench, and we covered the basic principles of the Amiga's GUI or Graphical User Interface. The basic controls are from the mouse, where the left button selects things and the right button activates menus. The left button also runs programs and opens disks for use, by double clicking.

The Menu Bar at the top of any screen can be activated with the right button on the mouse. By holding the button down and moving to the Menu Bar, you can select menu items by releasing the mouse button over the item.

Icons are tiny pictures which represent a program or a disk on the screen. You can have many screens on your display at one time, and these are layered so you can step between them using gadgets. Gadgets are little buttons on the screen that you can click with the mouse to make various changes to the windows.

And finally, we learned that windows can be flipped back and forth on the screen using the gadgets, and that they represent an opened icon.

3:
Workbench 2

Commodore surprised everyone when they shipped the Amiga A3000 and simultaneously launched Kickstart/Workbench 2. Now the Kickstart part of it is all in the ROMs of the Amiga 3000 and its recent descendants, the Amiga 500 Plus and Amiga 600, but the Workbench part of it is on the disk and this is the bit we're concerned with. Up till now we've been talking about Workbench 1.3, as this has until recently been the predominant system software on the Amiga. But Workbench 2 is now catching up, and although system 1.3 has a strong hold on the majority of the Amiga user base, 2 is vastly improved and will soon be in the majority of Amiga computers shipped into the home.

Workbench 2 is available as an upgrade for Amiga 500 and 2000 users. The kit contains a chip and a set of disks, which unless you are *au fait* with chip extraction and fitting, I'd leave to a dealer to fit for you. So how does it differ from WB 1.3, and what are the additions and benefits to the system?

Physical

For the most part as far as you are concerned as a beginner, the system won't have changed that much. It looks very different certainly, and this is one of the chief changes to the regular user. The gadgets, which appear on all Intuition windows, have changed position, shape and function, hopefully making the system easier and more pleasant to use.

The two back and front gadgets at the top right of the window have been changed for one single gadget. Click on it once and the window goes behind. Click on it again and it pops back to the front. Next to it there is an auto sizing gadget, which when clicked snaps the window to fill the full screen. Clicking the gadget again reduces the size of the window back to what it was before you clicked it the first time.

The arrows on the window slider bars have all been grouped together around the bottom right hand corner, along with the re-sizing gadget. You can still pull the sliders with the mouse too, but you can also slide them up and down a notch at a time with the arrows, as per 1.3.

Finally the close box has changed its looks, but its position and function hasn't altered at all. All the gadgets, and indeed the whole Workbench, has been given a new 3D look, with the gadgets and windows having the appearance of being raised from the surface of the Workbench screen, and highlights and shadows being picked out in the design. This new look is very easy on the eye, and makes picking out and using the gadgets you are looking for much easier. So much for the cosmetic changes, how about the operational ones?

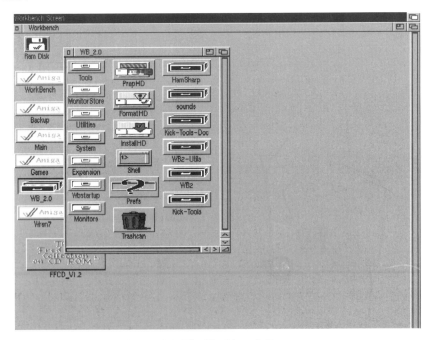

Figure 3.1. The Workbench 2 screen.

Operational

The operational differences between Workbench 1.3 and 2 are improvements in the way that the system works. (Table 3.1 shows you a list of the new menus available at the Workbench in the new version.) A lot of standard features present in other popular GUIs, like the Apple Macintosh system, have been brought in to Workbench, making it a state of the art Graphic User Interface.

When the system was re-written, it was done from scratch, whereas the majority of the commands and AmigaDOS parts of the system in 1.3 were written in C, Workbench 2 has been re-done in machine code. This affects the speed of the system, and this is not just to do with the fact that Workbench 2 works under and accelerated 68030 processor in the Amiga 3000.

The Workbench itself in Workbench 2 is in fact just another window, and can be closed, as with any other. The reason you would do this is to save the space that the Workbench takes up in memory, and although this feature has been available in certain programs before, this is the first time it has been implemented on the actual Workbench itself.

New folders can be created on the Workbench using a menu selection. This is different from 1.3, where you had to copy the Empty folder or drawer and rename it to have a new drawer on the disk.

Workbench 2 also allows you to leave files outside of their window, being still attached to the disk or partition they came from, but being able to be activated or run from outside the window. All you have to do is drag the icon outside the window onto the Workbench, and then apply the Icons/Leave Out menu selection. The opposite is Put Away, which is also in the icons menu. Also you don't have to press Shift and click on a bunch of icons to select them all. All you have to do is press the mouse button on an empty space in the window and drag a box around all the icons you want to select.

You have the ability in Workbench 2 to display the files in a window by name, size or by icon, and all the files in a subdirectory can be made visible and run from the Workbench. Running programs from a window, even programs which have no icon, and typing readme files etc is now possible with just a few mouse clicks. This brings the AmigaDOS interface a little closer to the surface, and it is now true to say that using the new system, both the Shell and Workbench allow you to access the same programs in a similar intuitive and simple way.

What's on the Menu?

New menus have been added to the Workbench in version 2, which add a great deal to the functionality and ease of use of the Workbench. Table 3.1 overleaf gives you a list of the new menus that are available on the new Workbench screen. Some are old familiar faces from 1.3, but others are definitely different.

Workbench Tools	Window		Icons
Backdrop	New Drawer		Open
ResetWB			
Execute Command	Open Parent		Copy
Redraw All	Close		Rename
Update All	Update		Information
Last Message	Select Contents		Snapshot
About	Clean Up		UnSnapshot
Quit	Snapshot-Window		Leave Out
		-All	Put Away
	Show	-Only icons	Delete
		-All	Format Disk
	View by	-Icon	
		-Name	Empty Trash
		-Date	
		-Size	

Table 3.1. The Workbench 2 menus.

The Window/New Drawer selection allows you to create a new directory on your Workbench, which is very useful believe me. After years of copying the Empty drawer and renaming it, you can now generate one simply by selecting a menu option. You can also Unsnapshot a previously Snapshot icon, so its location is no longer fixed in the window.

But the most important change is the way you can view the icons and programs on the disk using the Workbench. This is the most powerful improvement to the system, and as you can see from the Table, a number of options have been added to help you. Show/Only Icons is the normal state of affairs. But now you can Show/All, which enables you to see files on the disk which are normally not visible on the Workbench. Not only can you see them, but you can run them too, if they are an executable object that is. You can also view by icon in the normal way, or view as text sorted by name, date or size. This means that instead of looking at a window full of icons, you are looking at a sorted list of the programs on the disk, as if it were a directory. But unlike a dir on the Shell, you can click on each name on the window and launch the program as if it were an icon.

So now the Workbench is as powerful as the Shell, and make no mistake about it.

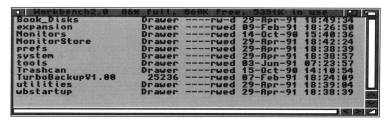

Figure 3.2. Viewing files sorted by name.

Shell

The Workbench 2 Shell program is different from the 1.3 Shell in a few respects, and some of these are basically just improvements in the functionality of the system. For example if you do a directory and it shoots off the top of the window, the window can be resized and the missing part will be re-displayed. This is called smart refresh, and it's a very useful feature which can save you a lot of time and hassle.

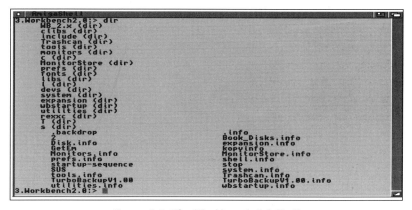

Figure 3.3. The Workbench 2.0 Shell.

Preferences

The Preferences program has been replaced on Workbench 2 with a series of separate programs in a Preferences directory. The prefs are more complex, with certain cosmetic enhancements, like patterns on windows and backdrops, and the ability to select the fonts you use on the Workbench.

You can select one pattern for the Workbench backdrop, and one for the windows. This means that the windows will stand out against the backdrop a little more sharply, and look more pretty into the bargain.

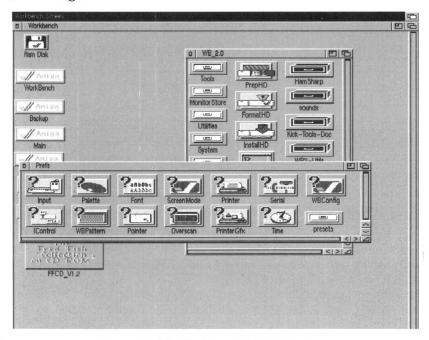

Figure 3.4. The Workbench 2 Prefs directory.

ARexx

In response to many cries for assistance, Commodore have added ARexx to the new system, and this means that you can not only have ARexx running and passing information between programs, you can also create your own ARexx ports for other purposes than those specified by the creators of your software packages.

Display Modes

Workbench 2 has been out on the Amiga 3000 for some time now, and its launch provided us with the first look at what Workbench 2 has in store for Amiga owners. Because the Amiga 3000 uses a multisync monitor, it is able to use other display modes which would cause interlace flicker on a normal Amiga. Not only does the normal interlace mode not flicker like crazy, but using the new Amiga Enhanced Chip Set there are also four new screen modes (the productivity and SuperHi-res modes) which deliver 640x480, 640x960, 1280x200 and 1280x400 respectively. The flexibility of the new display chip enables you to create any new resolution mode in between the old lower and new upper resolutions, for display on any multisync monitor.

So Workbench 2 is a real advance in Amiga computing, and takes us neatly into the 90s with a world class computer which can bandy resolutions and power with the best of them.

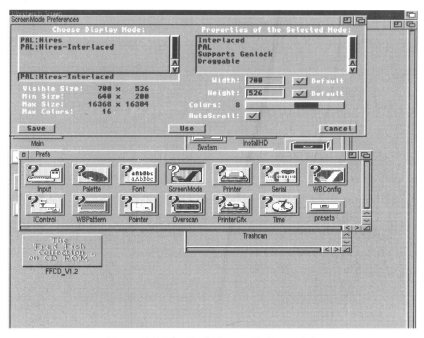

Figure 3.5. The Prefs ScreenMode module.

Note for 2000 Users

Conventional Amiga users can of course access flicker free Amiga graphics by employing a multisync monitor and either MicroWay's Flicker Fixer or the new Commodore 2320 display enhancer, both of which are circuit boards which slot into the video slot of an Amiga 2000. Once the monitor has been fitted, you can use the interlace modes without the flicker, and this is done by upping the scan rate of the machine and using a display which not unlike the VGA standard on the PC. Obviously it isn't VGA, but it is close enough that you can use a VGA monitor instead of a multisync. This means you can't use the normal Amiga resolution without switching to a normal Amiga monitor, but it can be done.

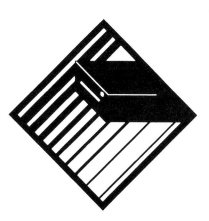

4: AmigaDOS

If you own an Amiga, then you obviously need to know all about the Workbench, as this is the standard way of getting at all the programs and files in your disks. But it's also essential that you aren't afraid of using AmigaDOS from time to time, as this is one of the most powerful ways of using your Amiga.

When you start your Amiga, you are usually faced with the *Insert Workbench* prompt. At this point you have a choice, to insert the Workbench disk or another program disk. If you insert the Workbench disk you see the Workbench, a full WIMP environment. But this is only one way of accessing the Amiga's power. The other is the CLI, or Command Line Interface. This is a more traditional interface based on AmigaDOS, the Amiga Disk Operating System.

But what is AmigaDOS? Many sources will tell you rather confusingly it is the Amiga's Operating System, and although strictly speaking this is true, it isn't the whole story. In the broadest sense it's the software that provides a link between your keyboard and the chips at the heart of the Amiga.

One part of AmigaDOS is a bit that you can't see, the part of the computer that carries on behind the scenes, shifting stuff around and making things available for you to use in the system. The visible part is shown through the Shell window, and is the set of commands which you type in to make the Amiga do things.

But don't confuse AmigaDOS with a programming language, because it isn't. You can't just type programs into the Shell and run them. No siree. If it helps to keep it stuck in your mind, think of it more of a housekeeper, which you can get to do tasks around the house, the house being the Amiga in this case. This is different to a programming language like BASIC, which is more like a working horse or dog, a thing which can be trained to do different jobs. Or you can see AmigaDOS as an admin department in a factory, and a programming language as a machine in the factory. Whatever way you slice it, AmigaDOS is only good at a very narrow band of tasks, and except in very exceptional circumstances cannot be programmed to do anything else.

Using AmigaDOS

You get access to AmigaDOS by double-clicking on the Shell icon. Then you are issued with a *prompt.* This is an on-screen figure which is the visual equivalent of the Amiga saying *"Yes? Did you want me to do something?"* On the CLI it appears like so:

        1.>

or on the Shell it is:

        1.SYS:>

(In fact the number 1 above may vary so you could and might get 2.SYS> or something similar – don't worry.)

At the prompt you can type any AmigaDOS command and the computer will act upon it as soon as you press Return. You can create lists of AmigaDOS commands, using a text editor of some kind, and execute them using the Execute command. These lists are called *batch files*, and as we'll see later on they can save a lot of time. But let's not jump the gun.

The Structure of a Disk

When you are using the Workbench, running programs and sorting through the various directories (called drawers on the Workbench) of the disk you are working with, the process used is that of pointing and clicking the mouse. In the Shell, the interface with AmigaDOS, all the input required from you is textual, ie you type it in. When you use Workbench it is still AmigaDOS which accesses all the files and programs on your disk when you use Workbench, but it does this in the background, using Workbench as its interface. Under AmigaDOS we refer to Workbench drawers as directories. There is no physical difference between them, it is merely the way that they are talked about depending which interface you are using.

Looking at a Workbench window displaying the contents of a disk you will see that a lot of the icons are shaped like drawers, that is to say something that you can put things in, and that is in fact their purpose. Drawers on a disk give you places to store programs or files. Information is stored in the drawers in much the same way that you would put papers and documents in a real drawer in a real filing cabinet. When you double-click on a drawer it opens out into a window displaying the contents of that drawer. The reason that AmigaDOS uses drawers is because it is operating what is called a *hierarchical filing system,* which is a *long-winded* way of saying that it has many levels and a structure based on drawers and files, all of which can be nested together to form a filing structure.

The only difference between a real drawer and a drawer on the Workbench is that a drawer on the Workbench can contain other drawers within it. It is possibly easy for you to imagine folders within other folders within a filing cabinet for the different levels of the filing system. An item that you are looking for may be inside one particular drawer and within that drawer the file you are looking for may be within a folder in that drawer. The method that the computer uses to find that file, and how you would describe where that file is, is as follows:

```
firstdrawer/seconddrawer/file
```

This is how AmigaDOS would look for the file in Shell and this is how you would describe to AmigaDOS how to get to it.

Back to AmigaDOS

Once you have opened an AmigaDOS window through the Shell, you are presented with a prompt as described before. This prompt normally has a number at the beginning indicating that this is the first or second Shell window opening. You can in fact open multiple Shell windows and perform different tasks in each one under the Amiga's unique multitasking operating system. Multi means many, and task means job. So the Amiga can run several jobs at once.

In AmigaDOS the names of the drawers and the files contained within them change slightly. AmigaDOS describes the disk windows you see on Workbench as *directories* and the drawers as *subdirectories* to indicate the different levels of the filing system for each disk. For example, if you put a disk into the drive and type:

```
dir
```

(short for directory) and press Return, this action commands the computer to display a directory or catalogue of the files on the disk in the currently selected drive. What you see is what we call the *Root* directory, that is to say the first level of the file system.

Think of this as being like the contents page of a book. For example, Table 4.1 is a root directory of a typical version 1.3 Workbench disk:

```
Trashcan (dir)
    c (dir)
    Prefs (dir)
    System (dir)
    l (dir)
    devs (dir)
    s (dir)
    t (dir)
    fonts (dir)
    libs (dir)
    Empty (dir)
    Utilities (dir)
    Expansion (dir)
.info           Disk.info
Empty.info      Expansion.info
Prefs.info      Shell
Shell.info      System.info
Trashcan.info Utilities.info
```

Table 4.1. A directory of an Amiga disk

In this directory you can see a list of any files, programs and subdirectories that are on the root directory of the disk. If you type:

```
dir <subdirectory>
```

(where the <subdirectory> part is replaced simply by the name of a subdirectory on the disk). The computer will then be looking into that particular subdirectory on that disk. Due to this arrangement of directories and subdirectories, this structure is often referred to as the *tree* structure. The directories are all linked using a distinct hierarchy or order. Don't worry too much about this yet, as you will soon see from navigating around the directories how they all fit together on each disk that you work with.

(Note: As a beginner you won't have to have too much to do with this level of AmigaDOS to start with, but it's as well to try it out a bit to see what can be done. Sooner or later you'll see that certain programs will not be available to you if you cannot find or execute them from the Shell.)

Let's take an example of a disk called *MyDisk* and the sub directory called *Work*, in which is a file called *Document*. The way the computer would describe where this file is, is:

    `MyDisk:Work/Document`

This is what we call the pathname, as the instructions in the line above tell the computer exactly where to look to find the file and execute it. (Note: the use of the colon *: h*ere is to specify a disk by name. The colon is used to specify disks and what are called *devices* on the Amiga, like RAM: for the ram disk and PRT: for the printer, but we'll go into all this a little later on.) You could quite simply type:

    `cd mydisk:work`

to get there, and then any Dir commands you type will show you all the files in the directory called Work.

And by the way, the Shell is not sensitive to the case of a command, so you could type either of the following:

    `cd mydisk:work`

    `CD MyDisk:Work`

and get the same result.

The AmigaDOS Commands

AmigaDOS is there for you to perform various functions on the disk that you are working with. From the Shell you can format a disk (what on the Workbench is called *Initialise*), navigate around the various directories, create new directories to put new files in, and delete and copy files that you need in a different place or don't need any more. As I said before AmigaDOS can be seen as a housekeeper, a method of keeping your disks in order and examining files which are not accessible from the Workbench.

(Note: The reason some programs are not usable from the Workbench is that in order for a file to appear on the Workbench it has to have an icon file carrying the same name as the file followed by the postfix *.info* – the way an icon file looks on a disk when seen from the Shell. If a file has no .info file attached to it, then it will not appear on the Workbench. So in the case of a program which has no icon, like a piece of public domain software for example, then the program must be run from AmigaDOS by simply typing the name of the program.)

AmigaDOS is used by typing commands and pressing Return, that big *L-shaped* key on the keyboard. The commands are what we call keywords which AmigaDOS understands, and these are executed when you press the Return key after typing them in. There now follows a list of the most frequently used Shell commands for your use. A more detailed list of AmigaDOS commands appears in the appendices at the back of the book. Before we begin the alphabetical list let us cover some basic ground.

All AmigaDOS commands are located in a directory called C (for commands) in the root directory of your Workbench or program disk. (See the demo listing of the Workbench disk we did earlier.) The commands available to you on any one disk will all be in this C directory.

Amiga drives all have a number, with the internal drive being 0, and the first external drive being 1. The drives are specified in commands to AmigaDOS using the code dfx:, where x equals the drive number. The DF part stands for *disk floppy*, and by the same token any hard disk units you might have (these are optional and don't come with your system) are specified in a command by the letters DH0 or DH1, etc. This is of course calling the drive *disk hard 0*.

For example, to display a directory of the internal disk drive which comes with your Amiga, that is the main drive from which you generally boot your system, you type:

```
dir df0:
```

This tells the computer to look at drive df0. If you wish to look at the first external drive that you may have attached to your system, you would type:

```
dir df1:
```

This tells the computer to do a directory of the first external disk drive.

Changing Directories

If you wish to draw the computer's attention to a particular disk drive and stay there, so that you don't have to specify which disk you want to look at all the time, then you must use the CD command, that is CD for *change directory*. To turn the computer's attention to drive df1, that is to say the external disk drive, type:

```
cd df1:
```

From then on if you type any AmigaDOS command, all dirs, copys and deletes will happen on drive df1, because the computer's attention is focused on that particular drive. If you wish to return the attention of the computer to the disk in the internal drive you merely type:

```
cd df0:
```

and this will redirect the computer to the internal drive.

If you have commenced a directory and the computer is taking a long time over it you can break out of AmigaDOS commands by pressing and holding the Control or Ctrl key and pressing the letter C on your keyboard. This breaks you out of the command and returns you to the prompt.

A lot of AmigaDOS commands require more than just the command to be entered at the prompt. Any extra words or letters needed after a command are called *parameters* and are usually entered after putting a space between the command and the parameter. Any parameters needed are listed in the entry on that particular command in the list following shortly. Before we begin the list of most often used AmigaDOS commands, let's just have a quick word about the difference between the CLI and the Shell.

When the Amiga first came out the only interface supplied for use with AmigaDOS was the CLI or Command Line Interface. However, when issue 1.3 of the Workbench came out, another interface was supplied called the Shell. The Shell is essentially the same as the CLI, although it has a lot more editing and convenience features added. For example, in the CLI, if you enter a command in error or miss out one of the parameters, you have to retype the whole line correctly from scratch.

In the Shell however all you have to do is press the up arrow key on the cursor keys on the keyboard, the line will be retyped for you and you will be allowed to re-edit the line and execute it with Return. The cursor keys up and down allow you to select from the last few entries from the keyboard to enable you to re-execute any past commands again, simply by pressing the up and down arrow keys to select the recently typed line you want.

The left and right cursor keys enable you to step backwards and forwards through the line you have currently lined up at the prompt to edit it. The Shell also has other features like telling you at the prompt which is the currently selected disk and directory, enabling you to see at all times where you are. The CLI has the same prompt all the time, just a number, so sometimes it's difficult to tell which directory you are currently looking at.

Another interesting point about the Shell is the ability to make certain AmigaDOS commands resident, using the Resident command. This makes life very easy for single drive users, as certain often-used AmigaDOS commands can be placed into memory, meaning that the C directory need not be in the boot drive when these commands are typed. Although Resident has many benefits as far as speed of execution is concerned, resident commands do take up memory which can be a consideration for 512K Amiga users!

Common Commands

Here are a list of the commands available at the AmigaDOS prompt. As I said before, full details of the kinds of commands available can be found in the appendix on AmigaDOS.

(Note: If you type a command and the computer refuses to execute it, flashing the screen and even printing up an error code, then the command you typed may not be on the disk you're using. Check in the c directory of your disk, as this is where all the AmigaDOS commands on a boot disk are stored.)

CD

This command changes the current directory, as if you are shifting the computer's attention to another disk, or even another drawer (or subdirectory) on the same disk. The cd command works like this:

```
cd <disk or directory>
```

You can cd to another disk by using the name of the drive like so:

```
cd df0:
```

meaning look at the disk in drive df0: whatever it is. Alternatively you can cd to a specific disk that isn't in the drive yet, by stating its name followed by a colon, like this:

```
cd extras:
```

The colon tells the computer that you are looking for a specific disk, rather than a file or folder on the current disk. If you forget the colon, then the computer will assume that the file or drawer is on the currently selected disk. If you want to switch the current directory to a drawer on the disk you have in the drive, you do this like so:

```
cd comms
```

If the directory is a subdirectory inside another subdirectory, then you can get to it like so:

```
cd docs/letters
```

where for example the drawer called Letters is inside the directory called Docs.

COPY

Copy does exactly that, copies files from one disk to another. To copy files, you just have to type:

```
copy <disk/file> to <disk/directory>
```

So if you had a file called Pete on a disk in df0: which you wanted to copy to drive df1:, you would type:

```
copy pete to df1:
```

Notice that I didn't say which drive Pete was on, because we had already CDed to the disk in df0:

DATE

Typing Date at a prompt shows you the date and time according to the computer's on-board clock. To set the time and date you type:

```
date <date> <time>
```

for example:

```
date 12-feb-92 12:30
```

or whatever the time and date is. If you just want to change the time, then type:

```
date 12:30
```

and if it's just the date which is wrong, then just do:

```
date 12-feb-92
```

The computer knows what the numbers mean. If the figures are separated by dashes, it must be the date, and if there's a colon between them then it's the time!

If you have a memory expansion and battery-backed clock in your computer you can load and save the time from the clock to the computer using another command called SetClock.

DELETE

This command deletes or removes a file from your disk. If you want to get rid of a file type:

```
delete <file>
```

For example if you had a file called KillerBob, and wanted to get rid of it, you would type:

```
delete killerbob
```

The drive will whirr a bit, and the file will be gone. Magic, eh? It is obviously not a good idea to do this willy nilly, as once a file is deleted it cannot be recovered easily. So use this command with care, and check what you're rubbing out before you do it.

DIR

This command gives you a directory display, also known as a catalogue, of what is on a particular disk. If the command is typed on its own, then the computer gives you a listing of the currently selected directory. If you add a specific directory path to the command it will list that directory on screen. Like this:

```
dir <path>
```

where the path points to the directory or disk that you want to see a listing of. For example if you want to see what's on your external disk drive, you type:

```
dir df1:
```

If you want to see what is on df0:, you type:

```
dir df0:
```

If you want to see a directory inside the disk in df0:, like the C directory, then you will type:

```
dir df0:c
```

The command is one quick way of checking out what is on a disk. If you want to see more detail on what is on a disk, like the size of the files and stuff like that, then you need to use the List command instead.

DISKCOPY

This is another command which is really self-explanatory. To copy one disk to another, you need to type:

```
diskcopy <first disk> to <second disk>
```

like so:

```
diskcopy df0: to df1:
```

This is handy for making backup copies of disks you want to use. The benefit of doing this rather than formatting or initialising a disk, naming it, and copying the files across one by one are that diskcopy formats as it goes. So you can just slot in a blank unformatted disk and do diskcopy. The copy of the disk is called "Copy Of" and then whatever the name of the original disk was. (This is done to prevent the Amiga crashing, as it does if it has two disks with the same name in at the same time.) After you've removed the original disk, you can rename it to the original name, using the Rename option from the Workbench or typing Rename from AmigaDOS.

ENDCLI

If you have a CLI or Shell window open and you want to get rid of it and go back to Workbench, just type EndCLI on its own, and the AmigaDOS window will vanish.

EXECUTE

The Execute Command is for running batch files, or lists of AmigaDOS commands. To use just type:

```
execute <filename>
```

and the file will be run. All the commands in the batch file will be executed in turn, until the end of the list is reached. Batch files can be create using a text editor.

FORMAT

The FORMAT command is the AmigaDOS equivalent of the Initialise menu item. This prepares a blank disk for use with AmigaDOS. Unfortunately the command parameters are quite long winded, and you have to type:

```
format drive <drive> name <name>
```

like so:

```
format drive df0: name Empty
```

to format a disk in drive df0: and name it Empty. The line must be typed in full, and so you can't for example just type:

```
format df0:
```

as this will produce a reminder of the proper syntax.

INSTALL

This command makes a disk bootable, although it doesn't install Workbench on the disk. To make a bootable disk just type:

```
install <drive>
```

and a *bootblock* will be installed on the disk. This means that you can insert the disk at the prompt and the computer will start, but it won't load Workbench. This is a more complex operation.

(Note: The command which creates the Workbench is LoadWB, and in order for this to work you have to create a C directory on the disk for all the commands using MakeDir, plus a Libs directory and a S directory. Check the contents of the S and Libs directory on your master Workbench disk and you'll see what files have to be in them. See the command LoadWB for a full rundown on the essential files needed for a bootable Workbench disk.)

To use Install just type the command followed by the drive containing the formatted disk you wish to give a bootblock to. This can in fact be a disk with data on it, as the bootblock has its own space at the beginning of the disk. None of the data on your disk will be erased, so if you have a disk with some stuff on it, you can Install that too. Type the following to install a bootblock on df1:.

```
install df1:
```

LIST

List is a bit like Dir, in that it displays a directory of the disk, but it does it in a slightly different way. All the file lengths and dates when the files were created are listed, which may be useful to know. For example, typing List with the Workbench disk in the drive will give you something like this:

```
Directory "df0:" on Monday 17-Dec-90

Expansion.info    894   ----rwed 13-Aug-88   18:02:32
Trashcan          Dir   ----rwed 13-Aug-88   18:02:34
.info             70    ----rwed 13-Aug-88   18:15:51
c                 Dir   ----rwed 13-Aug-88   18:06:03
Prefs             Dir   ----rwed 13-Aug-88   18:16:15
System            Dir   ----rwed 13-Aug-88   18:16:10
                  Dir   ----rwed 13-Aug-88   18:08:12
Shell             empty ----rwed 13-Aug-88   18:08:18
devs              Dir   ----rwed 13-Aug-88   18:09:09
s                 Dir   ----rwed 25-Oct-88   10:30:03
Shell.info        405   ----rwed 13-Aug-88   18:09:36
t                 Dir   ----rwed 13-Aug-88   18:09:38
fonts             Dir   ----rwed 13-Aug-88   18:11:03
libs              Dir   ----rwed 29-Aug-88   18:14:35
Empty             Dir   ----rwed 13-Aug-88   18:11:48
Utilities.info    894   ----rwed 13-Aug-88   18:11:51
Disk.info         370   ----rwed 13-Aug-88   18:11:55
Prefs.info        894   ----rwed 13-Aug-88   18:11:57
System.info       894   ----rwed 13-Aug-88   18:12:01
Empty.info        894   ----rwed 13-Aug-88   18:12:05
Trashcan.info     1166  ----rwed 13-Aug-88   18:12:09
Utilities         Dir   ----rwed 24-Oct-88   19:29:36
Expansion         Dir   ----rwed 3-Aug-88    18:13:31
10 files -              13 directories - 39 blocks used
```

As you can see the directory is full of files that were created in 1988, in August, which was when the final release of Workbench 1.3 was copied onto the master disks for duplication! You even have the exact time the files were created, and the size in bytes. The bit about "rwed" means that the files are readable, writable, executable and deletable. (See Protect command in Appendix B.)

LoadWB

This command loads the Workbench. In most cases you won't need to employ this command, as the Workbench is loaded for you when you use your master Workbench disk. But there will come a time when you will want to install Workbench on a disk, so that it pops up and allows you to run your own programs from Workbench.

In order for LoadWB to work, you need to copy the file called Icon.Library from the libs directory on your Workbench to a directory called Libs on your new disk. (Create all the directories using MakeDir and copy the files across using Copy.) You need a C directory containing the CLI commands LoadWB and EndCLI. In order for the LoadWB command to be executed automatically on bootup, it needs to be in a *batch file* called *startup-sequence* in a directory called S. You can make this with a text editor like ED, and it needs to look like this:

```
LoadWB

EndCLI
```

And finally the disk should be given a bootblock using Install, and if you want the disk to look the same as your master Workbench disk, you need to make a directory called Devs and copy across a file called *system-configuration* from the Devs directory on your master Workbench disk.

This is a very basic minimum Workbench disk, and is only any good if the programs you need to run have all the data they need internally. That is to say if the programs need to run any Amiga libraries for maths etc, then they won't work unless you copy all the libs across. But this is all the basic minimum stuff to make a disk that will boot.

Obviously if you want to use the CLI then you have to copy the Shell program and icon over, along with all the files that make the Shell work, like NewShell and Prompt in the C directory, a file called Shell-Seg in a directory called L, and the file Shell-Startup in the S directory. These can all be copied over from the Workbench master disk. Once everything is where it should be, you can click the Shell icon and get the Shell up on screen.

MAKEDIR

This command makes a new subdirectory on the disk. The usage is as follows:

```
makedir <new name>
```

For example if you wanted to create two directories on a word processing data disk, one for letters and one for articles, then you would do it like this:

```
makedir letters

makedir articles
```

and then when you do a directory, you'd see:

```
letters (dir)

articles (dir)
```

A directory made with makedir doesn't show up on the Workbench, as it hasn't got a .info file. You can create one of these using an icon editing program, or you can copy the Empty drawer from the Workbench disk, delete the directory called Empty using AmigaDOS, and rename the .info file from Empty to the name of your directory!

NEWCLI

If you are in a CLI then typing this will create a new CLI or task. A new CLI window will open up with the prompt:

```
2.>
```

or the next number on from the last CLI you had. You can type commands in the new window, and these are executed simultaneously with commands typed in other windows. Try opening three CLI windows and typing Dir in each one to see what happens. To close down any extra windows you've opened, type EndCLI.

NEWSHELL

NewShell is just like NewCLI, except that you get a Shell window instead of a CLI window. This means you have access to all the Shell editing facilities. NewShell is available from version 1.3 upwards.

RENAME

To rename a file just type:

```
rename <oldname> as <newname>
```

the drive will whirr a bit and the file will be called by the new name. For example if you had a file called Cooper and wanted it to be called Truman, you'd type:

```
rename cooper as truman
```

and when you type dir, you can see that the filename has been changed

RUN

To run a program all you need to do is type the name of that program. But if you want the program to multitask with the AmigaDOS window you have open then you have to type:

```
run <filename>
```

for example, to run a program called Mike, you would type:

```
mike
```

but if you didn't want the program to take over control of AmigaDOS, then you would type:

```
run mike
```

The CLI window shows a message to say it is opening a new AmigaDOS task for the program, and you then get the AmigaDOS prompt back.

SETCLOCK

To load and save the time on your Amiga to and from the battery-backed clock in your Amiga (if you have one) use SetClock:

```
setclock opt <load|save>
```

Using Load reads the real-time clock and tells your Amiga what the time is. Save sends the time you've set using Date to the clock.

TYPE

Many disks have text files or batch files (which are also just ASCII format text) on them. You can either load them into a text editor, or you can type them to the screen. Say you find, by displaying a directory, that there is a file called READ.ME on a disk. You type:

```
type read.me
```

and the file will be typed to the screen. If the text is more than a screen long, you can pause the typing by pressing the Spacebar. To continue reading the text, just hit the backspace key. (This is the little back arrow at the top right of the keyboard.)

You can also type program files to the screen using:

```
type program HEX
```

and the program will list itself in hexadecimal code, with an ASCII listing in the right hand column, like so:

```
0000:   000003F3 00000000 00000002 00000000  ................
0010:   00000001 0000004F 00000042 000003E9  .......O...B....
0020:   0000004F 286A0164 700C4E95 2401223C  ...O(j.dp.N.$."<
0030:   00000095 49FAFFEE 286CFFFC 2F0C2F02  ....I...(1../././
0040:   D9CCD9CC 200C6714 202C0004 E580B2B4  .... .g. ,......
0050:   08006C04 22340800 285460E4 2C010681  ..l."4..(T`.,...
0060:   00000032 91C8286A 0074700C 4E954A81  ...2..(j.tp.N.J.
0070:   670000E0 06810000 00322A2A 00702441  g.......2**.p$A
0080:   D5CAD5CA 2E01204A 20C62846 D9C7D9CC  ...... J .(F....
0090:   D9CC203C 474C0003 20C05480 B1CC6FF8  .. <GL.. .T...o.
```

Batch Files and the Startup-Sequence

Batch files are lists of AmigaDOS commands put together with a text editor which can be executed all in one go using the Execute command. One of the most-used batch files is the file *startup-sequence* located in the *s* directory of your Workbench disk. Why not Type it to the screen now, using the line:

```
type s/startup-sequence
```

This is a special setup file which auto-executes on bootup, setting up the Amiga for a Workbench! Figure 4.1 shows what this looks like.

This is the Workbench 1.3 version, but most other versions are similar. You can set up your own batch files to create automatic sequences of AmigaDOS commands for your regular use. Use of batch files, sometimes called *scripts*, is rather complex, and something which is covered in more depth in advanced textbooks like the rather excellent (I can say that because I didn't write it) *Mastering AmigaDOS 2* by Mark Smiddy and Bruce Smith, a two volume tome covering all aspects of AmigaDOS 2 and 1.3 (see Appendix E for full details).

```
Addbuffers df0: 10

c:SetPatch >NIL: ;patch system functionscd c:

echo "A500/A2000 U.K. Workbench disk. Release 1.3
version 34.20*N"

Sys:System/FastMemFirst ; move C00000 memory to
last in list

BindDrivers

SetClock load ;load system time from real time
clock (A1000 owners should

        ;replace the SetClock load with Date

FF >NIL: -0 ;speed up Text

resident CLI L:Shell-Seg SYSTEM pure add; activate
Shell

resident c:Execute pure

mount newcon:

;

failat 11

run execute s:StartupII ;This lets resident be
used for rest of script

wait >NIL: 5 mins ;wait for StartupII to complete
(will signal when done)

;

SYS:System/SetMap gb ;Activate the ()/* on keypad

path ram: c: sys:utilities sys:system s: sys:prefs
add ;set path for Workbench

LoadWB delay ;wait for inhibit to end before con-
tinuing

endcli >NIL:
```

Table 4.2. A typical Workbench 1.3 startup-sequence file.

Our Own Devices

Devices are a useful Amiga convention which, although a little bit strange at first, can be very useful to you. To make life easier, and to allow you to find things on a disk without having to know where they are first, the Amiga's operating system recognises certain global *devices*. A logical device, in terms of the Amiga, can be a directory, a disk drive, a partition on the hard disk, or indeed anything with a colon on the end. For example SYS: is the boot disk, C: is the c directory, RAM: is the ram disk, and PRT: is the printer specified in Preferences. Devices can be called up from the Shell, and you can redirect output to them like so:

```
dir df0: to prt:
```

will do a directory and send it to the printer. Or how about this:

```
dir df0: > ram:test
```

This will do a directory, but instead of listing it on the screen, it will list it to a file in the ram disk called *Test*. This is a text file and can be loaded into a text editor or word processor.

If in a program you get a requester on the screen, you can type df0: for drive 0, or df1: for drive 1, or dh0: for hard disk 0. But did you know you can type SYS: to change the directory to the boot disk? Or you can type RAM: to make it look in the ram disk? You do now. Typing PRT: won't do much, as the printer isn't a drive and so has no directories. If you type C: however, you will get the c directory, wherever it is. And the same goes for other important directories on the boot disk, like LIBS:, or L: or S: or even FONTS:. So Amiga devices are there to help you.

You can even direct attention to a disk that's not even in a drive yet, if you know it's name. Type:

```
dir extras:
```

to see what happens. That's right, a system request pops up asking you for the disk.

You can create your own devices too, using Assign. If you assign a program or directory like so:

```
assign mylibs: to df0:mylibs
```

Then you can type:

```
dir mylibs:
```

at any Shell prompt, and the directory you assigned will pop up! I wouldn't worry about this sort of thing too much. There is ample documentation on logical devices etc, and you only really need to know the basics to get you going. It won't affect your enjoyment of the Amiga if you never use them, but it's nice to know they're there if you want them.

Summary

In this chapter we learned about the CLI and Shell interfaces to AmigaDOS. We discovered what a pathname was, and that AmigaDOS isn't case sensitive. AmigaDOS commands are typed in at the prompt, and after you press Return the command is executed immediately. We learned about the most frequently used AmigaDOS commands, and had some examples of how they work. Batch files are text files containing lists of AmigaDOS commands, which can be run all at once using the Execute command. And finally we learned a bit about logical devices and what they mean.

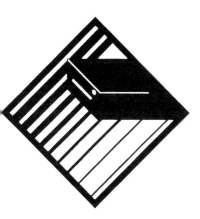

5:
The Ram Disk

Using Amiga programs will bring you into contact with something called the Ram Disk. This is a sort of imaginary disk drive using a portion of memory instead of an actual disk drive with a disk in it. The size of the Ram Disk is limited by the memory you have, meaning you can't store anything in the Ram Disk which is bigger than the memory you've got in your machine.

Why should you want to use the Ram Disk then? Well if you have only one disk drive on your Amiga, it makes a lot of sense to use the Ram Disk to copy things to other disks and as a sort of extra hand when you don't have time to format and label a disk when you have something to save.

But be warned, once you turn the computer off, the Ram Disk, like a program in memory, will be erased. So be sure to resave anything in your Ram Disk to a real disk before you turn off. Think of it as a temporary workspace, somewhere for you to do disk like operations without all the trouble of finding an actual disk to do it on. Using Ram Disk has advantages over a normal disk, mainly in terms of *access speed*, meaning that programs execute faster and that transfer of files to and from the disk is very fast.

Using the Ram Disk

The Ram Disk is automatically mounted by your Workbench disk when you boot up. The Ram Disk differs from normal memory in that the Ram Disk is treated as a disk.

Whereas in order to access a normal disk you would type its device name, like DF1: or DH0:, the Ram Disk is called the RAM: device. So to do a directory of the Ram Disk you would type:

```
dir ram:
```

at a Shell prompt. Any files that you have in the ram disk will show up as they would on a normal directory. There are certain files that the Amiga always keeps in the Ram Disk.

```
clipboards (dir)

env (dir)

t (dir)

tr (dir)
```

and these should be left there in case they are needed for temporary workspace. On some machines, especially those fitted with a hard disk, like a 2000, you will also find a file called Disk.info, and this is the drawer icon for the Ram Disk itself.

The Ram Disk doesn't have a size, in fact when asked it will always profess to be full. This does not mean that you can't put more in it, as it always expands to fill the size required, but only up to the amount of RAM you have fitted. In fact on creation, although it says it it full by the Full and Empty meter on the side of the disk window, it is in fact only about 1K in size. If you want to find out what size the Ram Disk is, then you can do so by typing the info command at a Shell prompt.

The Ram Disk is installed automatically when you talk to it using a AmigaDOS command. So even in a situation where the Ram Disk isn't present, you make it present by doing a directory or copying a file to it.

Once created you can add directories to the Ram Disk with MakeDir, and even create script files to transfer the whole of your C directory to RAM for faster AmigaDOS access. First you have to copy all the files over, and then all you have to do is type:

```
assign C: ram:
```

and there you have it. The only thing you can't do to files on a Ram Disk is add filenotes, but as practically nobody I know uses this feature, I can't see it standing in your way. I've never used Filenote in over five years of constant use, so to all intents and purposes the Ram Disk is identical to a physical disk.

Why Use RAM?

Ther are several times when using a Ram Disk is preferable to using a real disk. If you are capturing a buffer from a terminal program, the text is stored in small chunks with a long break in between each section being saved to disk. Doing this in RAM is safer because the Ram Disk doesn't have a magnetic surface to corrupt. The only thing if you fill up RAM you run the risk of a Guru error, crashing the machine and losing the text in the buffer. But, provided you have enough memory, you won't have any problems. It's a good idea to keep a copy of any files you have stored in the Ram Disk just in case this happens. Make regular backup copies to a real disk from time to time to make sure you won't lose them.

There is a way around some of the problems associated with the temporary nature of Ram Disks, and this is by employing a recoverable Ram Disk.

Recoverable Ram Disks

Some special versions of the Ram Disk are actually able to recover from a warm start, ie the CTRL-A-A three button reset This means holding down and pressing the Ctrl and two Amiga (A) keys together which will re-boot your Amiga. You need to do this if, for example, the keyboard *locks-up* and becomes unresponsive. This means that the Ram Disk will still be intact after a warm boot, enabling you to save things to it and get them back after a reset. This type of Ram Disk is called a *recoverable Ram Disk* or Ram Disk. There are some Ram Disk programs in the Public Domain, but the one most used on the Amiga is the RAD: device.

Totally RAD

The RAD disk is more like a real disk in use and functionality, as you can format it and it stays a constant size. Because it's so stable, you can even have it set up as the boot disk for your system, provided you copy all the requisite files from your Workbench and do the requisite assigns to the RAD disk.

The RAD is already set up in most of the mountlists on your Workbench disks, and so usually all you have to do is type:

```
mount rad:
```

and there it is mounted, and then all you have to do is refer to it using a Dir or a Copy command, and up it pops, just like RAM:. The disk will be called either Ramb0 or RAM_0, but you can change that to whatever you like, and just like a normal disk you can add directories and assign things to it. In fact it behaves just like a real disk.

To alter the size of the RAD, to make it the same size as a floppy for example, you have to alter the mountlist in your Devs directory using a text editor of some kind. The line you have to alter in the RAD: part of the list is the HighCyl number. When you start your Amiga, the mountlist entry for RAD will probably look something like this:

```
RAD: Device = ramdrive.device
Unit  = 0
Flags = 0
Surfaces = 2
BlocksPerTrack = 11
Reserved = 2
Interleave = 0
LowCyl = 0 ; HighCyl = 21
Buffers = 5
BufMemType = 1
```

So all you have to do to create a normal floppy style RAD is to alter the HighCyl number to 79. This will be impossible to load if you have less than about 2Mb of memory, so if you want to use a RAD disk in a 512K Amiga (getting rarer these days) you could set HighCyl to something like 4. Using the RAD as factory preset like the example above means you will have no spare memory for extra pages in your word processor or room for memory intensive programs like graphics or DTP packages. Obviously the more memory you have, the sweeter your Amiga will run, and the more fun you can have with things like RAD and other memory related Amiga tricks like multitasking, or running more than program at once.

Finally, if you want to get rid of RAD for any reason, the equivalent of popping the disk out of the drive (if it was a real disk), then you have to type in:

    remrad

at a Shell prompt. The RAD will vanish and inside the machine it will telescope down to a minimal size. When you reboot for any reason the RAD will be gone.

Note: To make the above mentioned changes you will need to use one of the Amiga's text editors. These are described in Chapter 12.

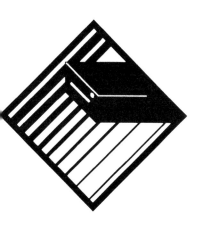

6:
Amiga Fonts

Letters on your Amiga screen appear in certain shapes and sizes, and the name for these different shaped letters is *fonts*. Fonts are designed to be as readable as possible, and to look good on a page or screen, although some fail in this respect it has to be said. The English way to spell fonts is founts but like most computer words, as computers are mostly made and designed in the US, the American word fonts has crept into common usage.

What are Fonts?

Fonts are sets of characters with a particular and distinctive design. (Notice the difference between the text of this book and the chapter name, for example.) All fonts are referred to in two ways, firstly by a name, which makes it possible to distinguish one font from another and secondly by a size.

The Amiga disks contain several fonts on them and these are listed in Table 6.1 overleaf along with the sizes available. Figure 6.1, also overleaf, shows how some of these fonts look when applied in Notepad.

As you can see, font sizes are measured in *points*, with one point being said to be 1/72nd of an inch. So a font which is 72 point (usually written as 72pt) would be exactly an inch in height. By the same token, a font that is 36 point should be half an inch in height. The most common sizes of font are in the order of 10-12pt and this is the size of the text you are currently reading!

Font Name	Point Sizes Available
ruby	8, 12 and 15
opal	9 and 12
sapphire	14 and 19
diamond	12 and 20
garnet	9 and 16
emerald	17 and 20
topaz	11
Courier	11, 13, 15, 18 and 24
Helvetica	9, 11, 13, 15, 18, and 24
Times	11, 13, 15, 18 and 24

Table 6.1 Fonts and sizes on Workbench and Extras 1.3.

The standard default, or system font, used by the Amiga is called Topaz. It's size is 9, and so the system font is sometimes referred to as Topaz 9. Because this font is always needed by the Amiga to display text and messages it is held permanently in the Amiga's ROM and this means that it can be used without access to the Fonts directory held on the Workbench disk. In addition the Extras Disk (Workbench 1.3) contains quite a few extra fonts, namely various sizes of Courier, Helvetica and Times. These fonts and several new ones can be found on the AmigaFonts disk in Workbench 2.

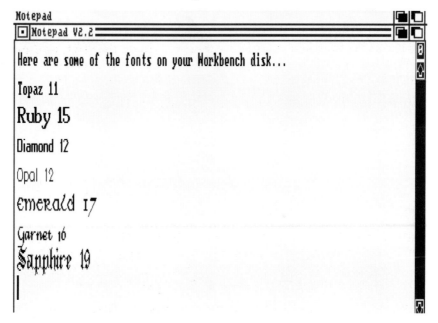

Figure 6.1. Examples of fonts.

These three fonts are possibly the most popular fonts in use around the world so you may find it useful to copy these onto your Workbench Disk. You may need to remove some other less-used fonts to do this. Alternatively, you can use them from the Extras Disk or copy them into the Ram Disk for use. More on this shortly.

The Courier font is different to the other fonts in that it is non-proportional or mono-spaced. This means that it uses the same amount of screen space to display all characters, in other words an *i* takes up as much space as an *m*. This can be advantageous when you wish to lay out columns or rows of text that need to line up below each other.

Font Storage

Fonts are normally stored in a Font directory and there is generally a file and a directory associated with each font. For example if you catalogue the Fonts directory on the Workbench 1.3 Extras disk (if you have Workbench 2 catalogue the AmigaFonts disk Fonts directory) you will find it holds the following files:

```
Courier (dir)

Helvetica (dir)

Times (dir)

Courier.font        Helvetica.font

Times.font
```

Each font is composed of two parts: a *.font* file associated with it which contains various bits of information about the font, and each font has a directory with it which contains the files for the different fonts themselves.

Displaying the Times font directory reveals the files:

```
11

13

15

18

24
```

and these are the font sizes available in the Times font. Each of these files contains the information for the shapes of each character you see on screen, and each file has to be different to appear the same shape at the various font sizes.

So Amiga fonts are easy to access on a disk, as they are just in a directory like any other. The fonts are organised which a directory called FONTS, within which are 1K files called, for example, topaz.font, sapphire.font and other sub-directories called by the name of the font, like topaz, sapphire etc. Inside these subdirectories are files named after the point size they represent: 11, 24, 18 and so on. So, the directory tree looks like this:

```
Fonts      (dir)
  Sapphire  (dir)
     9   10
     18  24
  Topaz     (dir)
     10  15
     24  48
  topaz.font sapphire.font
```

and so on for all the fonts you have on the disk. The files with the .font on the end are sort of headers which tell the system which font it is, what sizes are available and all that sort of info. The actual point size file in the subdirectory contains all the font information, the graphics of the letters themselves. The system knows where to find the fonts, as the pathname is specified using the ASSIGN command. The fonts directory has its own device name called FONTS:, and this can be called up to direct attention to the fonts in any application. If you want to use a fonts disk in another drive, all you have to do is:

ASSIGN FONTS: MyDisk:fonts

or something like that, replacing the word MyDisk with the name of the disk with the new fonts on. Obviously on a hard disk you can specify a new directory for the fonts, rather than another disk. This won't happen very often as the hard disk has space for just about all the fonts you will need. Then you'll be prompted to insert the volume (disk) you named and off you go, using the new fonts in your application.

The basic Amiga fonts are bitmap fonts, as I said just now, which means they are not scalable. (Unlike Compugraphic fonts, see Higher Resolution.) So you have to have the right size font on the disk, unless you want each letter to look like a small picture of an alligator. Like C directory commands and other utils, you can install any number of fonts on your disk or hard drive device, provided there is the room for them.

There are hundreds of font disks for sale in the private and public domain, and you can also define your own using any one of the PD font editors available. Most of these programs will store the font bits in their own little directories for you.

If you are clever and delete a number of useless files from your working copy of the Workbench, you will be able to copy all the fonts from the Extras disk onto the Workbench Fonts directory. If not, you can still use them. To be able to make use of the extra fonts, you must let the Amiga know where they are. Telling the Amiga to look elsewhere for fonts is done with the AmigaDOS ASSIGN command in a Shell like so:

```
ASSIGN FONTS: Extras 1.3:Fonts
```

Now the Amiga will look to the Extras Disk whenever it needs font information. However this does mean that the fonts on the normal Workbench disk are no longer available. The FONTS: device tells the Amiga where it can find fonts for use on the screen, so assigning it to a directory tells the Amiga where to look.

An alternative method is to copy all the fonts onto one disk (a hard disk is favourite) or simply into the Ram Disk. This following short script file would copy the three Extras disk fonts into the Ram Disk for use. The program could be extended to copy the Workbench Disk fonts as well, and be included as part of your startup-sequence in the S directory of your boot disk. Alternatively you could execute the file from the Shell using the Execute command:

```
MAKEDIR RAM:FONTS

MAKEDIR RAM:FONTS/Helvetica

MAKEDIR RAM:FONTS:Courier

MAKEDIR RAM:FONTS:Times

COPY FROM Extras 1.3:FONTS/#? TO RAM:FONTS

COPY FROM Extras1.3:FONTS/Helvetica/#? TO
RAM:FONTS/Helvetica

COPY FROM Extras1.3:FONTS/Times/#? TO
RAM:FONTS/Times

COPY FROM Extras1.3:FONTS/Courier/#? TO
RAM:FONTS/Courier

ASSIGN FONTS: RAM:Fonts
```

Now you will also find that font access is at least ten times faster as the font data is immediately available to the program from RAM, there being no time lost going through the physical process of reading the disk.

Other Sources

There are many ways you can supplement the number of fonts you have in your system, and these fall into two basic categories: commercial and PD. On the commercial side, you have a range of different options to choose from, including both regular single colour fonts and the new Colorfonts (note the American spelling), which are special eight colour fonts. The Colorfonts are mostly designed to simulate various materials like brick, metal or glass, and one of the chief examples of this type of font are the Karafonts range.

There are also a range of fonts in the public domain, fonts which have been designed by other users using font design utilities. My particular favourite is the one on the Metallion Utils disk (See Tricks With The System for details). Another one to look out for is the font called PenPal.font, which is a small font of slightly scribbly joined-up writing. There are many examples of this sort of thing, all you have to do is order a few PD catalogues from the ads in the Amiga-specific magazines.

Incidentally, following this line of thought there is a utility on Fish Disk 138 called MacFont which converts Mac fonts to Amiga, in case you're interested. If you have access to a Macintosh computer at work for example, you can convert the fonts to Amiga fonts using this program.

Installing a New Font

If you have a new font that you want to install on your Workbench disk or hard disk, then this is what you have to do.

If the font is archived in some way, unpack it using the arc, lharc, zip or zoo programs, whichever is appropriate. (See Comms and Modems Chapter 17 for more details about these archive programs.) You will be presented with the two elements of the font, the .font file and the files which go in the directory. So imagine you have a font which, for the sake of argument, we'll call Phil.font.

This is what you will have on disk:

```
Phil.font
8
10
24
```

Inside the FONTS directory on your boot device or disk you have a directory called fonts, in which is all the font data. You have to make a directory inside the fonts drawer to take the numbered point size files, in this case 8, 10 and 24. Simply type:

```
cd fonts:
makedir Phil
```

First you cd'd to the fonts directory making it the current directory. This means that every command you type from then applies to the fonts directory. Then you typed the MakeDir command, creating a subdirectory for you to copy the font files into.

Then you copy the files over from your disk containing the new font files. If the files were in df1: for example, you'd type:

```
copy 8 to fonts:Phil
```

This instruction copies the file called *8* into the Phil directory. Using *fonts:* instead of just *fonts* without the colon means that the Amiga will seek out the fonts directory wherever it is, rather than you having to type *df0:fonts* or something like that.

(Note: The reason you can do this with the fonts directory is that it has been Assigned. In the startup-sequence in your S directory the device FONTS: has been assigned to the fonts directory on your boot disk, so typing FONTS: at any time refers the computer to that directory right away. Assignments are always made to important directories like this. Read through your startup-sequence using a text editor or wordprocessor, and see if you can see what other devices have been created by the Assign command. In fact you can check the devices that have been created with the Shell, by typing Assign on its own. This gives you a handy list of what is assigned at the present time.)

Then copy the other files over to fonts too, with:

```
copy 10 to fonts:Phil
```

```
copy 24 to fonts:Phil
```

And finally copy the .font file over to the fonts dir with:

```
copy Phil.font to fonts:
```

and you're finished. Now, on any program which allows you to choose your font, you will get a requester up and among the choices will be a font called Phil. (Or whatever your font was called.)

Do 'Em Yourself

If the standard fonts you get with the Amiga start to bore you after a while, you can design your own fonts, using a program called FED on the Extras disk or any number of PD programs which do the same thing. Note FED is not supplied with Workbench 2 – but then you get a lot more fonts with it!

FED is a very simple program to use, and Figure 6.2 shows you the screen that you are presented with when you run the program.

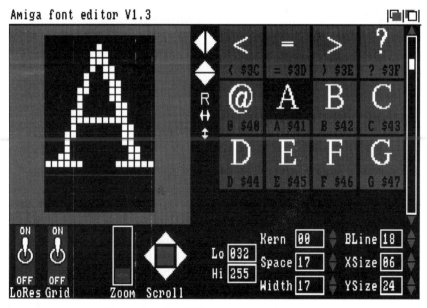

Figure 6.2. The FED program main screen.

To start with if you like a font but feel you'd like something different you can alter an already existing font, by loading it up and changing it. Or if you feel up to the design work involved, you can start from scratch. By and large it has to be said that the hassle of creating a new font isn't really worth it unless you really know you onions about design. Although FED is easy to use, it can't supply you with the necessary know-how of how a font fits together. Fun to play with, but try to find a font in the PD or commercial circles before you try to build your own.

Tricks with the System

There are a few interesting tricks that you can play on the system to get more interesting fonts on your screen and in all your programs. For example there is a way of altering the system font using a PD program called NewTopaz by a programmer called Metallion, which alters the system font, Topaz, to another shape. This means that all your text on the Workbench and programs is altered to the new font when you boot up. The program also features a font editor program and a sample of some of the fonts designed by Metallion himself.

The font editor is a bit simpler to use than FED, but the main strength of this program is its ability to tamper with the system's Topaz font, which you can't otherwise do. Metallion's Utilities disk is available from Amiganuts United. (See Chapter 20 for address details.)

Higher Resolution

The quality you get on the screen with bitmap fonts is superb, especially in higher resolutions. Okay for video applications but what about output? Well, this is not so hot, especially on higher resolution printers like lasers or inkjets.

The trick with the Amiga is that if you want better quality from your fonts, then you have several ways to go. AmigaTeX is one interesting way, as are the DTP alternatives, PageStream or Professional Page.

AmigaTeX (Radical Eye) is the Amiga version of the TeX (pronounced *tech* for some arcane reason) document processing language for mainframe computers. A document is prepared with special formatting commands embedded in the text file. Then it is fed into the processor and comes out as a perfectly typeset document. The fonts are contained on a multitude of disks, and cover all the major text groups. The pro of AmigaTeX is that it's usable on *any* printer, even a 9-pin Dot Matrix, up to a Postscript laser printer or imagesetter. The con is that it is a highly complex formatting language, and needs access to The TeX Book by Donald Knuth for you to learn it effectively.

Professional Page (Gold Disk) is the other option for high quality output. It too allows you you to run to more sophisticated printers, but not forgetting the low end 9-24 pin printers either. Pro Page 1.3 uses the Agfa Compugraphic scaled fonts to produce the highest quality output on any printer available, but only supplies two fonts. There are other Compugraphic fonts available for use with Pro Page and this is especially of interest to users or Workbench/Kickstart 2, as this supports the use of these special scalable fonts directly on the Workbench. This means that not only do you get a superb font on the screen at any size, but your output is antialiased and clean like the output from a DTP program.

Pagestream (Soft-Logik) also allows the use of scalable fonts, and the choices here are many fold. Pagestream allows you to use its own scalable fonts, or choose from Agfa Compugraphic, or even Postscript type 1 fonts. As a DTP program I prefer Pro Page myself, but like most things this is a matter of personal preference.

Colour Fonts

There is only one other type of font you need to know about as an Amiga user, the colour font. You need a special driver for these and this colour fonts usually comes on the disk or as a part of Deluxe Paint III or 4. ColorFonts are eight-colour fonts which look like textures or have shading on them. These are good for titling and other video applications, but usually look pretty poor when you use them in a DTP program. KaraFonts are a good set to start you off, but there are others around. Some Colorfonts are even animated, for special effects, and these are only for use with an animating paint program like DPaint III. The fonts move as they go onto the page, and are more what you'd call *anim brushes* like in the DPaint program.

Fonts are something you only have problems with on a few occasions, and choosing the right fonts for use in a bitmap drawing program like DPaint is tricky but not impossible. Shop around and see what is available in the public domain, and only then splash out for a commercial product if you can't avoid it, to get the job done.

Compugraphic Fonts

With the advent of System 2.0 you can add Compugraphic fonts to your Workbench, although quite why you would do this I'm not sure. At any rate the Fountain program is supplied for the conversion and installation of the fonts from CG to Amiga font format.

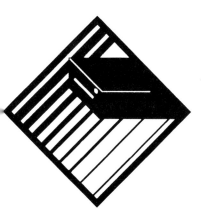

7:
Utilities
Drawer

The Utilities Drawer on your Workbench disk contains some very useful programs for you to use in your everyday dealings with the Amiga. This chapter gives you a quick guide to programs in the Utils Drawer, and a description of their various functions.

Some of the programs are to help your productivity, like the Calculator and the Clock, and others are more system orientated, like the More text reader. And don't forget, as the Amiga is a multitasking computer, they are at your disposal at all times. Just pull down the window you're working on (or click on the back and front gadget), open the Utils Drawer, and run the program you need.

Here is a roundup of what you find in the Utils Drawer.

Calculator

The calculator is just that, a calculator on screen that you can use like a normal pocket calculator. It works just like any other calculator, and to use it you can just click on the number buttons. Or by using the appropriate keys on the Amiga numeric keypad (to the right of the keyboard) you can tap in the numbers. To access the special functions such as CA (Clear All) from the keypad just press C and then A. The Return key functions as the = key.

So for example if you wanted to do 5+2 from the keypad, you would press the following keys in order:

5

+

2

Return

The CE key is a Clear Entry gadget and this allows you to delete the last entry you typed in, useful if you are tapping in a long list of numbers and type the wrong thing. So, if you meant to type 5*8 and actually entered 5*9 and you notice the mistake, you can type (or select) CE to remove the 9 and then carry on.

One key that isn't on calculators is the backspace or <- key. This allows individual characters to be removed from the currently typed number. So typing 1234567 and then typing a <- would remove the 7 from the number sequence. Hitting it again would remove the 6 and so on.

The +- key toggles the sign of the number, that's to say it changes it from a positive to negative value and vice versa each time you press the key.

Clock

This program displays a Clock on the Workbench. The clock can be run directly from the Workbench or CLI, and can also be made to display a digital clock, although when launched from the Workbench the clock automatically comes up in an analogue display. A Menu bar can be found at the top of the screen when the clock window is active. (You have to click on the window first.) This menu can be seen by moving the pointer up to the Menu Bar and holding down the right-hand mouse button.

There are five menus in all and these are summarised in Table 7.1 opposite.

Where menu options can be turned on and off, a tick is displayed next to the menu option that is currently active. The digital clock comes in two flavours. Digital 1 displays a two line window which displays the time on the top line. If the date option is on, then the date is displayed on the second line. If Digital 2 is invoked, then the time is displayed in a single line window. This is handy as it means that the clock can be moved onto the Menu Bar out of the way. If this option is in use and the date is turned on, then the date will be alternated with the time. This is rather annoying and I tend to avoid it. If an analogue clock is in use and the date is turned on, then it is placed under the clock at the bottom by the window.

Menu	Option	Details
Type		
	Analog	This gives you a clock with a face
	Digital 1	This gives you a digital clock
	Digital 2	another digital but smaller
Mode		
	12 Hour	This only affects the digital
	24 Hour	clocks, giving 12 or 24 hour readings
Seconds		
	Seconds On	This turns on the second hand or
	Seconds Off	if a digital clock, the seconds digits off
Date		
	Date On	This turns the date display
	Date Off	on or off
Alarm		
	Set	This sets the time you want the alarm to go
	Alarm On	and these two set the alarm on
	Alarm Off	or off as you wish

Table 7.1. The Clock menus.

Setting the alarm is straightforward. First select Set from the Alarm menu and a small window will appear. To set the hour click the pointer in the hour gadget box, ie over the hour counter. Use the up and down arrow gadgets to set the hour. Repeat the procedure with the minutes gadget and click on the AM/PM gadget to set the alarm for the appropriate half of the day. Select Use to set the Alarm. Selecting Cancel aborts the setting. Finally select Alarm On from the Alarm menu to enable the alarm. When the appropriate time arrives the screen will flash once and a high pitched noise will be produced on the speaker.

Clock From AmigaDOS

The clock can also be started from the Shell and, with the exception of the Alarm, all the functions mentioned above can be defined from the off. This is useful as it means that you can invoke the clock as part of your startup sequence, something that I generally do. The syntax of the command is:

```
clock [analog/dig][=<x>,<y>][,<w>,<h>][12/24][SECS][DATE]
```

As you can see all the options are optional and, if you omit any or all of the options, then the standard defaults will be used (these are the ones used when the clock is launched from the Workbench).

Most of the options are obvious. <x> and <y> determine where the clock is placed on the screen. <x> is the number of pixels from the left-hand side of the screen and <y> the number of pixels from the top of the screen. <width> and <height> determine the size of the box in which the analogue clock is to be displayed (these settings are ignored if an analogue clock is specified). When you enter this option there should be no space between the word *analog* and the equals sign. The default value is =10,15.

Try this example from the Shell (but close down any clocks that may be currently active before you do):

```
run clock digital2=350,0 12hour seconds
```

This places a single line digital clock on the top right-hand side of the screen. This fits nicely in the Workbench Menu Bar if it is active. The Clock Menu bar is now also available and can be used to change settings or set the alarm should you so wish.

ClockPtr

This program (not available in release 2) provides you with an on-screen digital clock on the pointer. This is a very clever little utility which changes into a digital display when you just need to just check the time. (Note: that this program will only work while the Workbench screen is active.)

To use it from the Workbench, just double-click on the ClockPtr icon to activate it, or to run it from the Shell just type:

```
run clockptr
```

Be sure to use the RUN command so that your Shell will remain active. Otherwise you will lock that shell. So use RUN, and the CLOCKPTR command will be run from its own CLI task.

To display the digital clock you should move the pointer outside a window onto the Workbench and click the mouse. To return the clock back to the more familiar pointer, move it into any window you like and click the mouse.

The clock will display the current time in hours and minutes. You can see the exact time in terms of seconds by moving the clock pointer to the very top left-hand corner of the Workbench screen. The display will change to show minutes and seconds. The current date can also be viewed by moving the clock pointer to the left-hand side of the screen, anywhere below the Menu Bar. The date is shown in the American format with the month given first, like this:

220

for example would mean February the 20th. The date and time will be read from the system clock which can be set using the SETCLOCK and DATE commands. (These are described in Chapter 4 and Appendix B.)

To turn the clock pointer off, simply double click on its icon in the Utilities drawer once again. If the program is being run from the Shell then simply enter the command:

BREAK n

where n is the number of the CLI process used for the command. This will have been displayed in the window after the RUN CLOCKPTR command was executed. For instance, a typical response would have been:

[CLI 2]

in which case the command:

BREAK 2

would terminate the program. If you cannot remember the task number then the AmigaDOS STATUS command can be used to list all currently active tasks.

CMD

CMD (pronounced CoMmanD and not *see-em-dee*) allows you to send all of your printer output to a file. This is called redirection and operates with parallel or serial printers. Why you'd want to do this isn't clear when you first begin to use computers, but you may need it some day, so here's what it does. If this gets a bit much for you just skip it. I've never used CMD, and can't see a reason to, so not knowing about it won't hurt you. But for the sake of completeness I'll tell you about it.

The program can be used from either the Shell or from the Workbench though the manner in which you use it is rather different. Let's look at its use from the Shell first. The format of the command is as follows:

CMD <Parallel/Serial> <Filename> [OPT s/m/n]

The device you wish to redirect must be specified in full as either Parallel or Serial and this will determine whether the information being sent to the PAR: or SER: devices are diverted. (Note: you can't just type PAR: or SER:, but the words *parallel* or *serial* only.)

<Filename> is the destination file which will be used to hold the data sent to the printer. It is standard procedure to use the filename CMD_File, to identify it as a product of a CMD redirection. If you are in doubt about what this command does, use the command and see what happens.

For details about how CMD works under version 2 of Workbench, see Chapter 3 which has all the differences from WB 2.

InstallPrinter

This program allows you to either install a new printer driver or to change an existing one. Full details on printers and printer driver use can be found in Chapter 16.

GraphicDump

This program dumps an image of the current screen to any printer you have attached to your Amiga. (The printer must be capable of producing a graphics image and so this program will not work with a Daisywheel type printer.) Because it can take time shuffling through Workbench windows, and for use of the program from the CLI, there is a ten second delay before the program takes a picture of the uppermost screen and prints it. This will give you time to re-arrange and position windows accordingly.

From the Shell the format of the command is:

```
GraphicDump [option/xdots:ydots]
```

As you can see, two sets of parameters are optional. [option] determines the size of the screen dump and these possibilities are given in Table 7.2.

Option	Result
TINY	Dump width is about 25% of that allowed by printer
SMALL	Dump width is about 50% of that allowed by the printer
MEDIUM	Dump width is about 75% of that allowed by the printer
LARGE	Dump width is 100% of that allowed by the printer
xdots:ydots	User definable printer size dump in absolute dots

Table 7.2. The GraphicDump options.

To enable the named options to work the Limits setting in Preferences must be set to Ignore. This is the default option so unless you have changed it for some reason you shouldn't have to do anything. If no option is specified the LARGE setting is used as a default.

Here are a few examples of use of the command:

```
GRAPHICDUMP TINY

GRAPHICDUMP MEDIUM

GRAPHICDUMP 320:100
```

In the last example, the size of the dump is specified in terms of the number of dots in each direction. In this case the resulting image dumped to the printer will be 320 dots wide by 100 dots in height.

From the Workbench the GraphicDump can be run by double clicking on the icon. After the ten second delay the screen dump will commence. By default the LARGE option is used.

More

More is a program that you may have already used several times without knowing, especially if you have been reading README files supplied with some applications programs or PD disks. If you haven't then a little explanation is in order.

More is an ASCII text file display program. That's a bit of a mouthful, but this just means that it allows text files (such as those created in ED, EDIT or some kind of word processor or text editor) to be displayed on-screen in a window. As with the other Utility Drawer programs, More can be run from the Workbench or from the Shell.

Double click on the More icon to launch the program from the Workbench. A window will appear on screen displaying various bits of information and ending with a prompt like this:

```
Enter filename or <Return> to exit

Filename?
```

If you press Return the program will terminate. If you enter the name of a suitable text file, including the device or path name, then the file will be loaded and you can read it. Use the startup-sequence file if you like, by typing:

```
s:startup-sequence
```

at the prompt. When you press Return at the end of the filename, More will locate the file and display it in the window. It is quite likely that the file will be too long to fit into the window, and if this is the case More goes into a page mode. It displays the first window (page) full of text and then stops. An inverted prompt appears at the base of the screen which looks like this:

```
More (86%)
```

This informs you that there is more text to see and that the program has so far displayed 86% of the text. To display the rest of the text press the Space key. The next page of text will be displayed, and so on until the prompt at the base of the screen changes to:

```
End of File
```

Of course if you have extended your startup-sequence file radically it may be too long to fit on two pages of the More window, in which case you will be presented with extra pages of text as appropriate to display the whole file.

If the text file you wish to display has an icon, you can tell More to operate on it directly from the Workbench. You do this by clicking on the More icon, holding down the SHIFT key, and then double clicking on the text icon you want to read.

Running More from the CLI is even simpler and the command to do is simply:

```
More <filename>
```

where <filename> is the name of the text file you wish to display.

More Commands

More has a number of key commands that it recognises which become useful when you are using it in conjunction with long text files. These are listed in Table 7.3.

Command	Effect
<SPACE>	Display next page of text
<BACKSPACE>	Display previous page of text
<RETURN>	Display next line of text
<	Display first page of text
>	Display last page of text
%n	Display from a point approx n% into the file
<CTRL-L>	Refresh display
/<string>	Search for <string> case sensitive
.<string>	Search for <string> non-case sensitive
n	Find next occurrence of the string
h	Display on-line help
q	Quit
<CTRL-C>	Quit
E	Edit using editor set in ENV:EDITOR

Table 7.3. More commands.

PrintFiles

This utility program provides a most convenient way of sending a series of files to the printer for printing. And it can be used from the Workbench or CLI. Taking the Shell for example, the syntax is:

```
printfiles [-f] <filename> [-f] [<filename>]
```

The <filename> part is the name of the file to be printed and this should include any directory path, like df0:etc, for safety. Any number of files can be specified and to make life easy it is generally best to place them all into the same directory.

The -f parameter is totally optional and puts the system into form feed mode. If this is placed before the filename then a form feed (or *paper eject*) will be made between each file, ensuring that each new file starts on a new sheet.

The program is very clever in that, if a file cannot be located, (either it doesn't exist or perhaps the wrong path has been supplied) it simply ignores it and moves onto the next file you told it to look for.

Now from the Workbench, you should first select the files you wish to print. To enable this to take place they must obviously have icons. (If they do not then the Shell will have to be used.) Assuming icons are available, select the first document to be printed. Then press and hold down the Shift key and select the additional icons to be printed. When all the files for printing have been selected, keep the Shift key depressed and double-click on the PrintFiles icon to start printing.

If you wish to use the formfeed *f* option then, before selecting the icons for printing, you should set the PrintFiles Tool Type box in Info. (See Chapters 2 and 9 for details about icons and tool types and the Info program.) It should read:

```
FLAGS=formfeed
```

select the Save gadget and then proceed. There are simpler ways of printing out, and with more control, like text editors and Word Processors. But as a quick'n'dirty way of printing out files, this is very easy to use.

Say

The Say icon provides a demo of the Amiga's Speech device and SAY command which is described in more detail in Chapter 11. When you run the Say program from the Workbench, two windows are displayed. The top one is called the Phoneme window, and the bottom window is called the Input window. The Phoneme window contains some instructions outlining the various options available to you. Type the following at the keyboard:

Mastering Amiga Beginners

Press Return and the Speech device will respond by saying the words you typed. (Turn the volume up!)

In the Phoneme window the following gibberish will have appeared:

MAE4STERIHNX AHMIY3GAH BIXGIH4NERZ

These are the phonemes that the Amiga actually passes to the Speech device to make the text sound more like the real thing. *Phonemes* are basic building blocks of speech, and although you can type the raw phonemes into the Amiga, it can translate normal English into speech. More about this can be found in Chapter 11, Making your Amiga Speak.

The Input window is in fact a Shell window, so press the up-arrow key to display the text once again, and press Return to execute the speech again. Its a good idea whenever you are entering text to the Say input window to try to write it phonetically, as it usually sounds better. Here is a short list of some words which you might like to try:

Why	Y
You	U
Are	R
Two	2
High	Hi
Low	Lo
See	c

You can probably think of some more yourself, but experiment for the best combinations.

Table 7.4 lists the options available from the Phoneme window and these all function as described in detail in Chapter 11.

Option	Effect
Option	*Effect*
-m	Male voice
-f	Female voice
-r	Robot voice
-n	Natural voice
-s##	Speed where ## is 40-400
-p##	Pitch where ## is 65-320
x <filename>	Where <filename> is a text file

Table 7.4. Phoneme options.

Pressing the Return key on a blank line quits the program and closes the two windows.

Notepad

Notepad (which is not available with Workbench 2) is a text tool which can be used for most document editing tasks. What it isn't, and doesn't pretend to be, is a fully-featured word processor, and it shouldn't be seen as one. If however you only use it for letters and similar small documents, then the notepad will be okay.

Notepad takes a little longer than most other tools to load, as one of the first things it does when it runs is look for the Amiga fonts directory and these can be used within Notepad. As it does this the following message will be displayed across the top of the Workbench screen in the menu bar:

        Notepad is Looking for Fonts

The process normally means searching for the current boot disk, your Workbench Disk usually, and then checking in the FONTS: directory to see what fonts are available for use. The subject of fonts is discussed more fully in Chapter 6.

When all this has taken place, the Notepad window is put up on screen. This is rather smaller than you would normally need for anything other than notes and will need re-sizing. Just grab the re-sizing gadget with the pointer and drag it down to make the window larger.

If you are not going to be taking advantage of the various Amiga fonts in your Notepad documents then the searching and loading process is a rather redundant procedure. You can stop it by entering the following into the Notepad Tool Types box using the Info program from the Workbench menu. Click in the tool types box and type:

        FLAGS=nofonts

Then when you boot the Notepad by clicking the icon, the standard system font (Topaz) is used, which is the default font.

Using Notepad

The best way to learn to use Notepad is to experiment. You should be familiar with the way in which Amiga menus work and the five menus that Notepad has associated with it offer a wide choice of options all of which are pretty self-explanatory.

To use Notepad just make it the active window, by clicking in it with the pointer, and start typing. The vertical black bar is the cursor and its position determines where each new character will be typed on the screen as you type it on the keyboard. Try entering this:

        Mastering Amiga Beginners

        The Indispensable Guide

You start the second line by pressing the Return key at the end of the first. Notepad is an inserting editor, and this means that if you position the cursor within one of the words in the text and start typing, the text to the right of the cursor will be shuffled up to make room for it. (This is the reverse of an overwriting editor, which simply erases the text by writing over it as you type.)

To position the cursor you can either move it up, down, left and right using the cursor keys, or more easily by clicking the mouse pointer at the point you wish the cursor to be positioned. For example, click the pointer to the immediate right of the word Amiga to place the cursor before the B in Beginners, and then type a dash -. The line will shuffle along to the right to give:

`Mastering Amiga - Beginners`

If you make a mistake then you can use the Del key to erase characters to the left of the cursor position.

This piece of text can now be saved. The Notepad Project menu contains the option Save, and this should be selected. (There is a quick-key short cut to this, Amiga-Amiga-S, and this has the same result. A requester appears, and you can insert the desired filename into the string box, by clicking in it and typing a filename like:

`RAM:Test`

You can press Return or click on the OK gadget. If you wish to abort the operation, click on the Cancel gadget. If you open the RAM Disk window you will see that the file has been saved to the Ram Disk with a special Notepad icon, which looks like a little page of text.

Add another line of text to the base of what you have done already:

`For all serious Amiga users!`

Now select save again. Nothing happens...well, in fact nothing *appears* to happen. In actual fact Notepad has re-saved the file using the RAM:Test filename you gave to it a moment ago. It remembers the filename. If you had saved this file to floppy disk rather than to the Ram Disk then you would have noticed some disk activity at this point.

Close the Notepad window by clicking on the close gadget. Now re-open the file by double-clicking on the Test file icon. This will automatically load Notepad once again and also load the text. In addition it also remembers both the size and position of the Notepad window when you last saved it and will size and position it accordingly. (The reason that the Notepad text knows to run Notepad again is that the default tool says Notepad. This was set when you saved the file. Clever, eh?)

The Save As option under the Save option on the Project menu allows you to do two things:

• Save a backup copy of the current file to another disk

• Change the filename if you want to keep your original file

When you select this option you go through the same procedure as for a Save operation. However, a new copy of the current Notepad contents are saved, leaving any previous saved copy intact and unaltered.

(Note: It is up to you to remember to ensure that you save the latest copy of your text before closing a Notepad window. Notepad does not provide any safety net for you, ie it doesn't ask you if you want to save your changes. If you close your window and have not saved any changes these will be lost. The moral of this story is ensure that you always perform a Save before closing a window, as the program might not be clever enough to rescue your work from destruction!)

Notepad Fonts

The Fonts menu will contain a list of the fonts that Notepad was able to find when you ran the program. If you specified NOFONTS in the Tool Types box then only Topaz will be present. However, you can ask Notepad to look for the fonts by selecting the Read Fonts option on the Project menu. Any fonts located in the fonts directory will then be listed in the Fonts menu the next time you look at it.

If you move the pointer slowly down through the font options on the menu you will notice that a few sub-menus are displayed. These menus list the various point sizes in which the font is available. (See Chapter 6 for a description of fonts and point sizes.)

By default, fonts affect the contents of the Notepad globally, that is to say all the text changes to the selected font. Select Ruby and 15 from the menu, and all the text in the current Notepad window will change to Ruby 15. However, if you look at the Format menu you will see a Global Fonts option. This gadget is normally ticked, to indicate that it is selected. If you select this the tick will be missing from the menu, and now fonts will not have a global effect. With the Ruby 15 font in use, move the cursor to the second line of text and select Opal and 9 from the menu.

Now only the text from the cursor position is changed to this font. The line of text above remains in the Ruby 15 face. Move the cursor to the third line and position it just to the left of the word Amiga. Now select Sapphire and 19. Only the words to the right of the cursor change to the new font. The point to remember then is that, with global fonts disabled, font changes affect all text *after* the cursor position. If you remember that you can't go far wrong.

If you want to reset the contents of a Notepad window to a single font then you should place the cursor at the start of text and select a new font. An alternative quicker method is to select Remove Fonts from the Format menu. This resets the font globally to the first font used in the text.

In addition to allowing you to specify the font in which text is displayed, Notepad also allows you to select the style of the text. Styles affect the way in which the text is displayed, and the Notepad Style menu offers five styles, these are: Plain, *Italic,* **Bold,** Underline, and NONE

The effect of each of these selections should be obvious. Text style is applied in a similar fashion to fonts. Position the cursor at the point you wish the effect to start and then select the style from the Style menu. The style is then applied to all of the text from the point of the cursor. Place the cursor at the point where you wish to stop the effect and then select Plain from the Style menu. Consider the following line of text: This is underlined now with italic. This is now plain.

The NONE option allows you to turn a single style off without affecting any others that might follow it. For example to turn only underlining off, place the cursor at the start of the text and select NONE. Italics remains active.

Moving Text

Notepad's Edit menu provides a number of facilities which will allow you to manipulate blocks of text. A block of text can be of any length, ranging from a single character to multiple paragraphs. There are three basic operations which you can carry out on a block of text:

Cut	Remove a block of text
Copy	Make a copy of a block of text
Paste	Insert a block of text previously cut or copied

Cut and copy are invariably used in conjunction with Paste, although Cut will occasionally be used by itself to simply remove a block of text. When text is cut or copied it is placed into a special area of memory or buffer, called the clipboard, and when text is pasted it uses the text in the clipboard. In this way text can be transferred or copied from one part of a Notepad file to another.

To enable text to be cut or copied it must first be marked and this is easy to do. Double click the pointer at the start of the text block. This will place a small orange block on screen at this point. Repeat the process at the end of the block. The block of text bounded by the markers is highlighted in orange. If you now select Copy, a copy of the marked text will be transferred to the clipboard. To paste the clipboard contents into Notepad, first place the cursor at the point where the text is to be pasted and then select Paste from the Edit menu. You use cut in an identical fashion.

If you accidentally mark the wrong section of text then the markers can be removed by selecting Cancel from the Edit menu. When text is copied and cut, it also takes with it any of the style attributes assigned to it. Style attributes which have been inserted within the block (ie after the first character or word of the block) will take effect and be applied to all the text following or at least up until the next style change. Text before any such changes will take on the style and font of the preceding text.

Equally, if you are cutting a section of text which contains embedded style changes these will be removed from that particular area leaving the text to revert to any previously assigned styles. Bear this in mind as this could have a drastic knock-on effect. As a matter of course it is always best to perform a save before you make any drastic block alterations, just in case it goes wrong. Then you can always re-load and start again from the point prior to the operation.

An alternative way to mark text is to use the Mark place option which can be found on the Notepad Edit menu. Place the cursor at the start of the point you wish to mark, and select Mark place. Move the cursor to the end of the text to be marked and repeat the process.

If you have marked a section of text and change your mind then you can clear the marked area by selecting the Cancel option from the Edit menu. However, remember that Cancel only affects the text from the cursor position so you may need to re-position it prior to cancelling.

Tabbing

If you are entering text that needs to be arranged in a tabular format, using the tab key can speed things up. The tab key is pre-set so that each tab stop is eight characters from the previous one. Thus pressing the tab key once will position the cursor eight characters in from the left-hand edge of the Notepad window. Pressing it again will move it a further eight characters in, ie 16 in total from the left-hand edge of Notepad, and so on.

Find and Replace

The Edit menu also provides some useful tools for locating and, if required, replacing words or phrases, in Notepad text. The options all centre around Find. If you select this you will be presented with a small string gadget dialogue box. The orange cursor will be positioned in the first gadget box and it is here that you should type the word or words that you are trying to locate. Note that the find routine is case sensitive so you must be sure to use the correct mix of upper and lower case letters. Press Return and the cursor will move into the Replace gadget box. Here you can enter any replacement text. There are three button gadgets below this. Cancel terminates what you are doing. Next will search for your Find string in a forward direction from the cursor position and Prev will search backwards, ie from the current cursor position to towards the start of the document. If the Find word or text is found then the cursor will be positioned at the start of it. Nothing more will happen at this point.

If you wish to replace the found text with the replacement text then select Replace from the Edit menu. This will delete the text located with Find and substitute the Next text. If you then wish to seek out the next occurrence of the text for possible replacement then select the Find Next or Find Prev option as appropriate.

Notepad Pages

So far we have concerned ourselves with just the front page of Notepad. This in itself can hold a good deal of text but it is just one of ten pages of *paper* which can be used. The current page number is always displayed in the top right-hand corner of the Notepad window just above the up-arrow gadget. To change to a new Notepad page all you have to do is to click on the very bottom left-hand corner of the Notepad window, which is represented by an icon of a page with its edge turned over. This will then move you onto page 1 of Notepad and the page number has changed accordingly. Moving onto new pages is done in the same manner, and there are ten in all numbered 0 to 9. To move back a page you click on the current page number.

There is a limit on the number of lines on each Notepad page, and the exact number will depend on the size of the font you are using. With the standard default font you should be able to fit in the order of 160 lines on the page, and this number will decrease as you use bigger font sizes.

Short-Cuts

You may have noticed already that the Notepad provides a number of hot-key short cuts to its various options. These can be quite time-saving and as there are not that many you will probably pick them up quite quickly if you wish to dispense with the services of the menu options. As with most other hot-key short cuts you will be required to press Amiga key and then the other specified key to emulate the menu option in question.

Printing

Printing from Notepad is not at all complicated assuming that you already have your Printer driver installed, have edited Preferences accordingly and are all switched on. If you have not already installed a printer driver then you will need to do so. (Full details on how to do this can be found in Chapter 16.)

Notepad offers two forms of printing which are defined in the Project menu under the heading of Print As. When this option is selected you are presented with a further sub-menu which provides three further sub-heads, namely: Graphic, Draft, and Form-feeds

For the purpose of proof-reading your text it is best to select the Draft mode of operating. Then you print, your text will be printed as plain text using the printer's system font. When you wish to print out in a final form and take advantage of any fonts and styles that you have used in the text then select Graphic. The final option Form-feeds will eject the paper from your printer at the bottom of each page, which can be important if your text spreads over several Notepad pages. Depending on how your printer is itself configured, this may or may not be required. It is best to try out printing with this option on and then off to see what best suits your printer configurations.

Once you have selected the print mode you are ready to print. This is done by selecting Print from the Project menu. This provides four further options as follows: Auto size, Small, Medium and Large.

These options are really only relevant if you have the graphics print mode enabled. The Auto size option will try to print out the contents of the Notepad at roughly the size you see them on screen; the Small option produces a printout at about 25% of the width of the paper, while Large will try to use the full width. Medium fits in between the two. Again it is worth having trial runs using each option so that you can get a feel for what their corresponding output is.

Notepad Defaults

I mentioned earlier that one way of saving your favourite Notepad setup is to save a dummy file. However you can use the Notepad Info box to configure these items more permanently. To do this quit Notepad, select the Notepad icon and then select Info from the Workbench menu.

To define a new position for the Notepad window you use the Tool Types string gadget and set the new position using the WINDOWS tool type. For instance, I prefer to have a wide Notepad window across the base of the screen. To configure this as the default click on ADD and then enter:

> WINDOWS=015,125,500,125

These numbers define the position of the window on screen as measured in pixels. They correspond as follows: 015 Left edge of Notepad, ie 15 pixels in. 125 Top edge of window from top of screen. 500 Width of Notepad window. 125 Depth of Notepad window. Select the Save button and then re-launch Notepad. At first the Notepad window is displayed in its normal default position but should then relocate to the new position within a few moments.

It is also possible to select the default font used by Notepad. To do this you must use the FONTS tool type. Select Notepad info once again and then click on the ADD gadget and type:

> FONTS=ruby.12

and click on Save. This will make the Ruby 12 point font the default font. You can, of course, specify any font and size you wish.

There are a few other items that can also be configured as default and these can be added to the Notepad Tool Types as you wish. They are listed below.

> FLAGS=draft

This sets the Print As menu option to draft as default. It is normally set to Graphic.

> FLAGS=formfeed

This selects the form-feed option by default.

> FLAGS=global

Selects the Global fonts option as a default.

> FLAGS=local

De-selects the Global fonts option so that it is not enabled by default.

FLAGS=nowrap

Disables the wordwrap option as a default.

Summary

So that's the Utilities drawer. Although there are many Public Domain programs which do better jobs of the various tasks covered by the utils drawer, the ones in Utils are *free,* so you can play with them until you get something better.

8:
State Your
Preferences

One of the best things about the Amiga's graphic interface is that it can be readily customised to suit your taste, and not just twiddled to be compatible with whatever peripherals you might have. All this customisation is done using a program in your Prefs drawer called Preferences. If you have a machine running Workbench 2 then the method for running and using Preferences is very different, so please consult Chapter 3 on Workbench 2.

Preferences provides a suite of easy to use tools to allow you to customise the way in which your Amiga looks and works. Using Preferences, you can configure how your computer looks when it starts up, and after that each time you switch it on or re-boot using the CTRL-A-A warm start. The configuration is saved to your Workbench Disk *devs* directory as a file called *system-configuration*, which the Amiga then refers to each time it boots. This is automatic, and although you can put system configuration on a disk in the root directory (if there is no devs directory on the disk), if there is a devs directory then the Amiga will look in there first. You don't have to configure the Amiga to this, as the means to look for and load the Preferences has been coded permanently into the system software.

You can change your Prefs settings as many times as you like to suit your needs, and even your ever-changing moods, and you could even have a variety of

Workbench Disks, all configured in different ways to suit a number of different environments, acting as a kind of colour coding so you know which Workbench you have in your system at a glance. The Prefs Drawer contains a number of interesting icons, all looking equally important, but let's concentrate on the program called Preferences itself. Double-click on its icon and the Preferences program will be launched. Through its screen control panel, Preferences allows you to define a number of different settings, and these are:

Reset All

This button gadget is the ultimate safety net. If you click on this button it will restore all of the Preference Tools' original ROM settings, which are held internally and can be recalled at any time. (Note: these are the manufacturer's settings and may contain some settings not compatible with your setup.) So this means that you can play around as much as you like with the settings on Prefs, as you can always get the original settings back.

Last Saved

This restores Preference Tool settings in much the same way as Reset All. The difference is that the settings used are the set that were last saved to disk. (Obviously this option is only relevant once you have saved new settings to disk.) So this undoes everything you've tinkered with in your current session on the computer.

Date and Time

Immediately below the Last Saved option are the date and time gadgets. If you have a real time, battery-backed clock fitted and this is already set, then chances are that the date and time displayed will be accurate. If not you can change the time and date here, using the up and down arrowhead gadgets. Before the date, month, year or time can be set, you must first select the item you wish to change by clicking on it. To change the month, click on the month, and as you do this you should see a white box flash over the month gadget. The month item is now selected, and so you can alter it by pressing on the up or down arrow head gadgets. The date, year, hour and minute gadgets are altered in exactly the same way.

Change Serial

This gadget takes you to a further Prefs menu, which enables you to define the way the Amiga's serial interface, the RS232 socket at the back of the machine (usually used for serial printers or connection to the phone via modem) is accessed. We'll talk about this in detail in a moment.

Text

This is a simple choice between 60 or 80 column text. This specifies the number of characters displayed on a line of the screen. 60 character screens are good for Amigas which are running through a TV set, as the characters are larger and less prone to be too fuzzy to read. The usual setting is for 80 characters per line, as this gives the maximum amount of text per line viewable on a monitor.

Key Repeat Delay

This is a slider gadget, meaning you move it by dragging the slider (in this case the white spot) either left towards *Short*, or to the right towards *Long*. This sets the length of delay until a key is repeated, if you keep the key pressed. The shorter the delay the quicker the key press is repeated. (Note: setting the delay to the shortest period makes the keyboard almost unusable. You can try this just for fun if you like!)

Key Repeat Speed

This makes the keys on the keyboard repeat much more quickly. Drag the slider gadget towards *Fast* to increase the repeat speed and towards *Slow* to decrease the speed.

Workbench Interlace

This gadget should generally be set to off. However, if you have a multisync monitor and trademark you can take advantage of the interlace mode on your Workbench, which offers a higher screen resolution screen by doubling the number of lines. This means you can fit more on the screen, giving you access to more icons and bigger windows. If you only have the standard Philips or Commodore monitors, then forget using this mode.

Mouse Speed

This gadget runs vertically with boxes numbered 1, 2 and 4. This allows you to set how far you have to move the mouse across the desk to move the mouse pointer across the screen. Set to 1 if you wish to keep your mouse movements to an absolute minimum. (It's a bit like gears on a bike, really.)

Double-Click Delay

This slider gadget allows you to set the length of time that can separate a double-click from two single clicks. Drag the slider up to increase the length of time between clicks. In this way a double-click can be two leisurely single clicks. Alternatively, dragging the slider down decreases the delay and means that the two clicks have to be pressed very rapidly in quick succession to be recognised as a double-click.

Display Centring

The large rectangle in the centre of the screen, containing the small right-angled gadget, can be used to centre the display on the monitor. This is done by clicking on and dragging the angled gadget until the screen is centred to your satisfaction. As you move the gadget, the whole screen moves around, so you can accurately match the corners of the Amiga screen to the corners of your monitor screen.

Colour Palette

The Workbench colour palette at the base of the Preferences Tool allows the Workbench colours to be changed. The 4096 colours of the Amiga palette are defined in terms of Red, Green and Blue, and this is what the R, G and B sliders are for. Dragging these in either direction and in various combinations mixes the colours that make up the Workbench. The four boxes of blue, white, black and orange can be selected to select which colour the sliders are altering. Clicking on *Reset Colours* will reset them to the default Workbench settings. You will spend a lot of time changing the colours on your Workbench when you first get your computer, as this is one of the most novel and addictive customisation processes on the Amiga. You will gradually settle on a colour scheme that appeals to you. My screens are all a sort of blueish grey, which is much easier on the eyes than the garish purples and pinks that I used to change them to!

Change Printer

This option allows you to alter your printer configuration, and this is gone into in a bit more detail later on in this chapter.

Edit Pointer

This option allows you to edit the on-screen pointer, and again this is discussed in more detail in a moment.

Cancel

If you make changes and then change your mind, click on this gadget to cancel the changes you made. The Preferences Tool will be closed, and none of the changes you made are saved to disk.

Save

Selecting this gadget saves the changes to disk and quits the Prefs program. There is no need to re-boot the computer to see the changes, as they are made right away. The Preferences Tool is then closed, while the changes are saved to disk.

Use

This gadget closes the Preference Tool and effects any changes that have been made. It doesn't however save the changes to disk, and so the changes are only made to the computer until it is switched off, or a new set of preferences are set using the Prefs program a second time.

Other Preferences

The Prefs drawer contains several other icons and these allow direct access to three of the items mentioned briefly above in the description of the Preferences Tool. They are the Printer, Serial and Pointer icons, and they cut-out the need to first have to open the Preferences Tool to use them. In addition there is CopyPrefs, which enables you to make backup copies of your current Preference settings to extra disks if you wish to ensure continuity across your range of working environments. The Serial and Pointer icons are discussed below, while Chapter 16 contains a complete guide to installing a printer for use on your Amiga.

The Serial Tool

You get to the Serial Tool by double-clicking the icon in the prefs drawer. (You can also get to it from inside the Prefs program itself.) The Serial Tool allows you to define how information is sent to and read from the Amiga's serial connector. Although this can be important when it comes to *communications* or *comms*, accessing a bulletin board using a modem connected to the phone line, mostly these settings are dealt with by the terminal program you use to drive the modem. Where the settings in the serial tool are important is if you intend to use a serial printer. Communications are covered in Chapter 17, which outlines several of the terms used here, and printers are covered in Chapter 16. Anyway, for your information here is what it all means, simply put.

Baud Rate: Pronounced *bawd* or *bowd*, this determines the number of bits that are transferred through the serial interface in one second. The default setting for this is 9600 baud, ie 9600 bits per second (bps) and this equates to about 1200 text characters per second. Fast, huh? The up and down arrow gadgets on the tool can be used to change the setting to another baud rate. There are eight possible values and these can be cycled through simply by pressing either of the gadgets. The eight baud rate settings are: 31250, 19200, 9600, 4800, 2400, 1200, 300, and 110. (Note: the fastest normal modems you can get only go up to 9600, but MIDI interfaces use the fastest setting of 31250!)

Buffer Size: The serial buffer is an area of reserved memory in which data is placed prior to being transmitted or after having been received. By default this is set to 512 bytes. The buffer size can be increased or decreased by using the arrow head gadgets accordingly. There are six possible buffer sizes as follows: 512 bytes, 1024 bytes, 2048 bytes, 4096 bytes, 8000 bytes, and 16000 bytes. The advantage of using a large buffer is that the serial data can be stored in memory, which is quicker than having to read or write it to disk every few hundred characters. Of course any incoming data may need to be copied to disk at the end of the serial transfer. This buffer is usually set by the modem or terminal software, anyway.

Read Bits: Each character that is received via the serial connector is composed of a number of bits, normally it will be either seven-bit characters or eight-bit characters.

Write Bits: Each character that is transmitted via the serial connector is composed of a number of bits, normally it will be either seven-bit characters or eight-bit characters.

Stop Bits: A stop bit is used to signify the end of a character that is either being transmitted or received via the serial connector. There are normally one or two stop bits added onto the end of the character.

Parity: Parity checking is a method by which software can detect if there has been an error in serial transmission. Parity may be either Even or Odd or it may not be enforced.

Handshaking: When two systems are in communication with one another via a serial connection, then there must be a system whereby one can inform the other that it has finished what it is doing. For example, when receiving data, one Amiga may wish to inform the other not to send any more data as its buffer is full. Then it might want to signal that it is ready for more data. This mode of signalling is generally called *handshaking*, and the mind picture of what goes on is quite clear I think. Handshaking can be XON/XOFF or RTS/CTS, or in fact none. This gadget allows the mode of handshaking to be selected.

Cancel: Quel Surprise! This gadget closes the Serial Tool without saving any changes you might have made. Note that you do not exit back to the Workbench but go to the Preferences Tool.

Save: This gadget saves any changes you made and closes the Serial Tool. (Note: You do not exit back to the Workbench but go back to the Preferences Tool.)

Pointer Tool

The Pointer Tool allows you to custom design your own pointers. This is done by using the pointer editor, and double-clicking on the Pointer icon brings up the Pointer Editing Window. (You can also get to this window by clicking on the Edit pointer button in the Prefs program itself.)

The editor gives a magnified view of the Pointer, showing exactly how it is constructed of small square points on the screen, which as we know are called *pixels*. The image itself is surrounded by a number of button and slider gadgets.

Restore: This is the safety net or panic button, and allows you to restore the pointer you had before, should you decide you don't like what you've done and want to start from scratch again.

Clear: This removes the current contents of the Pointer Editing Window, clearing the way for you to start from scratch.

ResetColor: This button resets the pointer colours to their original values. (Note: The four pointer colours can be completely different to the Workbench colours!)

Set Point: Every pointer has a single pixel which is called the Point. This is a special pixel which is used as the *hot spot* of the pointer. This is what you click on an icon you are selecting when the mouse button is pressed. It is displayed on the Pointer Editing Window as a small square inside a standard pixel. This gadget allows you to set the Point. To do this click on Set Point and then click where you want it in the Pointer Editing Window to define it. (Note: it's a good idea to put the point at the corner of a pointer design, as this makes it easier to use. Sounds obvious, but you'd be surprised how many people bury it away in a huge icon, then wonder why they can't click on anything accurately enough.)

The sliders across the base of the screen allow the red, white and blue components of the pointer colour to be set. The four colour bars across the sliders can be used to give you the correct setting for any of the four base colours displayed. ResetColor restores any changes you may make here.

To alter the points in the Pointer Editing Window first select the colour you want to use, clicking on any of the four colour gadgets and mixing using the RGB sliders. Using the mouse, position the pointer on the editing window and click to place a pixel in the desired position. If you make a mistake simply erase the point by drawing over it in the background colour (normally blue but of course it may be a different by now!).

The four boxes down the right side of the Pointer Editing Window provide you with different coloured backgrounds, to give you an indication as to how your new design will look against the other screen colours.

The OK and Cancel buttons have the effect you would expect, of either saving the new changes to disk or exiting without saving. In either case you don't return directly to the Workbench screen but to the Preferences Tool. (Note: Remember to use Save to exit here if you have made any changes you wish to keep.)

CopyPrefs

This Workbench tool allows you to copy your current Preference settings to other disks. (This is for use on systems which require a boot disk or boot partition on a hard disk. If your system Autoboots, then there is no need to copy the Prefs settings.) To make a copy, insert the disk to receive the new copy into the internal drive and double click on the CopyPrefs icon and the system-configuration file is copied to the devs directory. CopyPrefs moves a copy of the file from the Devs directory on the Workbench Disk to the new disk. For this reason be sure that a Devs directory exists on the destination disk prior to copying.

Preferences and the CLI

Preferences can be run from the CLI. One of three options can follow the command which specifies the Preference window you wish to open. The format of the command is:

```
preferences [pointer/printer/serial]
```

so if you type:

```
preferences printer
```

the program will open the Printer Preferences window. The command Preferences on its own will open the standard preferences window as if you had opened the icon from the Workbench.

9:
Making
Icons

On almost every Amiga disk you come across you find the Workbench has icons representing programs on the disk. We know that when you click on the icon with the mouse pointer you launch (or in other words run) the program the icon represents. We also know that icons are seen on the disk from the Shell as files ending in *.info*. So the icon for the disk is usually called *disk.info* and the icon for the trashcan is called *trashcan.info*. Icons also have a type, depending on what the icon is used for. It can either be a disk icon, a drawer icon, a tool icon, a project icon, or a trash icon. Disk and trash icons are obvious, but what are the others? Let's look at all the icon types in turn and then we'll look at how you can make your own.

Icon Types

The first type is the disk icon. This is an icon representing a disk that you insert in any drive. When you put a disk into a drive, the icon will pop up on the Workbench. The icon for your disk can be found using the Shell, and will be called *disk.info*, whatever your disk is called on the screen. If you double-click on the disk icon, a window will open up showing you the contents of the disk, as icons. An example of the disk icon type is the Workbench disk icon.

The next type is the drawer icon. This literally represents a drawer in the memory of the Amiga and it can be opened and closed, and program icons can be put into it. When you click on a drawer icon, it opens out into a window, not unlike the disk window. More often than not the drawer icon is shown as a little picture of a drawer, just to keep it clear what the icon is. The *.info* file for the drawer icon will have the same name as the drawer itself. An example of a drawer icon is the System drawer on the Workbench disk.

A tool icon represents an actual program, something you can run. If you double-click on this icon, you will run the program. Like the drawer icons, if you look on the disk using the Shell, you will see the tool icons as *.info* files with the same name as the program.

The project icons are files created with tools, so the files you make with the Notepad program are projects. Project icons cannot be opened or run, and can only be double-clicked to see them if the program that created them is around on the disks you have on your system, and the computer knows where to find them.

The trash icon is a special variant of the drawer icon and, only this icon can't be moved from the disk window. You put files in here that you want to trash, and select the Empty Trash icon from the Workbench Menu Bar.

Table 9.1 is a listing of a disk using the Shell's Dir command, showing the files, directories, and the icons as *.info* files. The reason the other directories don't show up on the Workbench is that they have no *.info* files attached to them. Figure 9.1 is a screen shot of the same disk as seen from the Workbench.

```
Tools (dir)
  l (dir)
  devs (dir)
  s (dir)
  c (dir)
  Prefs (dir)
  System (dir)
  t (dir)
  fonts (dir)
  libs (dir)
.info             Disk.info
Prefs.info        Shell
Shell.info        System.info
```

Table 9.1. Directory of a disk.

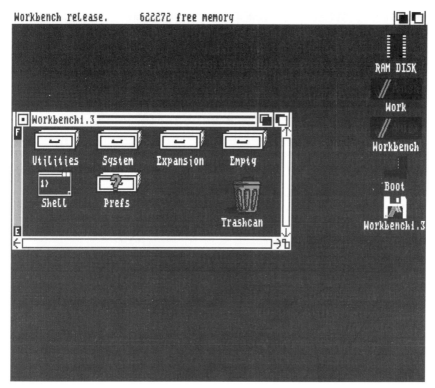

Figure 9.1. How the listing in Table 9.1 looks on the Workbench.

Making Your Own Icons

If you like the icons you have on the disks you use, fine. Skip this chapter and we'll say no more about it. But if you make your own programs with Hisoft BASIC, AMOS, C or another programming language, then eventually you'll want to make your own icons.

The best way of doing this is with an icon editor of some kind. There are lots of these around, and there is even one free with your Amiga. But the best ones are in the PD, and the best of these in my view is IconMaster. But first let's check out the one you get for free, called IconEd.

IconEd

The icon editor you get free with the Amiga is on the Extras disk and is called IconEd in Workbench 1.3 and Icon Edit in Workbench 2. To start the program you simply double click on the icon and the program will begin. When the program is up and running, you will be faced with the main screen, which looks like Figure 9.2.

The idea is that you can draw on the big image of the icon, and this will be converted into a small icon for you to save to disk. IconEd has nine boxes or frames on screen, all of which can contain Icon images. If you click on one of these frames, you will put what is in that frame into the main editing window on the left.

To load an icon from disk all you have to do is type on the requester line which icon you'd like to load, and the icon will be loaded into the current small window on the right, and a big image you can edit will appear in the big edit window on the left. What you type into the requester line can be just the name of the icon, or a proper AmigaDOS pathname, so:

```
disk

df0:disk

df0:trashcan

df2:iconed
```

will all do, provided that's where the icon file is of course. The program automatically appends the .info part of the filename, so you don't have to type it. This is a little bit cumbersome to say the least, because you have to be accurate in your specification of the file you want to edit, where a more advanced program like Icon Master will give you a file requester with a listing of the files available. But it's better than nothing.

To edit the file you simply select the colour you want to draw in from the Menu Bar, and then draw on the big frame with the mouse. Simple. To erase an area of colour you have to draw with the background colour, whatever that may be (usually blue).

The major drawback about IconEd is that it doesn't allow a simple menu selection of icon type. So you have to either manually change the icon type, or just re-edit an icon of the same type. Other than that IconEd is a good enough basic icon editor if you have nothing else to fall back on, which brings us to my icon engine of choice, Icon Master.

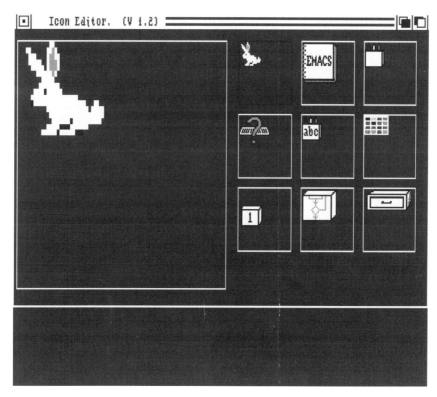

Figure 9.2 IconEd main screen – this has been redesigned for Workbench 2.

Icon Master

You can get a copy of Icon Master on the support disk which to compliments this book, or you can get it from just about any PD library.

The thing that makes Icon Master better than all the other programs of a similar type is that it is more like a proper graphics package in looks and in use, so that means that you can just draw the icons rather than the usual rather unforgiving *keyhole surgery* approach used by other PD programs and the free one you get on the Extras disk. Also it allows you to import IFF brushes like those saved out from DPaint, meaning you could even use digitised images, shrink them, save them out as brushes and then use Icon Master to create an icon out of them.

After you start the program by double-clicking on its icon, you can see the main screen, with buttons to select icon type and all the other switches like executable etc. From this screen you can see the two images, primary and secondary, of the currently loaded icon, and this gives you an idea of the animation in that particular icon. (Before you load any icons the program uses a default set drawn by the creator of the program.) If you click on the primary icon, you can preview the two-frame animation that will occur when the icon is clicked. If you click and hold the button on the icon image, you can see the secondary image, Let go of the button and the secondary image will vanish, showing you the primary image again.

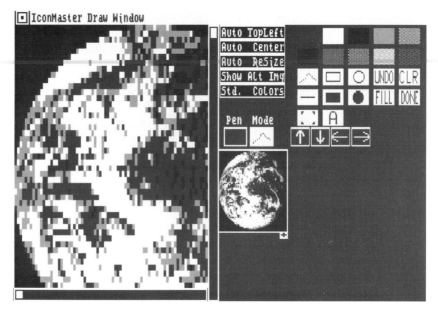

Figure 9.3. Icon Master main screen.

When you select Edit Primary or Edit Secondary Image, you are presented with IM's magnified and normal size icon windows, plus a palette of the colours available to you. Some of these colours are actually tones, mixtures of dots of two colours. So although you only have four colours available to you, you have a number of tones you can use to shade and liven up your icons.

If you've used a graphics program like DPaint then using the tools for Icon Master will be second nature. The broken line tool is freehand drawing, the straight line is the line tool, and the four black triangles are the brush tool, just like DPaint. Yes, you can grab an area and print it onto other areas of the icon, just like in a real graphics package! To select the colour and tools you want to draw with you can just click on the colour patches or tools and you're there.

To swap the colours on the icon, especially useful if you've imported from DPaint brushes, you use the Menu Bar menu to swap the colours on your currently selected icon, either first (primary) or second (secondary) image. The colours are numbered 0 to 3, as Workbench only generally works in 4 colours (Workbench 2 systems work in up to 16), and the colours are laid out in that order on the toolbox 0, 1, 2, and 3. So for example if you've loaded a digitised image in from DPaint, and the colours are all wrong for a normal Workbench you can swap say colour 0 and 3, to make it more normal looking.

When you are finished editing the icon image, you can click on done and you'll be returned to the main screen. There you can save the image back to the .info file you got it from, if you loaded it in in the first place. Or *Save As* something or other if your icon is one you've made.

Icon Master is by far the best program for icon creation, especially for Workbench 1.3 users, and it's PD which makes it even better. Version 2 has its own problems, but these are covered in more depth in Chapter Three.

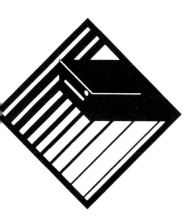

10:
Introducing
AmigaBASIC

One of the most interesting things you can do with your Amiga is program it. Although this might sound like a daunting task, it is actually very easy. All you do is type in a series of commands and run then. Simple when you say it like that, anyway. This chapter is designed to give you a grasp of the concepts behind programming in BASIC and then send you off to explore for yourself.

One of the easiest ways to start programming when you are a beginner is BASIC. BASIC is a programming language, and the name is an acronym for Beginners All Purpose Symbolic Instruction Code. BASIC is basically (ahem) a set of words which are interpreted by a BASIC interpreter program to be instructions that the computer understands. These words are strung together as listings, lists of commands to be executed in order, and the listings of words are called programs. (Note: The word *program* is always spelled with a single *m*, as the origins of the language are American.)

When you run a program, the computer reads each instruction in turn, and performs whatever function it is told to by each instruction. When the program finishes, the computer stops doing what you told it to do and returns to readiness.

You can run programs, and you can save them to disk. Once on the disk they can be loaded from the disk each time you want to run the program, rather than you having to type the whole thing in again. Also programs can be loaded and re-edited, to correct any mistakes to allow you to adjust any bits of the program that aren't as you like them, and then the program can be saved.

You can't just load any old program into a BASIC interpreter and edit it, however. Most programs on the Amiga are written in Machine Code, and so are not BASIC programs. Machine Code is the computer's native language, and is very difficult to learn, so you can only edit programs from other sources if you know what you're doing.

You can however load other BASIC programs that have been already written. These can be re-edited and saved as your own unique version of the program. So before you try to load a program into BASIC, make sure it is actually a BASIC program. Most BASIC programs in the public domain have a *.bas* after their filename, which should give them away.

There are many reasons why you should want to program in BASIC. You might need to run up a little program that you can't buy, a program to solve some problem you have, or to help you with your homework. Or you might like to run programs that you get from other sources. Or you may just like the mental exercise of programming, which is one reason people tinker with computers in the first place. Whatever reason you want to program, here is how to do it.

Overview

AmigaBASIC is no longer supplied free with the Amiga 500 Plus or 600 so users should check out HiSoft BASIC and AMOS for their programming needs. AC BASIC and True BASIC can also be found from certain suppliers. The AmigaBASIC interpreter (supplied free on the Extras disk on Amigas up to the 500 Plus) is a version of the popular MicroSoft BASIC used in many other kinds of computers. So you can take any MicroSoft compatible program (within reason) and run it.

The AmigaBASIC program has an icon, so to start the interpreter just double-click the icon and after a while you're in. The program has two windows, an output window where all the direct commands are typed, and a listing window where you type your program listings. Direct commands are executed immediately, so you can test a line out by typing it into the output window. The main use for the output window is for loading and saving your programs, and doing directories of your files.

You do this by typing the word:

```
files
```

in the output window. You will see a directory of the disk in your df0: drive, and a very non-standard format it is too. MicroSoft aren't generally well-known for their Amiga programs, so this accounts for why they didn't follow standard Amiga conventions when designing this program.

As well as the output window, there are also some menus at the top of the screen in the Menu Bar. These are called Project, Edit, Run and Windows. Project allows you to load and save your programs without having to type the whole LOAD command into the output window.

The Edit menu contains Cut, Copy and Paste commands for editing and moving around the text of your programs. If you select a piece of your program to cut and then cut it, that part of the listing is removed from the listing window and placed into a buffer in memory until you want to paste it back at some other point in the program. Copy does the same thing as cut, places the selected text into a buffer, but copy doesn't remove the selected text from the program. And finally Paste lets you paste a cut or copied buffer back into the program listing at the cursor.

And the Run menu has some menus for running and fault-finding with your BASIC programs. You can run them with the Run selection, stop them with the Stop menu item, you can Continue the program after you've stopped it, you can Suspend a program (a bit like a pause button on a tape recorder), and you can turn the Trace function on or off. Trace allows you to see which line a program stops on if it hits an error. The final item on the Run menu is the Step selection. This allows you to step through the program a line at a time to see if the program is working in the way you wanted it to. (More complete instructions on how to use the AmigaBASIC program are in the book *AmigaBASIC* that comes with BASIC.)

So that's what you've got to work with, how do you go about writing BASIC programs. First read this chapter to familiarise yourself with the concepts of the language. Then check Appendix C which has full descriptions of all the BASIC keywords and their meaning, with examples.

Writing BASIC

BASIC is a computer language that was designed with the new user in mind, and so all the commands are in English rather than slightly nonsensical code words. So if you want to print something on the screen, you type:

```
PRINT "Hello World"
```

which in this case prints the words in the inverted commas to the screen, which will look like this:

```
Hello World
```

BASIC used to be constructed using line numbers, where each line of the program would be preceded by a number. So a program would look like this:

```
10 PRINT "Hello World"

20 PRINT "This is the Amiga"

30 GOTO 10
```

Although you can use line numbers in AmigaBASIC, it's not necessary. The programs will run in the order you type them. The reason that BASIC used to have line numbers was as points of reference for loops (see the paragraph headed *Loops* for more information). This is where the computer can go back up the program and do certain things in the program over and over, like a calculation repeated many times. In AmigaBASIC you can put a number next to a point of reference, but there is a much more clever way to build your programs, and that is using *labels*.

Labels are names given to sections of the program like so:

```
main:

PRINT "This is the main program"
```

If at any point in the program I wanted to go back to that part of the program, all I'd have to type is:

```
GOTO main
```

and the computer would know which part of the program I meant. Alternatively, I could have called the main program line 10, by putting a figure 10 at the front of the line.

Variables

Programs use *variables* to stand for various figures and letters or words. The reason that the programs use variables is that they stand for things that vary each time the computer program runs.

To represent numbers you can have variable names up to 40 characters long, like:

```
a

andy

AndYesTheTimeIsNow

23Skidoo
```

These are all legal *numeric* variable names, numeric as in *numbers*. The other type of variables you need to worry about right now are those that represent letters, like:

```
a$

andy$

AndYesTheTimeIsNow$

23Skidoo$
```

You will notice that these variables are exactly the same as the examples I gave you just now, except for one thing. They all have a dollar sign at the end. This indicates that the variable is used for holding letters, and these are called *alphanumeric* variables, or more commonly just *string* variables.

In a BASIC program you tell the computer that:

```
something = a variable
```

by saying LET something equal something. In a BASIC program it would look like this:

```
LET a=10

LET a$="Amiga"
```

If you type this short program in and run it, you get nothing out, as all the program does is give the values to two variables. Now if you use the PRINT statement after these commands, like so:

```
LET a=10

LET a$="Amiga"

PRINT a,a$
```

The output from this program when you run it would be like so:

```
10      Amiga
```

A bit of a nonsense program that, but you get the gist. Variables can be anything you like, and you can use them to do calculations and print out the results:

```
LET a=1

LET b=1

PRINT a

PRINT b

PRINT a+b
```

And so you have there a rudimentary example of the most expensive non-portable calculator in the world.

The Colons

Two of the most important characters in the BASIC language are
the colon and semi-colon, the : and ; symbols respectively. These
perform some very useful jobs in BASIC, and in different ways. The
colon is used to use a lot of BASIC statements on one line, like so:

```
LET a=1: LET b=1: PRINT a: PRINT b: PRINT a+b
```

This is the same program I just did, only this time it's all on one
line with the colon separating the BASIC statements.

The semi-colon is a lot more subtle, being used in PRINT
statements to separate strings and variables. Like in this pair of
lines:

```
LET a$="Phil South"
PRINT "The winner is ";a$;"! Give him a big hand!"
```

where my name is inserted into the line. When you run it, sure
enough, my name is part of the sentence when it appears on the
screen. Try adapting the line to LET a$ equal your name.

All this just goes to show variables can be fun, which is really
strange because call it algebra and stick me in a maths class and I
find it really dull. (No offense meant to any maths teachers out
there by the way!) So you can use them to add information to parts
of the program.

Another way you'd use the semi-colon is like in the PRINT
statement below:

```
howdy:
 PRINT "Hi, I'm Phil. Fly Me. ";
 GOTO howdy
```

This will repeat the same thing over and over, but the odd thing is
it is all on the same line! The semi-colon is interpreted in this case
as telling the computer not to do a new line after it has printed
whatever the string is I'm printing, but to stay right there.

The Comma

The comma is used in the same way as the semi-colon, but instead
of leaving no space, the comma sort of tabs across the page like on
a typewriter. I can't think of very many uses for this, and besides
you can use the TAB(x) command, where x equals the spaces you
want to tab. Like a lot of commands in BASIC, TAB is a hangover
from the days when computers didn't have screens but were
displayed by teletypes, which were basically just typewriters which
printed out the text onto rolls of paper.

Looping

I mentioned before that you could create loops in your programs, and this is how you do it. There are two types, IF THEN commands and GOTO.

IF THEN tests a variable before it branches back or forward to the label you give it. For example:

```
main:
    INPUT "Type a number";number
    IF number=10 THEN finish
    GOTO main


finish:
    PRINT "Got it!"
    STOP
```

The bit of the program called *main* tests the number you type in, and if it is a 10 then the program goes to the label *finish* and prints the message. If you don't type a 10, then the program goes around again, asking you to type a number. It will do this forever until you get it right, or until you press CTRL-C. There that's one type of loop. The other kind is more direct.

If you say:

```
    GOTO main
```

The computer will go to, or GOTO, that label or even line number, as in:

```
    GOTO 10
```

The computer doesn't argue, test any variables or say it's got a bone in its leg and it can't possibly. No, it just gets itself off to that label or line, and no messing. (Note: If you say GOTO hell to an Amiga it will say that there is no such label as hell. Which is a comforting thought, really.)

Routines

In computer speak, *routines* are any part of a program that does a specific job, one of the many separate tasks that make up a program. These are also known as *subroutines*, a smaller part of the biggest routine which is the program. It is a good idea to think of any program you write in terms of the subroutines which govern each job, so you can program a different subroutine for each bit of the program. For example you could have one subroutine which introduces the program by printing a welcome message:

```
welcome:
    PRINT "Welcome to the test program"
    RETURN
```

like that. Then you could write a subroutine which does one job:

```
calc:
    INPUT "First number please: ";a
    INPUT "Second number please: ";b
    PRINT "The result is: ";a+b
    RETURN
```

and another subroutine that does another job:

```
naim:
    INPUT "What is your name: ";a$
    PRINT "Hello there, ";a$;". My name is Amiga."
    RETURN
```

and a subroutine that chooses which subroutine you want to run:

```
choose:
    PRINT "Do you want me to add two numbers, or call
you by name?"
    PRINT "Type a 1 for Calculate"
    PRINT "Type a 2 for Name"
    INPUT "Make your selection: (1 or 2)";z
    IF z=1 THEN GOSUB calc
    IF z=2 THEN GOSUB naim
    RETURN
```

And finally you can have a main program which calls the other routines in turn:

```
main:
    GOSUB welcome
    GOSUB choose
    GOTO main
```

Now string it all together and you get a program. Add a little REM statement here and there, and you have a really nicely structured and documented program:

```
' Name And Calc By P South
'

main:
```

```
    GOSUB welcome
    GOSUB choose
    GOTO main
'

choose:
    PRINT "Do you want me to add two numbers, or call
you by name?"
    PRINT "Type a 1 for Calculate"
    PRINT "Type a 2 for Name"
    INPUT "Make your selection: (1 or 2)";z
    IF z=1 THEN GOSUB calc
    IF z=2 THEN GOSUB naim
    RETURN
'

welcome:
    PRINT "Welcome to the test program"
    RETURN
'

calc:
    INPUT "First number please: ";a
    INPUT "Second number please: ";b
    PRINT "The result is: ";a+b
    RETURN
'

naim:
    INPUT "What is your name: ";a$
    PRINT "Hello there, ";a$;". My name is Amiga."
    RETURN
```

The REM statements (you can either type REM or use a symbol) are commands that are not actually executed by the program, and that is because they are REMarks or comments on the program. Like so:

```
REM This is a remark...
'   So is this, but in an abbreviated form.
'   And none of these three lines will be executed
by the computer.
PRINT "But this one will!"
```

If a program doesn't have comments in it, in the form of REM statements, then it is much harder to read. Also if the program has no title in a REM line, then it may be hard to figure out what the program does without running it. You can learn a lot about a program simply by reading the REMs.

Backtracking a little, you will notice that the word Name has been replaced by the word *naim* in the last program. This is because NAME is a reserved word in BASIC, one of the keywords used to make the Amiga do things. I have used naim because if you say it out loud, it sounds the same as name. If you need to use a keyword as a label, use a phonetically similar word, as any word will do as a label. The Amiga is much more forgiving where spelling and pronunciation is concerned.

(Note: Don't worry about reserved words, as the computer will tell you if there is an error due to a reserved word being used as a label etc.)

The place you can use a reserved word is within the inverted commas of a PRINT or INPUT statement. So:

```
PRINT "Name"
INPUT "Name";naim$
```

is okay, but:

```
LET name$="Phil"
```

is not allowed.

Load and Save

Loading and Saving from AmigaBASIC is done by typing the LOAD and SAVE commands into the output window. To Load a program called BallBlazer type:

```
load "df0:ballblazer"
```

And provided the program is in the root directory of df0:, the program will load. If the program is in a directory called Games, then you'd have to type:

```
load "df0:games/ballblazer"
```

in order for the program to find it. It's a good idea to do a directory using the files command to discover where the programs you want to load are.

To save programs just type:

```
save "df0:MyProgram.bas"
```

or whatever you want to call the program, *Fred.bas*, *Calculation.bas* or even *MyFavouriteGame.bas*, whatever you like. I make it a rule to save my BASIC programs with a *.bas* on the end, just so I know what I'm looking at on the directory.

ASCII Text

The standard format of text files on a computer is the ASCII format, pronounced *ass-key*. AmigaBASIC can read programs in ASCII format, but stores programs in its own format. To SAVE out an AmigaBASIC program in ASCII format to load into a wordprocessor or another BASIC interpreter, simply save with a ,a on the end of the filename.

Programming Hints

1. Pay attention to the structure of your programs.

2. Always plan what you are going to do in advance and write it down on paper.

3. Divide the tasks of your program into subroutines and write each subroutine in BASIC on its own. Test it out on its own and save it as ASCII.

4. When you have all your subroutines written, create a main program to call up all the subroutines in turn.

5. Bolt all the routines together in a wordprocessor or text editor.

6. Test the program as a whole by loading it into AmigaBASIC.

7. Re-edit the program to iron out any bugs and save it as a whole program.

8. Keep lists of your variables and what they all do. If possible put them all in a REM statement at the beginning of the program so other people know what they all are.

9. In fact, put a lot of REM statements into your programs, so that when you come back to a program the next day you can see what part of the program is what.

10. Finally, practice makes perfect. Fool around with the AmigaBASIC program just to see what happens, and type in any listings you see. Even old fashioned ones with line numbers will work, so get some books out of the library and try out some programs.

The most important piece of advice is don't try to learn too much at once. Take it all a stage at a time and you'll pick up more about using BASIC than trying to cram it all in at the first sitting. Refer to the notes on the BASIC keywords in Appendix C and try them all out. And have fun!

Other BASICs

AmigaBASIC is far from being the be all and end all of Amiga programming. In fact there are other BASIC programs on the Amiga which do a much better job of it. AMOS from Mandarin Software is one that you really should look at after you've become a little bit more proficient in BASIC programming. This allows you to do all manner of clever stuff with graphics and sound that are impossible with standard AmigaBASIC. Another such program is Hisoft BASIC, which is a compiled BASIC. Compiled means that you can write a program in BASIC as normal, but then it is compiled into machine code to make it much faster and more powerful.

There are other ways of programming your Amiga, like using an authoring package like CanDo or AmigaVision, and these are sometimes easier. They use simple icon based interfaces, and although they are very simple to use, they really unleash the power of your machine.

Books On BASIC

For those of you who want to go further into BASIC, there are some very good books on BASIC around. Firstly I must mention my own *Mastering Amiga AMOS* which provides a complete guide to this tremendous programming environment which is rapidly becoming the most popular way to program the Amiga. Back to BASIC itself and my favourite book is *Illustrating BASIC* by Donald Alcock. It's a nice simple guide, and although I learned BASIC at college, I'd have never got a grip on it if it wasn't for this book. Another nice tome is *The Little Book Of BASIC Style* by John M Nevison, which goes into how to write programs so that they are nice and tidy.

Also I would say that there are a great many books containing BASIC listings for you to type in, and two of my favourites, although rather old by now, are *BASIC Computer Games* and *More BASIC Computer Games* both by David Ahl. Anyway, for more books on BASIC and related topics check out Chapter 23 for my guide to further reading.

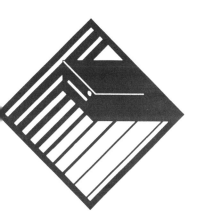

11:
Making Your
Amiga Speak

Unlike any other computer I can think of, the Amiga has a speech synthesiser built-into it. Not only that but it has the built in ability to read a text file and speak it through the speakers in your monitor. The computer's voice is very easily customised, and can be high-pitched a feminine, deep and male, or neutral like a robot. And all these features are available in both AmigaBASIC and the AmigaDOS Shell.

Before you can make your Amiga speak you should first consult Chapters 4 and 10 about Amiga-BASIC and AmigaDOS, just so you will fully understand the processes used to create the voice.

Firstly, don't be too disappoint-ed at the way the Amiga speaks. It doesn't talk like the robots and computers on Star Trek, or something like that. Speech synthesis has moved on some way in the last few years, but it's still not as flexible and express-ive as a real human voice. You can get the computer to produce very intelligible speech, and a lot of fun it is too. But nobody will mistake it for a real human voice, no way.

The Amiga's voice is made up of BASIC building blocks of sound called *phonemes*, and these are put together to make words. If you program in the raw phonemes you can make speech in any language, German, French, even Japanese. There is a device in AmigaDOS called the *narrator device*, and if the file *narrator.device* isn't in the devs (or device) directory of your boot disk, you won't get any speech out at all. The narrator device takes the phonemes in and spits out human speech.

Speech In AmigaBASIC

To get the Amiga to say something in BASIC you can go several routes, the easiest of which is using the TRANSLATE$ keyword. Try typing the following into AmigaBASIC:

```
main:

INPUT "Type something you want me to say: ";a$

SAY TRANSLATE$(a$)

GOTO main
```

run this and anything you type will be translated and spoken by the Amiga. (Make sure the sound is turned up!) To see the phonemes that make up your typed sentence, simply add the line PRINT TRANSLATE$ like so:

```
main:

INPUT "Type something you want me to say: ";a$

PRINT a$

PRINT TRANSLATE$ (a$)

SAY TRANSLATE$(a$)

GOTO main
```

This program speaks the text and prints out two lines which look like this:

```
This is your Amiga speaking

DHIHS IHZ YOHR AHMIY3GAH SPIY4KIHNX
```

The second line is the phonemes which make up the spoken version of your text. Although this looks like nonsense to you and I, the narrator device understands it and generates the speech.

The TRANSLATE$ command saves you the trouble of learning all about the phonemes and with this command all you have to do is supply the text for the TRANSLATE$ command to read. Sometimes the computer will translate something you type and it will sound really muffled and unintelligible. To get around this problem, you must type in the text you wish to translate more phonetically, the way it sounds rather than the way it is spelled. My name for example sounds like *fieel* when you shove it through the translator. I get around this by typing *FIL* instead of *PHIL*, as this sounds more like my name when the Amiga says it. So, experiment to get the best sounding words in your sentence.

Speech Modes

There are a number of features you can use to alter the way the Amiga's voice sounds. These are called the modes, and they are employed in AmigaBASIC using what are called *mode arrays*. There are bits of data held in a DATA statement somewhere in the program, which control the pitch, speed, sex and quality of the voice. Each number in the array, added to the SAY command using the READ DATA commands, stands for one of the parameters of the SAY command. Each number controls a variable, like the numbers on a dial on the front of a stereo. Each parameter can be set to a number, and these settings have a noticeable effect on the voice that the Amiga produces.

The format for the SAY command is like so:

```
SAY "<string>"
```

```
or with the mode array added:
```

```
SAY "<string>",<mode array>
```

In most cases you will add the TRANSLATE$ command too, otherwise you need to type in the relevant phonemes for the words you want to produce. Here is an example of using the mode array. It has been set up in a variable called BOO%, and if the words I wanted to say were *Phil is great*, I would type:

```
SAY TRANSLATE$("Phil is great"),BOO%
```

(Modest soul, aren't I?) The modes for the various settings are taken from the variable BOO%, and the words are spoken using that voice.

Table 11.1 gives you a list of the different parameters you need to set to alter the default settings for the Amiga's voice.

Parameter	Range	Use
pitch	65-320	The pitch of the voice in Hertz. The default setting is 110, which is a medium-pitched male voice.
inflection	0-1	0 means the voice has inflection, 1 means the voice is a robotic monotone.
rate	40-400	Speed of the voice in words per minute. Default is 150.
voice	0-1	Gender of the voice, 0 for male, 1 for female.
tuning	5000-28000	Sampling frequency, which can be thought of as the quality of the voice. Default is 22200.
volume	0-64	The loudness of the voice. Default is 64.
channel	0-11	Assigns the audio channel for the voice.
mode	0-1	Synch mode. 0 means that BASIC will wait for the Say command to finish before the program continues. 1 means the voice will start, and the program will continue underneath it.
control	0-2	Control mode. This is a trifle complex. If the mode is mode 1, then the control mode can be activated to control how the voice is processed in the face of multiple Say commands. If it equals 0 then the first Say command is processed then the next one and so on. If it equals 1 then the Amiga stops processing voice statements altogether. But if it is equal to 2, then the Amiga chops off the first statement and goes straight on to the next one. I can't see you using this mode much, but at least you know what it does now.

Table 11.1 SAY parameters.

When you use the voice, you usually just leave the channel assignments to the default value, which is suitable for most tasks. But for certain programs you might like to have some kind of stereo control over the four channels, two on each side. If you already have a piece of music or a sound effect playing in one of the other channels for example, or if you want to get a stereo panning effect. Table 11.2 gives you all the parameters for the channel assignments.

So you have an idea of the kind of voice you want, how do you program it in BASIC? It's easy. Try the following program:

```
FOR D=0 TO 8: READ BOO%(D): NEXT D

SAY TRANSLATE$ ("Hi Phil, thanks for teaching me
how to speak."),BOO%

DATA 250,0,130,1,22200,64,10,0,0
```

Value	Channel(s)
0	0
1	1
2	2
3	3
4	0 and 1
5	0 and 2
6	1 and 3
7	2 and 3
8	Any left channel
9	Any right channel
10	Any left or right pair of channels
11	Any single channel

Table 11.2. Channel assignments for Voice.

The first number in the DATA statement is the pitch, which is quite high at 250. The next number is the inflection, which is turned on with 0. The next number is the rate of speech, which in this case is 130 words per minute, slower than the default setting. Next is the gender, which is set to 1 for a female type voice, where the voice has been modulated for a more female sound. Next is the sampling rate, which is set for the default rate of 22200. The volume is set to 64, and the final two values for mode and control settings have been set to 0 to keep them out of your hair.

Using Phonemes

Instead of using the TRANSLATE$ command you can just type SAY followed by a string of phonemes. For example:

```
SAY "DHIHS IHZ YOHR AHMIY3GAH SPIY4KIHNX"
```

makes your Amiga speak the words *This is your Amiga speaking.* Table 11.3 shows a list of available phonemes for you to use in your AmigaBASIC and AmigaDOS programs and batch files.

Phoneme	Sounds like
IY	ee in beet
EH	e in bet
AA	a in carnival
AO	a in talk
ER	ir in bird
AX	a in about
IH	i in bit
AE	a in bat
AH	u in under
UH	oo in look
OH	o in border
IX	i in solid
EY	a in made
OY	oi in boil
OW	ow in low
AY	i in hide
AW	w in power
UW	w in crew
R	r in red
W	w in away
M	m in men
NX	ng in sing
S	s in sail
F	f in fed
Z	s in has
V	v in very
CH	ch in cheque
/H	h in hole
B	b in but
D	d in dog
K	c in Commodore
L	l in yellow
Y	y in yellow
N	n in men
SH	sh in rush
TH	th in thigh
ZH	s in pleasure
DH	th in then
J	j in judge
/C	ch in loch
P	p in put
T	t in toy
G	g in guest
Q	en in kitten (glottal stop)
QX	e in pause (silent vowel)
RX	r in car

Table 11.3. List of Amiga phonemes.

Placing stress on a syllable using phonemes is done by adding a number after the phoneme, like so:

KAE5T

where the A in the word CAT is stressed. The number between 1-9 indicates the amount of stress to be placed on that one syllable.

Finally, a full stop at the end of a string makes the voice prop in pitch at the end, and a question mark causes a rise in pitch. These changes in pitch mimic the natural speech method of indicating a question or the simple end of a sentence. Type these lines into your AmigaBASIC:

SAY TRANSLATE$ "Hello how are you."

SAY TRANSLATE$ "Hello how are you?"

noting how the second one sounds like a question.

Speech in AmigaDOS

Using speech in AmigaDOS isn't actually very different. All the things you've learned using the speech facility in AmigaBASIC will stand you in good stead. The AmigaDOS command for speech is still Say, but the way you use it is slightly different. The phonemes don't work, as the AmigaDOS Say command automatically translates for you. So if a piece of speech is wrong you have to spell it phonetically to alter it.

To make Amiga speak using the Shell all you type is:

`say Hello world`

You can add some simpler parameters to the command, using the options listed in Table 11.4.

Option	Meaning
-f	Use the female voice
-m	Use the male voice
-r	Use the robot or neutral voice
-p<number>	Set the pitch of the voice
-s<number>	Set the speed of the voice
-x<file>	Get the Amiga to read a text file

Table 11.4. Options for using the Amiga Voice with the Shell.

So for example if you wanted to duplicate the speech we did earlier on, you would type:

```
say -f -p250 -n -s130 hi phil, thanks for teaching
me how to speak.
```

which would give us the same speech as the AmigaBASIC example. The one thing that the AmigaDOS version of Say can do which the AmigaBASIC version cannot is to read a file automatically. Using the -x option, you can feed a text file into the narrator device, and out will come a spoken version of the text file. To use the same voice as above to speak a readme.doc file on disk df1: for instance, you would type:

```
say -f -p250 -n -s130 -x df1:readme.doc
```

and sit back while the Amiga reads you the file, saving you the bother of loading it up into a text reader or a wordpro and reading it yourself. Only Amiga can do this.

Scripts

Using speech in AmigaDOS means you can get the computer to talk to you in your startup-sequence. Using a text editor to edit the startup-sequence file in your S directory, simply put in a Say command a couple of lines before the end, followed by your message and parameter settings, and you can have your Amiga greet you vocally every day when you start it up, like so:

```
...
Echo "Hello, Phil. How are you today?"
Say hello phil, how are you today?
LoadWB
EndCLI
```

remembering to put the say command after the Echo which prints it to the screen, so you see the text at the same time you hear the voice.

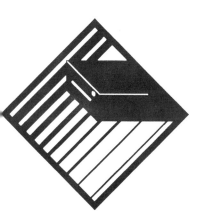

12:
Text Editors

When you are programming for the Amiga, be it in C or BASIC or just a little batch file, a good text editor is what you need. I use a text editor as opposed to a word processor for all my writing and correspondence, but then that suits my needs. All I need to do is bang in the words, spell check and count them. If you need to do more than that then you'd best look at the chapter on business programs, Chapter 18, to see what word processors will suit you.

On the subject of text editors, what are they good for? Well, for an example you can use them to type in your BASIC programs if the slow speed of the editor in AmigaBasic gets you down. Then all you have to do is load it into AmigaBasic to run it. To export it out again all you have to do is use the ,a command, but see Chapter 10 about that.

With your Amiga you get three free text editors, which are ED, EDIT and MicroEMACS. Both ED and EDIT are in the C directory of your master Workbench disk, whereas MicroEMACS is to be found on the Extras disk.

ED

The ED program is described as a screen editor, and this is the most commonly used text editor on the Amiga, due to the fact it is very small in memory and is available from any Shell prompt. The program isn't suitable for letter writing or anything like that, as it doesn't wrap the text around at the edge of the screen. But, as a very plain editor for getting programs or batch files together, it's hard to beat, especially as it doesn't cost anything and you own it already if you have an Amiga.

The program is started from the Shell by typing:

ed

followed by the filename you wish to edit. If the filename can't be found on the disk, a new file will be created with the name you chose. So to edit your startup-sequence type:

ed s/startup-sequence

The filename here includes the pathname, or the route you have to take through the directories on the Workbench disk to find the file. As the startup-sequence is in the S directory, then this is what we have said to the Amiga with that command: Look in the S directory, and load startup-sequence.

Once the file has loaded you are presented with the file in the ED editor (see Figure 12.1). You can edit the file just by moving around the file using the cursor keys on your keyboard, and typing into the file.

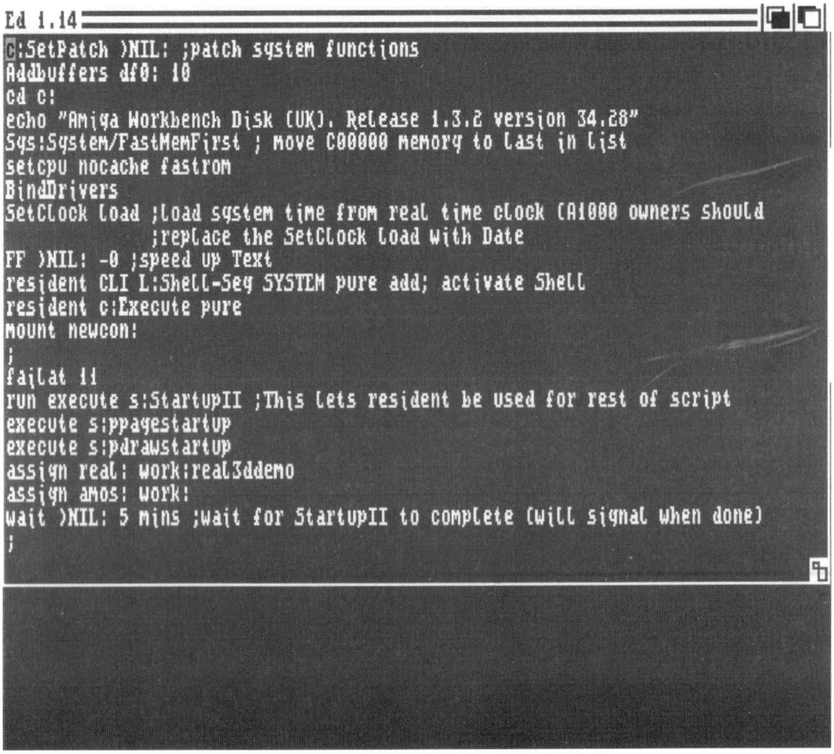

Figure 12.1. ED in use.

Many of the commands in the ED editor use combinations of keys with the CTRL key. Table 12.1 is a list of control key commands.

Hold down CTRL key plus:	
A	Insert line (also you can hit Return)
B	Delete a line
D	Scroll the text down 12 lines
E	Jump to top or bottom of file, toggles between the two
F	Change character between upper and lower case
G	Repeat last extended command
H	Backspace and delete
I	Move cursor to next TAB
M	Same as hitting the Return key
O	Delete word
R	Sends the cursor to end of previous word
T	Sends the cursor to start of next word
U	Scroll text up 12 lines
V	Verify screen
[	Extended mode (same as ESC key)
]	Jumps cursor to start or end of line

Table 12.1. ED CTRL key commands.

As well as the control key commands there are extended mode commands. Extended mode is entered by pressing the ESC key, and you can tell you are in extended mode because there is a little asterisk (the * symbol) at the bottom of the screen. As you type commands into the extended commands line, the commands appear next to this asterisk. Extended mode commands are for formatting but also more important things like loading and saving your documents. Table 12.2 has a list of the most used commands.

Command	Action
A/<string>/	Insert the text after cursor position
B	Move to the bottom of the file
BE	Mark the end of a block at the cursor
BF/<string>/	Search back through text for the string
BS	Mark the start of a block
CE	Move cursor to the end of a line
CS	Move cursor to the start of a line
D	Delete line
DB	Delete marked block
DC	Delete character at cursor
F/<string>/	Find the string
IB	Insert marked block at cursor
IF/x/	Insert file x from disk at cursor
J	Join line with next
M n	Move to line number n
Q	Quit without saving
S	Split line at cursor
U	Undo changes on current line
X	Quit and save

Table 12.2. The ED extended mode commands.

Some of these commands require a little explanation. Blocks can be marked in the text, so you can cut and paste sections of the text and put them elsewhere. Select the start of the block using ESC then B then S and press Return. Then move the cursor to the end of the block and press ESC, then B then E and Return. The block is then marked. You can cut it out of the text with ESC DB. Or you can paste it somewhere else using ESC IB. Using text search commands to find the word *phil* for example, you press the ESC key to get the prompt, and then type:

```
F/phil/
```

The file will be searched and the word found, if it is there that is.

ED is a reasonably basic text editor, but it will do for most tasks, as it has what I would call a basic minimum set of commands for a text editor.

EDIT

Edit is another program which resides in your C directory. This time the program is referred to as a line editor. The difference between a screen and a line editor is that a screen editor allows you to edit text over the whole screen, whilst a line editor is based on single lines. Edit is too archaic and is only really of interest to people raised on the likes of EDLIN on the PC and VI on UNIX. Delete it, that's my view. It's too complicated and it's sitting there wasting your disk space.

MicroEMACS

A much more modern piece of kit altogether is the MicroEMACS program on the Extras disk. This is an alternative screen editor to ED, and the principle difference is that MEMACS (as it is called) is mouse operated rather than relying on complex commands. And whereas ED is purely Shell based, MEMACS can be started from the Workbench by clicking on its icon.

You can see from the screen (Figure 12.2) that the layout is fairly straightforward, and all the commands are made from the menus. MEMACS is a little easier to control than ED, but some of the commands are little bit obscure. READ a file is less clear than LOAD, and how would you interpret VISIT a file? This is the point really, the program is really designed for people who are familiar with the EMACS text editor on larger computers. Although I wouldn't advise you to use it, there's no reason why you can't tinker around with it. Who knows, you might discover that you like it. But for my money, you are better off using ED.

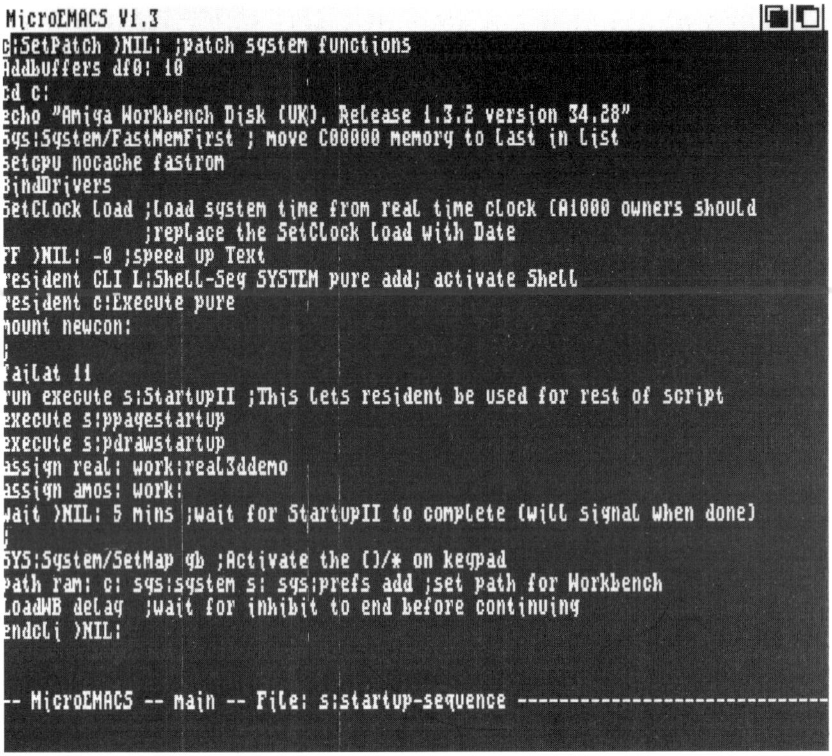

```
MicroEMACS V1.3                                              ▣▢
c:SetPatch )NIL: ;patch system functions
Addbuffers df0: 10
cd c:
echo "Amiga Workbench Disk (UK), Release 1.3.2 version 34.28"
sys:System/FastMemFirst ; Move C00000 memory to last in list
setcpu nocache fastrom
BindDrivers
SetClock load ;load system time from real time clock (A1000 owners should
               ;replace the SetClock load with Date
FF )NIL: -0 ;speed up Text
resident CLI L:Shell-Seg SYSTEM pure add; activate Shell
resident c:Execute pure
mount newcon:
;
failat 11
run execute s:StartupII ;This lets resident be used for rest of script
execute s:ppagestartup
execute s:pdrawstartup
assign real: work:real3ddemo
assign amos: work:
wait )NIL: 5 mins ;wait for StartupII to complete (will signal when done)
;
SYS:System/SetMap gb ;Activate the ()/* on keypad
path ram: c: sys:system s: sys:prefs add ;set path for Workbench
LoadWB delay  ;wait for inhibit to end before continuing
endcli )NIL:


-- MicroEMACS -- main -- File: s:startup-sequence ---------------------
```

Figure 12.2. The MicroEMACS screen.

Best of the Rest

Or even better yet, why not get one of the excellent Public Domain text editors? They are available from all the best PD houses, and are clearly marked as a text editor. TextPlus is a very good example of what you can expect from a PD text editor. Alternatively you can even buy one. I know your heart sinks every time someone says they can solve your problems if only you'd spend some more money. But actually text editors are very cheap in the main, being around £30-50 or thereabouts, so you don't stand to lose much. Even though there are some very cheap and even free text eds, I'd still try before you buy. And have a really proper go at it before you part with anything, as text editing needs to be a smooth operation if you want to get any sense out of the other end.

TextPlus

TextPlus is a very sophisticated text editor written by a German programmer called Martin Steppler and placed into the public domain. The program is now up to version 3, and the current version is getting to look more like a wordprocessor.

The colours of the program are a nice sort of Workbench 2 grey, which obviously teams up quite well with your system if you run 2.0. Cosmetic things aside, the menu commands on the program are a bit less hard to figure out than those used in something like MEMACS, and so are more suited to the production of both text and programs. I know of at least two people who typed their University thesis on TextPlus without a hitch, and that was almost as many words as there are in this book in both cases. So big files like novels aren't a problem.

Formatting the text is easy, and you can justify it so that the left side is straight, or the right side is straight (I never figured out why any one would want this!), or both sides are straight. There are options for bold type, underline and italic, and although the program is PD it looks and feels like a professional program. Not only that the program prints out too, unlike a lot of programming editors. TextPlus is a first rate program and you can get get it from most PD houses. Try Amiganuts disk 1047, if you want to go right to it!

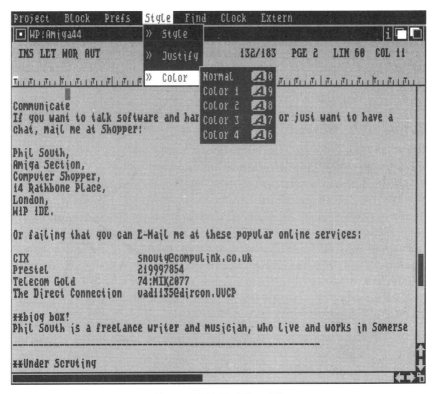

Figure 12.3. TextPlus 3.0.

Transcript (including TransEdit)

As I write for a living I really do need a good text editor, and for a long while I couldn't find one on the Amiga that didn't come free with graphics, a lot of useless features and a whole pile of snags. I even threatened to start using the PC (perish the thought)! But in the end I did find one which was trouble free, rock solid and generally brilliant.

Transcript was written by the Canadian software house Gold Disk, who brought you Professional Page, Professional Draw, Comic Setter etc. If you have to spend 90% of the time you should be working tinkering around with the wordprocessor to make it do what you want it to do, then it's not what I'd call a professional product. Almost all the wordprocessors and text editors I have used over the last few years have had one feature I really wanted, and a whole lot I didn't want. What you want from a wordprocessor is to crunch the basic text, count the words, format it for printing or save it to disk as a clean ASCII file for porting into a DTP program. Nothing more, nothing less. And that's exactly what you've got with Gold Disk's Transcript.

All the *added value features* are all useful, not go-faster stripes like on other processors. And it's cheap, just a whisker under £40. It does a word count when you press A-Shift-?, it has a comprehensive 90,000 word spelling checker (albeit in American) and it will format your pages any way you like, either using the Print output requester or by the use of embedded formatting commands, not unlike the dot commands you get in PC wordprocessors.

As well as doing all the basic stuff quickly and guru free, it even does mail merge, headers and footers and macro keys without a shudder. Everything about Transcript is about speed and ease of use. The file requesters will stop if you push the buttons, not like some which churn on and on until they've read the whole disk. It is a program designed for people who write, and this much is apparent from the way the features have been organised. It's fast too, which means no waiting around for text to reformat itself, but most of all it's fully Amiga-ised, which means it's multi-tasking and can operate happily with any other program in memory.

Transcript was written by Chris Zamara and Nick Sullivan, who you may not realise spent the rest of their lives being the editors of the late Transactor for Amiga magazine in Canada (which is why it's called Trans-script I suppose!). The package includes TransSpell, the 90,000 word spell checker, and Transedit, a memory efficient cut-down version (a text editor for programmers or those for whom memory is at a premium), plus example files and readme files to update you on the latest versions of things. TransSpell is a very intelligent spelling checker, treating words in the way you would yourself. Okay, so it is an American dictionary, but a few weeks of spell checking should weed out the *colors* and *theaters*, as you can add your own user dictionary as you go.

There is only one scroll bar on the screen to indicate the size of your document, and that is along the *bottom* of the screen. Novel idea, that, but logical as it allows the *full* width of the screen to be used for words. Of course, grabbing the scroll handle with the mouse scrolls you through the document.

If you want to write a lot of words, like a novel or something, then TS is the one for you. If you want to write letters then go for something with a flashier output (or buy a flashy printer). But for most text crunching applications, from writing articles to books, Transcript is still my engine of choice, even in the light of many other wordprocessors with more *features*.

Now there are few features not included in Transwrite, like graphics and fancy fonts. But it's not a low end DTP program. It's a word engine and it doesn't make any excuse about that. If you want graphics etc, then paste the words from Transwrite into Pro Page, and print out. More importantly it actually meshes with Pro Page as an *on-line word pro*. So you can actually access it automatically from later versions of Pro Page, and it will multi task quite happily as an *on-line* editor. In fact I heard that in the latest version of ProPage, you get an editor like TransWrite free with the package.

TxEd

The only other text editor I know and approve of is TxEd by MicroSmiths. I have no idea where you might pick this up from but look out for it as it is a very good solid *programmers* text editor. I know people who prefer CygnusEd as a text editor, but I've never seen that properly and so can't comment. I like TxEd because it is small, quick and powerful. I have it installed in my C directory on the hard disk, and so it's always on call whenever any scripts want writing.

Summary

Text editors are a matter of some argument among Amiga types, and in fact computer types in general. Some say they like such and such, but when all is said and done it just down to personal preference. Don't just take my word for it, test as many as you can to find your favourite.

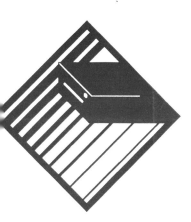

3:
ound
nd
raphics

When you first buy your computer, you are impressed by the sound and graphics that the demos have. The big problem is that it is often very hard to get that same quality of work out of the Amiga without a lot of help. The Amiga has many different display modes and resolutions, low res, high res, interlaced low res, interlaced high res, 64 Halfbrite and HAM. The Amiga also has stereo sound system, capable of recording and playing back sound samples at very respectable quality. But what do you need to help you harness all this power? Programming in BASIC is one way, but only very crude results can be obtained by this route. So here is a sort of jumble sale of hints and tips and creative options, with advice on what to use to get more sound and graphics out of your Amiga.

Sound Sampling

One of the most interesting pieces of hardware you can get for your Amiga is a sound sampler. My particular favourite is the Perfect Sound 3.0 made by Sunrize Industries in the USA. The box containing the sampler is very small, about the size of a large matchbox, and it plugs into the parallel port behind the Amiga, on one end of the box is the plug which goes into the Amiga. On the other end are two phono plugs, ready for attaching a stereo audio cable.

Once you run the piece of software, you can take in a sound from an amplifier or tape recorder, and sample it into the

Amiga. Once in the Amiga, the sound can be edited and played back in a variety of ways. The editing is all mouse driven, so you can select a part of the sound with the mouse and cut it out, reverse it or just zoom in to see what it looks like. This machine is perfect for creating sounds to use in MED or Soundtracker. Or perhaps music isn't on your mind. Perhaps you just want to sample things for fun. Or even sound effects for your own films and videos.

As a sort of PS to all this, you may also like to know that a full specification 12 and 16 bit music sampling package has just been released by the self-same manufacturer as Perfect Sound. Musicians take note that not only is this CD quality sampling, it can also sample and edit direct to a hard disk.

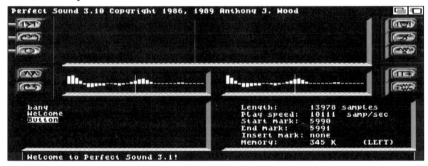

Figure 13.1. Perfect Sound editor.

Music and MIDI

MIDI stands for Musical Instrument Digital Interface, and it is a serial communications standard for musical instruments. The practical upshot of which is that, if you connect a MIDI interface to your computer, you can use the computer as a sequencer to make music with any MIDI synthesiser. All you have to do is get a synth, MIDI interface, two MIDI leads, and a sequencer program for your Amiga. You connect the MIDI leads up to the synth and the MIDI box, and load the sequencer software. You can then run the program and produce music on your computer.

MIDI for Beginners

MIDI is simple, even I can use it. But there are several things you ought to bear in mind before you launch yourself into it.

Firstly, you're going to need a MIDI sound source, like a synthesiser Casio CZ series, Roland MT-32 plus MIDI keyboard or a multitimbral module, like the Cheetah one, or Yamaha's many FB-01, TX7, TX81Z or DX11 devices. This is the most important bit. There's no point in buying MIDI packages unless you've got a decent device with more than one sound on it! If you're lucky you can pick up these devices for around £250 to £850. And you needn't buy new either, as second-hand can be picked up very easily through music magazines or from the weekly classifieds. You're still looking at a fair bit of outlay. My optimum system would be a Roland MT-32 at about £200 second-hand, and a new Roland MIDI keyboard for about £150.

Now if that hasn't put you off, you next need the MIDI interface. The Datel MIDI box specification is as high as anything on the market. Sure, it hasn't got a single bell, whistle or value added feature, but it does do MIDI. The problem comes when you add MIDI devices to it. (It's like the old joke, which has it's own version in most service industries, that "This (job) would be alright, if it weren't for the public". As anyone who's got their hands dirty with serial communications of any kind will tell you, there's no such thing as a standard.

For example, Casio keyboards use a special MIDI mode to play four separate sounds at once, MONO MODE 7, I'm reliably informed. Now how is your average MIDI package going to know that is what you want?

Take another example. To dump the sounds from the Casio into the Amiga, so you can save the sounds to disk, requires that you switch off the keyboard and reset the CZ Master program in between each attempt. You can't do it repeatedly as the poor keyboard gets confused and locks up. The problems are with minor incompatibilities between what the Amiga calls MIDI and what the keyboard in question wants to receive.

Okay, so there are problems. But in the light of that, what hints and tips can I give you?

1. Most important. MIDI sends along 16 channels, and in order to avoid any lock-ups, you must keep a track of all these channels and what they are doing. Write it all down on a piece of paper!

2. In most cases MIDI devices ignore data which they don't understand, (one way of making a standard of sorts, I suppose) but it's advisable to make sure you know the capabilities of all the devices you're driving, and match them as far as possible. For example, certain expensive keyboards are *velocity-sensitive*, in other words the sound gets louder the more you hit it. There's no point in sending this information to a non-velocity-sensitive device.

3. Keep your leads tidy. Sounds obvious but many's the time I've plugged the wrong leads in because I've just let them trail all over the place. Labelling them with stickers is a good wheeze.

4.	You can make your own MIDI leads for about quarter the price of shop-bought ones, and it's very easy. You need two 5 pin DIN plugs at 50p each and a length of two core screened cable, at about 25p a metre. Then you wire it together like so:

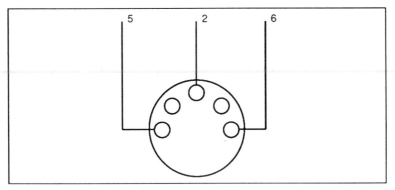

Figure 13.2. MIDI plug.

The two cores go onto pins 4 and 5, and the mesh is soldered onto pin 2 as an earth. Don't get the 4 and 5 wires crossed, though!

Music X 2

One of the best music programs for the Amiga, although by no means perfect, is Music X 2 by MicroIllusions. The program works in a very intuitive way, using controls based on video and HiFi: play, rewind and pause etc. The tracks you create can be shown as bars and blobs, or in a more conventional tabular form. The tabular form is called an Event editor, and this is a very accurate method of inputting musical data. You can just type it in, although it's best to play it in from your keyboard.

The beauty of making MIDI music is you don't have to be a real musician to use it. You can play tunes slowly, and then speed them up. You can put the notes in one at a time and worry about the timing later. Or you can even put any old notes in, in the right rhythm, and worry about the actual notes later. In the bar editor you can move notes around with the mouse, and this is by far the best way of editing music, especially for someone who knows what they want, but doesn't have time to go and learn musical notation for the next five years.

Soundtrackers

There is a very special way of making music on an Amiga, using sound samples and MIDI and that is with the use of what we call *soundtrackers* or just *trackers*.

There was an original tracker actually called Soundtracker, but this is long gone now, in the wake of a huge wave of copies, re-writes and new versions. The beauty of Soundtracker was that it used a very simple interface, and sound samples on two or three disks, to produce music. The music was written on the screen in columns, and as the tune was played, the columns (the four tracks of the piece) scrolled up like the paper roll on a Player Piano.

One of the most famous new trackers was Noisetracker, an updated version of the original program, and also Games Music Creator, a tailor_made program for producing music for games programs. But by far the best tracker ever made is MED 3.0, written by Teijo Kinunnen. See Chapter 20 for more details about MED, as quite surprisingly for a program of this quality, it is actually public domain!

Trackers are easy to use now, and using them you can create stand-alone music files. First you save off the music as a *module*, as they call it, then you run it through a PD program called Module Processor which turns the module into an executable program. You can then run the music file just by clicking on an icon. Both MED 3.0 and Module Processor are available from Amiganuts. (For address see Chapter 20.

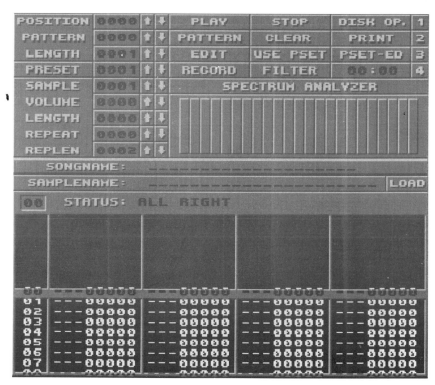

Figure 13.3. The original Soundtracker.

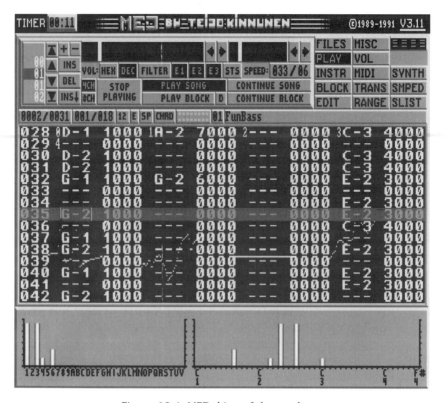

Figure 13.4. MED, king of the trackers.

DTP – Desktop Publishing

Amiga users often get big ideas about doing desktop publishing and graphics on their machine. But so often, as is the case with DTP especially, even if you only want to make a simple newsletter on a dot matrix printer, you find you run out of memory before you start. Using Professional Page 3.0 is like this, especially on early A500 machines with small amounts of chip memory. You boot the disk and as soon as you type a word, the outline fonts clog your memory up and you can't even open a requester to shut the thing down. But don't worry, because help is at hand. Gold Disk, the very firm who wrote the Professional Page program, did a new version of its popular low end DTP program, Pagesetter, and called it Pagesetter II. How very original.

With this program you can do page after page of superb text and graphics, and all on that tatty old Epson printer you were about to pension off. Unbelievably, you can produce reasonable output on a Preferences printer. The reason for this textual bliss is the rather smooth and tempting Agfa Compugraphic fonts that have been included with the program. Yes, these are the very same CG fonts that you get with Professional Page 3.0, only they've been unshackled from the complexities of a Post-Script based program, and allowed to run amock in a smaller, much more manageable machine. Although you can run it with the normal old fonts, you get the option of using the two CG fonts, (CG)Times and a Helvetica clone called (CG)Triumvirate.

People who are familiar with Professional Page will feel right at home with Pagesetter II. Although PageSetter is more of what you might call Personal Publishing rather than proper DTP in my book, you can actually produce professional-looking results in a short time and on usually feeble equipment. The CG fonts look great and even the dithering on the IFF files is more than acceptable. (Be warned the best IFF files are contrasty ones, so please set your Preferences to recognise fewer colours as black, using the threshold setting.)

Although you boot up in medium res by default, you can easily select interlace mode from a menu. Pagesetter II is a multitasking program too, and will happily sit around in memory while you do something else. It doesn't steal too much memory for itself either, and if you haven't got much, it even allows you the option to turn workbench on or off.

So don't be fooled into paying a lot of money for a wordprocessor with pictures, when you can have a very creditable DTP program for the same price!

Okay, so that's DTP covered, or is it? There's just one more thing you need to get you to DTP heaven, and that's clip art. You have to draw the pictures or scan them in to a DTP package, but what if you can't afford a scanner or a digitiser? The answer is you buy some disks of clip art and you just import them into your document. What's clip art? It's professionally produced drawings, saved to disk in a format that Pro Page or PageSetter can read, and you can use the pictures in your documents. *eclips* is just such a set of clip art.

These disks are structured clip art drawn using Professional Draw, on a wide range of useful subjects. All you do is select the import *structured clip* menu option and voila! There you are.

The thing about using structured clip art is that it gives your DTP more punch. The pro quality line art in these clips is jaggie free because the lines are drawn in the mind of the computer and the printhead of the printer. So they stay smooth at any scale, because they are redrawn afresh every time. The lines are mathematically drawn, you see, rather than being fixed bitmaps, like an IFF picture from Deluxe Paint. So they look good on any printer, and even on a dot matrix they are smooth and professional. They are automatically drawn using the highest resolution your printer can deliver.

The eclips package contains four disks with over 300 separate pieces of structured artwork, covering every subject you can think of; animals, arrows, Amigas, bears, balloons, bicycles, carrots, donkeys from a to z. Most things you could think of are there, and even if the exact thing you think of isn't in the selection, you can usually find something that is just as good, if not better. The artwork is all in black and white, but if you want colour, and you have the facility to print it out in full colour via separations, you can recolour them. What you have to do is paste the artworks into Professional Draw and recolour them there. Then save them off again and paste them into Professional Page. Obviously there's no point pasting colour art into Pagesetter 2, as it only works in black and white.

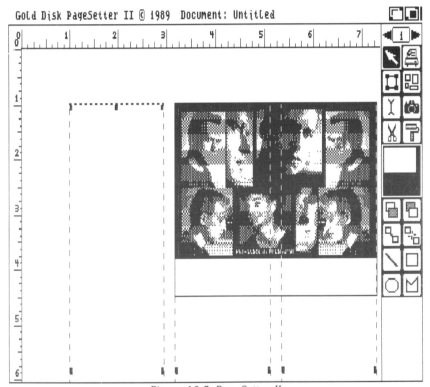

Figure 13.5. PageSetter II.

Painting and Animating

There are a clutch of programs which form your BASIC Amiga users' software tools. Obviously we have Deluxe Paint III for graphics and animation, DigiPaint 3 for HAM graphics, Professional

Page 3.0 for DTP, Music X for MIDI, Soundtracker for Amiga music, and Perfect Sound for sampling. But few people would think of using The Director for animation. DPaint and Disney Animator are obvious choices, so why choose the Director then? Well, it's one of the most useful programs going, that's why.

Yes, The Director is an animation program, and although far from being user friendly at first, is actually very easy to use. It takes the form of a subset of the BASIC programming language. Here's an example:

```
print "Here we go..."
load 1,"picture1"
getkey a
load 1,"picture2"
getkey a
load 1,"picture3"
getkey a
load 1,"picture4"
getkey a
load 1,"picture5"
getkey a
load 1,"picture6"
getkey a
pause 20
end
```

This program first prints *Here we go...* in the CLI window. Then it takes the named files from the current directory and displays them one after the other, but only after you press a key.

A great many demos and utilities have been written with the Director. Joel Hagen, artist extraordinaire, made his famous RGB, Focus and Probe demos with it, and not only that but Eric Gustafson's famous disk three PD Star Trek game was written with it, too. In fact although the program was designed as a sort of DeskTop Video product, it actually has applications as a programming tool, like a sort of multimedia authoring tool. For example, even some of the tools in the Director Toolkit, were written using the program itself.

Although the Director is essentially a version of BASIC, the program you write is actually compiled by the main program. Once a program has been written, it is transformed by the Director program into a short machine code file, which can then be shown, or *projected*, using the Projector program. What you do is write your program into a text editor. Then type:

```
director <filename>
```

where the filename is the name of your program. All the IFF brushes, pics and sounds you want to use must be in the same dir as your program. The Director runs through the animation slowly to compact it, and then saves it to disk. (Note: This means that if you list the files on a Director'ed demo, you can rip the graphics and sound from it!) When the compilation is finished, your original source file is joined by a file called:

```
<filename>.film
```

which is a compacted version of your instructions. You can then delete your source code file and then run the .film file using Projector. This runs the .film file and shows all the pics as you want them to be, with wipes, sound and even animation.

The range of commands is varied and even includes functions to control the blitter chip for faster turns of speed. You can select an area on screen to be clicked by the mouse, thereby creating menus and interactive movies. You can make a Computer Aided Learning disk, which drags the pupil by the nose through a complex web of graphic data on a certain subject, and all the operator would have to do is simply click the mouse on the screen, wherever he was told to.

The Director is cheap, fast and powerful, and if you can program in BASIC you already know how to use it. Demos are easy, as are presentation graphics, short educational films, and even utilities, if you can spend the time on them. Graphics are all you need, so all you have to do now is learn how to draw or buy a digitiser.

Another program of a similar quality is the Mandarin Software program called AMOS. This is also a BASIC-based programming language, and this one supports sound samples and tracker scores too! I'll talk about AMOS in more detail in a moment.

Digitising

To get graphics of your own into a multimedia or animation program, you can spend years going to art school and learning how to draw. Or you can draw already perhaps, but you can't draw with the mouse, a common problem. So you have to digitise.

Digitising is all about grabbing images using a video camera or video recorder, and what this means is that anything you point the camera at is going to be grabbed as an IFF file. There are three options here, the DigiView Gold by NewTek, the VIDI Amiga and RGB Splitter by Rombo, and the ColourPic and SuperPic machines by JCL.

DigiView was the very first Amiga graphics digitiser, and it works by taking the output from a black and white video camera and feeding it into the parallel port of your Amiga. Once the program is running, any image on the screen can be grabbed into memory. It's vital if this is a still image, as the grabber takes a few seconds to grab. Colour images can be made using the same software and a b/w camera. Yes, a black and white camera. You hold red, green and blue filters over the lens and take a separate exposure for each colour component. The computer then fits all these components together and makes a colour picture.

DigiView is a high quality digitiser, but works best when you point the camera at a still photo or drawing. This means you are best advised to buy what photo shops call a *copystand*, which is a base board with a column, onto which you fix the camera and a pair of lightbulbs. This means you can digitise any material like photos, drawings, paintings, in fact anything flat. The DigiView also has the distinction of being the only digitiser that works with the HAM-E 256 colour device made by Blackbelt Systems.

The Rombo VIDI Amiga is more versatile than the DigiView, although most times I've tested them the Rombo came off worse in terms of quality. The VIDI is more of a frame grabber, as it performs best grabbing screens *on the fly* as they say, from moving video. The machine is fitted to the parallel port again, and this time you can take the output from a video recorder. The VIDI grabs screens very quickly, and in fact when you press the grab button on your keyboard, you have the last 20 or so frames stored in memory. This is obviously nice for digitising animation. But grabbing so fast usually means that you are sacrificing quality. However, you can get a similar quality out of the VIDI as you can expect in DigiView, by the simple process of buying the VidiChrome colour kit and the RGB splitter box. This allows you to grab colour frames, and if the frames you are grabbing are from a video camera, then the quality is much better.

The ColourPic and SuperPic are real top of the range gadgets. Inside the boxes you have a real frame store, and this means you can run realtime video through it and store a frame of colour video in the machine. This is frozen in the memory of the ColourPic, and then it can be grabbed at leisure by the digitising software. The quality you get out of ColourPic is astonishing, much like you'd expect out of a still frame digitiser like DigiView, but from moving video! Okay so the ColourPic and SuperPic are expensive, but the quality they deliver is superb. The SuperPic version of the device comes with a built in *genlock*, meaning you can also overlay Amiga graphics over an incoming video signal. This can form the basis of your own DeskTop Video setup, for adding titles and special effects to your home videos.

So that's digitising. Are there any better or cheaper ways of getting outside graphics into your Amiga?

Figure 13.6. Digitised picture made with VIDI Amiga.

Scanning

If you're a graphics or DTP person, then one of the biggest bugbears of your life is getting real life graphics into your computer for treatment. As most people who draw on computers come from a paper and pen background, sometimes they begin to think it would be nice to just scoot the mouse across a picture on the paper and wallop! Well, you can, if you use a hand scanner like the Geniscan from Datel.

The scanner itself looks not unlike a mouse, but with a fat end, like a hammerhead shark. Inside is a scanner light, green like all the best photocopiers or fax machines, to give you the best contrast with even coloured pictures. On the underside of the scanner is a wide rubber roller, plus two small polythene ones. It looks as though the scanner would easily slip and make your scanned pictures all wiggly, but in practice this is not the case. The scanner rides smoothly across surfaces, as long as they are flat and the rubber can get a purchase. On the side of the unit is a little flush mounted button, which you press when you want to scan, plus a selector switch for line art and grey scale, and a contrast knob marked *light-dark*, the purpose of which is I think self-explanatory.

The software is a little spartan, but it gets the job done, allowing you to scan IFF files into your Amy in 100, 200, 300 and 400 dpi, which is not a bad resolution in anyone's language, when you think that your average laser or inkjet is only 300 dpi. With it you can scan a screen at a time, or more than one for bigger subjects. As you stroke the scanner across the image underneath, the picture rolls onto the screen like a blind being drawn down. The light on the scanner goes on and off, controlled by the software, only illuminating the image being scanned when the software is receiving.

Adjusting the light and dark wheel gives you a lot of say about how much detail you get in the finished scan, and the resolution is enough to pick up the finest tracings of pen on the paper. If you want IFF files from drawings or tracings, you can do a lot worse than this device.

Fractals

You may have heard about fractals and how they can generate graphics on computers, but you may not have considered that you can use them on your computer. It's a common misconception that you need a very powerful machine to create imaginative computer graphics that look like real objects or places. In fact using PD programs like MandelVroom, FracGen and Turbomandel, you can create and view the most beautifully detailed fractal shapes on your computer, even on a base-level machine without much memory.

In fact you can go much further than that, if you purchase a program like Vista or VistaPro.

A New Vista

Virtual Reality has come to be a bit of a buzz phrase over the last few months. Along with the language of cyberspace and cyberpunk literature, virtual reality is a couple of words that almost any cellphone-toting technobore can flip out over dinner without a blink. And yet so few people actually understand what it all means. Real worlds within the electronic fabric of a computer. Real landscapes that you can create and roam around, all seeming very solid, and yet the mountains and the trees only exist in the computer. No human eye has ever seen these sights before. And like the synthesiser before it, fractal geometry allows us to do with landscapes what we did to sound, create a mood or place that wasn't there before in nature.

About a year or so ago I happened across a fractal demo which showed a flight through a mountain range. The *camera* flew through the trees and across the surface of the lakes so smoothly, it seemed like a jet was racing through the Rocky Mountains, and the thing was so real. You could just about make out the jaggy aliasing, due to the fact that the mountains were made out of triangles. But the effect was amazing, and so it should be with about 300 frames of animation. At the bottom of the screen the legend said that the program used was a forthcoming product, from a firm called Hypercube Engineering. I'd forgotten all about it until Vista arrived. This was the forthcoming product mentioned in the demo, and with Vista you can create and view fractal landscapes, and even make animations.

Vista is more than a fractal landscape engine, allowing you to create random landscapes at the touch of a button. Included in the package are files created from US Geological Society Digital Elevation Model files, a digital representation of the various heights in an area of land. About 40% of the USA and various astronomical bodies have been converted into DEM files, and eventually all of these files will be made available to Vista users. These DEM files are turned into Vista format by its creators, which means you can load in a real landscape and walk around it. Supplied on the disk are DEM files for:

• El Capitan in the Yosemite Valley, California

• The Half Dome formation, again at Yosemite

• Crater Lake, Oregon

• Mount St Helens, Washington (Before and After)

• Olympus Mons, Mars

The files cover some of the most stunning views in the US and Olympus Mons is a view of the biggest volcano in the Solar System, on the planet Mars. One very interesting feature is the view of Mount St Helens, before and after the famous eruption of 1980. This is a great idea, this packaging of famous landscapes for the computer, and I hope they get a few more data disks out a bit sharpish, as I've already used up the first lot!

After you've loaded up all the DEM files, you can start to create your own. All you have to do is either hit the F button at the bottom of the screen. Or you can type in a number to make the scape. I tried my birthday, which in numbers is 100360, in case you want to tap it in yourself (or send me a card). This created a nice little atoll which you can see in the accompanying picture. Once you have a landscape, you can save the data as a .scape file, or even a file for use in Imagine ray tracer. Obviously if you want

want to save a huge mountain range into Silver and render it, you've got to have a large amount of memory, so watch it. After you've got the mountain you want, you can smooth out the contours for a nice even landscape, or exaggerate them to make it spiky. You can also change the colour, which in the case of Olympus Mons is red, red, red or red. For normal 'scapes you can make the grass and tree lines green, the rocks beige and the snow white, for a natural-looking landscape. But if you're feeling silly, you can colour the scape any range of psychedelic hues you wish. As well as using shades for the earth and sea/lakes, the program shades them a little too, to give the impression of reflections in the water and even haze on the horizon.

There are four different resolutions you can render at using the program, lower resolutions with size 8 or 4 polygons, and higher *finished* resolutions with size 2 or 1 polygons. Other neat features are really odd things like the fractal music you can play while rendering. This music is a musical version of the values of the polygons being used to make the picture. (Californians. Don't you just love 'em?)

The technical among you will probably like to know that the program features 4 billion different fractal landscapes for you to discover. Just tap in all the numbers you can think of and there you have it. When you've done that you should be very old indeed. What else? Although the program displays pictures in 320 x 200 pixel HAM mode, the pictures are defined internally as 24 bit pictures with 16 million colours. This means if you have the professional version of the program you can render the landscapes to a 24 bit graphics card, like the Harlequin from Amiga Centre Scotland.

Vista is fast, flexible and fun, the 3 Fs. And best of all it's currently number one in a field of one. So if you want to draw fractal mountains, take a picture of your birthday island, or just take a stroll on Mars, Vista is the only way to fly.

Figure 13.7. My birthday rendered as a landscape.

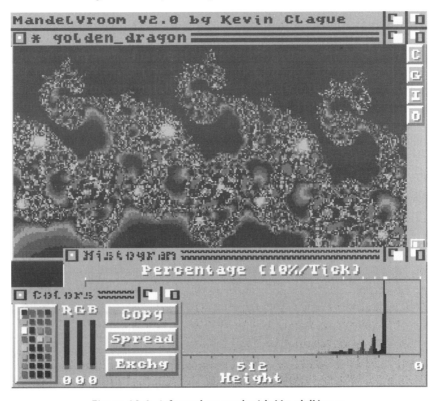

Figure 13.8. A fractal created with MandelVroom.

AMOS Does Everything

Now after all that about graphics and sound applications, here's the last word about a package which does it all. AMOS is a way of programming your Amiga to do everything you ever wanted it to do, using a simple to understand programming language that you can learn in minutes.

The language is in fact BASIC, the single simplest computer programming language ever designed. So if you know BASIC, you know enough to be up and running in about 20-30 minutes. If you don't know BASIC, then it's very simple to learn. (See Chapter 10 for more about BASIC)

Having said all that, what is this AMOS thing all about? Well, normal BASIC interpreters, like the one you get free with your Amiga, are slow. AMOS is fast, very fast. And it does things that you shouldn't be able to do using any form of BASIC. You can do those neat multicoloured bars, like on machine code demos, you can load and manipulate IFF screens, Soundtracker, Sonix or Game Music Creator music scores, and you can scroll screens of graphics smoothly and professionally. This really shouldn't be possible on an Amiga, and not only does it do the impossible but it does it on any Amiga, from the base-level single drive unexpanded A500 right up to the top of the range Amiga 3000. How the program does this is using extensions to BASIC, commands which do more than normal ones, and AMOS Animation Language (AMAL). But more of the details in minute.

Included in the package you get AMOS BASIC, a sprite editor, a three hundred page manual, 80 example programs, sprite files and AMOS Club Newsletter. On disk you also get some fully-fledged programs to let you know the power of the program. There are two arcade games, called Magic Forest and Amosteroids, a graphic adventure game called Castle AMOS, and an educational program called Number Leap.

The two disks are the master AMOS disk and a Data disk, containing the demo programs and the demo games. AMOS is definitely being pushed as a games creator, and these show what it can do. Castle Amos is a graphic adventure game, which gives you a graphic for each location and displays text in a scroll-shaped window which slides down when you need it. The graphics are nicely done and the game slick and playable. All the other programs on the disk are demonstrations to be used with the AMOS manual.

AMOS is easily installed on your system. The disks are non-copy protected to allow easy back-ups or installation on your hard disk. For HD users there is actually a neat little INSTALL program on the disk written in AMOS, just to show how versatile it is. Okay so you can do this with a simple batch file, but they're out to PR the program, aren't they, so you can't blame them.

Using AMOS is simplicity itself. You have two modes of operation after you've started the program, the editor, where you write programs, and direct mode, where you type bits in to execute immediately.

The command set has been made as simple and idiot proof as possible with commands like MUSIC to start a piece of sequenced music. A grounding in conventional BASIC isn't essential but does give you a big advantage over a non-BASIC user. The language is a nice structured format like AmigaBasic or Hisoft BASIC, where there are no line numbers (unless you want them) but labels. You can type in and run any normal BASIC program and it will run.

The editor is a joy to use. I hate to have to say that, but this time it's true. I've never used a language with such a friendly editor before. All the commands you need for manipulating your programs are on a big menu at the top of the screen. Certain buttons are on display which you can click on, and there is another bank to use if you hold down the right mouse button. From this menu you can load, save, test, merge and run programs, as well as a number of other functions. The menu options are also available on the function keys, with the first bank being the straight keys, and the second needing the aid of the SHIFT key. As you use the editor you have a constant display of how you're doing for memory, handy if you're working to a tight K budget.

There are a lot of very easy to use commands for memory saving, like CLOSE WORKBENCH for example, which saves you 40K. You can even free up memory by using CLOSE EDITOR, which frees up another 28K. You want to get rid of the mouse pointer? Just say HIDE. To get it back say SHOW. To change the shape of the mouse pointer say CHANGE MOUSE. To get a status of the mouse buttons say MOUSE KEY or MOUSE CLICK. The command to limit the mouse pointer to an area of the screen is simple too, just say LIMIT MOUSE, and give the co-ordinates. Reading the joystick is similarly trouble free. The business of manipulating sound and graphics have also been taken apart and reduced to their BASIC building blocks. You have three built-in sound affects other than the normal BEEP, and these are BOOM, an explosion, SHOOT, a gun firing, and BELL, a simple bell tone. If these aren't enough for what you want, you can also trigger individual IFF sound samples. To play a sample from a sample bank (they love having banks of things in AMOS) you type SAM PLAY. To play a raw sample from the Amiga's memory, type SAM RAW. To play a sample looped over and over, just type SAM LOOP.

It's all so cool and logical you keep wanting to say "Of course, it's obvious! Why haven't we thought of doing it that way years ago?" Music is played from banks as well. Like to play a bit of music, you type MUSIC and then the number of the sequence. This sequence could have been created in Sonix, Soundtracker or GMC, it doesn't matter. You can even define and play your own synthesised notes using the PLAY, WAVE, SAMPLE, and SET ENVEL commands.

The Amiga has a filter on the audio channels which muffles the sound. This is for preventing you hearing the jaggies in the sound, but all it does is make everything sound muffled. You can turn the filter off by typing LED. The *audio anti-aliasing filter* (as it is called) will go off and so will the LED power light on the Amiga. The test program to show you the difference goes like this:

```
Load "AMOS_DATA:MUSIC/MUSICDEMO.ABK"

Music 1

Do

    If mouse key=1 then led on

    If mouse key=2 then led off

Loop
```

This means it plays the tune then, lets you turn the filter on and off with mouse buttons.

If sound and control options are easy to get at, then so are graphics. To load an IFF screen into memory you say LOAD IFF. Try that with AmigaBASIC! And to save an IFF file just type SAVE IFF. If you want to do something, say it in plain English and you'll be close to the AMOS command, it seems. Screens can be loaded, moved around in memory, scrolled around the screen, and can make use of a battery of special effects like APPEAR, FADE, FLASH, SHIFT UP, RAINBOW, and ZOOM.

This on its own would all be very impressive, but AMOS doesn't stop there. You have access, with the same level of simple high-level commands, to the Copper and the Blitter, enabling you to contrive dazzling effects of your own. This is what makes AMOS so exciting. Not the party tricks, but the real raw unfocussed power of the thing, letting you get right into the soul of your Amiga and call the shots.

As you can probably tell, I'm more than a bit impressed with AMOS. It's everything a good program should be, fast, user-friendly, compact, powerful and most of all cheap. The whole thing costs just £50 at last count. That's right, a powerful programming language that anyone can use and it's just fifty quid. And the AMOS compiler will be out by the time you read this. This program will compile your AMOS programs into stand-alone machine code, and speed them up more than a tad.

With AMOS no avenue of exploration is closed to you, unlike the case with AmigaBASIC which allows you freedom inside narrow parameters. The future of AMOS is secure, with expansion modules being planned for release into the public domain and a lot of support in motion already, generated by its sister program on the ST called STOS. The multimedia aspects of the program are there to be explored by some bright spark. Let's all get into high level languages again, that's my view. I can't count in hex in my head, anyway!

14:
Good
Software
Guide

There is a lot of very good software out there for the Amiga now, but sometimes it's hard to see what's hot and what's not without a little help. So I thought it'd be a good idea to review some of my own current favourites in software, to give you something to go on as to what you might need to buy once you've got your Amiga system up and running.

Software falls into some more interesting categories nowadays, rather than the boring old leisure and business. There are categories for games, creativity, music, graphics, desktop publishing, multimedia, accounting, presentations, desktop video, and many more which even I don't know about! Here is a stack of short reviews of the very best software I've come across in recent months. Some I use now, some I don't use any more, but all of them are good programs, and have been of use to me at some stage when using the Amiga, albeit for just the one job. As always these products are on the move; newer versions may crop up, and better programs may come along, but as of right now these are my choices. If you really want to buy anything from this list, check the ads in the current Amiga-specific magazines for prices, availability etc or ask your local dealer.

Deluxe Paint IV

A real classic, and something that every Amiga user should go out and buy right away. Dpaint IV is a graphics and animation program, using the mouse to let you draw on screen in anything up to 64 colours. Using a variety of excellent tools you can draw on the screen, and grab areas of a picture as *brushes*. These brushes can then be used to draw on the screen. This is a very startling effect, and very hard to describe without having the package in front of you. Equally stunning is the program's palette control, allowing you to cycle the colours at any speed.

As well as being a first-class drawing program, and very easy and intuitive to use, Dpaint IV is also an animation program. (This feature was added for Dpaint III, and DPaint versions 1 and 2 didn't have it!) The screen is seen as a series of pages which can be flipped back and forth to draw, the different frames of the animation. Once drawn, the animation can be saved out in the standard ANIM format to be played back by a variety of different programs, like PageFlipper, Disney Animation Studio etc.

The really neat thing about DPaint is that it is good to use even if you can't really draw. You can doodle with it for hours, invoking all the different tools and swirling them around, cycling the colours and drawing in the mirror mode until the cows come home. It's a highly creative and absorbing pursuit, and one which only the Amiga can give you for the price.

DPaint is my first choice of graphics software, for just about any purpose. It creates everything from ordinary bit-mapped graphics to ANIM files. I'm never far away from it.

Although DPaint II was very good, it couldn't handle HAM or Hold And Modify mode. Dpaint IV can. In this mode you have access to all 4096 colours of your Amiga at once on the same screen, and it is this mode that is used for most digitisers, enabling them to render images that are almost photographic quality.

Deluxe PhotoLab

The best companion program to Deluxe Paint is Deluxe PhotoLab and, although it is no longer published, you might be able to pick one up secondhand. This is a suite of three programs allowing you to Paint, Colour and create huge printouts of your IFF pictures, HAM or otherwise.

What Deluxe PhotoLab allows you to do is not only paint in any resolution up to HAM, but also exchange an IFF graphics file to some other display format. So if you have a low resolution HAM image from a digitiser, you can take the HAM off it and render it in 32 or 64 colours for DPaint to handle. This is good as it enables you to use other graphics in your own art, even pictures from HAM slideshow disks. (See Chapter 20 on the Public Domain for details about these.) Although you can draw with Deluxe PhotoLab, it is really to be treated as a sort of filter through which you can put pictures created by other means.

Also using PhotoLab you can create huge printouts using the Poster program. If you wanted a picture six feet square, you could get one using this program. It does this by printing out the usual A4 sheets, but each sheet is a part of the larger picture, meaning you can stick them all together and make the big picture suitable for framing, or even papering your wall!

Spectracolor (Oxxi)

HAM programs were all the rage a little while ago, as they showed all 4096 colours that the Amiga is capable of on the screen at the same time. Digi-Paint and Spectracolor grew out of this fad, and they are the only two programs that are still around after the dust has settled.

Spectracolor is a big and complex program, with a lot of very nice features to help you draw in HAM mode. You can draw with any colour you can imagine, and all the colours can sit pixel by pixel on the screen. The trade off here is that, as with all HAM pictures, the effect can be a little bit woolly, due to the way HAM is rendered. But for paintings, as opposed to drawings, the effect is very good, allowing you to get very subtle graduations of colour, just like mixing colours on the artists palette.

Also Spectracolor is unlike any other HAM package in that it does animation. Although this is a very memory intensive exercise, the effect can be very impressive indeed.

Digi-Paint 3 (NewTek)

Just like Spectracolor, Digi-Paint 3 is a HAM painting package, and is a superb way of creating graphics in HAM mode. As well as a mind-boggling array of effects, the program is much faster than Spectracolor, and has a separate program called Transfer 24 which allows you to alter files to suit any other paint program and make overall changes to the pictures you make, in the way of palette, number of colours etc. This means you have a program a bit like Deluxe PhotoLab which can chop files about in just about any way you like.

As well as all this I personally find Digi-Paint to be much more user-friendly, and I like the speed of its interface. It lacks the animation potential, but I've never needed that anyway. There are plenty of animation programs that fit into less memory, besides.

The Animation Studio (Disney Software)

A great animation program from the home of great animation. The program is one of the very few to feature traditional animation techniques on a computer, and it works very well. Although you can create the artwork in The Animation Studio, it is much better to create the key frames in something more technical like DPaint, and use TAS to clean up the animation and make an honest ANIM file out of it. The disks also feature a lot of digitised Disney characters in motion for you to study various aspects of animation technique.

Protext 5.5 (Arnor)

Protext is in use in just about every Amiga-based environment I've ever seen. Some of the Amiga magazines use it to tap in their words, and friends I have swear by it as the very best fully featured Amiga wordprocessor in the world and it's from England. Although I don't use it, I appreciate that it is a very good program, and one which users who have come from a PC computer to the Amiga will feel most at home on. I don't use it myself, as I don't really need all those features.

excellence! 2.0 (MSS)

A superb graphic word processor, using the Amiga interface to the full. excellence! (always spelled with a small *e* and an exclamation mark) is a graphic wordprocessor, in that it prints out exactly what is on the screen as a graphic, rather than just pumping the words out as text to the printer. In this way it's more like a Mac wordprocessor in looks and operation, with a range of very interesting features. Not least of these is its ability to grammar check your work. Yes, it will check your grammar to see if you've made a really BASIC mistake, although it's not a substitute for a good editor (thanks – ed). Spell checking is available too, and it also allows you a check spelling as you type. There is a thesaurus built in too, but all these features don't really come cheap. It does have a WYSIWYG (What You See Is What You Get) display, and uses all the Amiga fonts. And it allows you to paste graphics into your documents too! Drawbacks include the fact that it's an American English spell checker and so it needs a few months of use to get it into normal English.

ProWrite 3.0 (New Horizons)

A similar proposition to excellence! in essence, a graphics based wordprocessor. Although less memory intensive, and with fewer features, the program has a lot to offer, and makes just about every bit of text look impressive. Works well with both dot matrixes and inkjets, and even has a separate program for output to PostScript printers.

Transcript/Transwrite (Gold Disk)

A simple no frills word processor, originally designed to be a text editor for Professional Page, but actually quite efficient in its own right. I use it to create all my text, even these words you are reading in fact, and I find it just great. All I really need from a word-processor is to be able to type words in, spell check them and count them. If you want fancy formatting and graphics, then you'd best look at one of the others.

You can print out and even mail merge from this program, so it does just fine for letters, and as it was designed with DTP packages in mind, the text is free of the returns and control characters what other programs generate. This means my text can be sent on disk to the magazines I work for and they can just flow it into the page.

So for BASIC text editing on anything from a book down to a three line letter, here's the best option. (Also available as TransWrite and the Article Editor that comes free with Professional Page 2.0)

Access! (PD)

A public domain comms program that I used for a while. Not bad at all, but unfortunately NComm wasn't far behind! Try this one before you buy one. Its a very colourful program, and yet features all the right download protocols for you to get started. If you've just bought a modem then this is a nice simple introduction to comms.

NComm (PD)

Another PD comms program and in my opinion the best one with all the best features, including YModem and ZModem, plus all the other bells and whistles. The program stores a list of phone numbers for you to dial, and dials them automatically from a menu selection. You can edit and save your phone books, and although less colourful and simple than Access!, it is actually a more sussed-out program. I use it all the time, and it's never let me down. It's a shareware product, which means that although you can use it free of charge for a while, you have to send some money to the authors if you intend to use it for ever. This isn't too much trouble, and you get free updates when the program goes to a new version.

Deluxe Video III (Electronic Arts)

A brilliant video making package, and provided you obey the rules it holds more moving objects per bit of memory than most other packages. MovieSetter comes close, but I still prefer Old Faithful.

The really neat thing about DVideo is that it is very user-friendly, and now that it supports MIDI and has buttons that you can push on screen, it's more of a multimedia program, allowing you to create everything from a video title to a presentation to a point of sale program. You make videos by dragging the different events like graphics and effects around as little objects with arrows on them. The arrows point to a time line along the screen, so you can accurately edit the timing of events. The program also allows you to distribute your animations and video using a PD player program, which means you can give someone a disk containing your video and they can just plug it into their system and off they go.

Broadcast Titler 2 (Innovision Technology)

For broadcast quality titling there isn't much in the way of alternatives. Sure you can bang off some video titles in DPaint and whizz them around with DVideo, but the quality will be a little bit crunchy for the most part, and if the quality of the text is what you're after, then there are only two programs to looks at. At the low end there is Big Alternative Scroller, which I will go into in a minute, but at the high end of the spectrum we have Broadcast Titler 2.

This is a big program with some very neat scrolling tricks in its repertoire, and very smooth scrolling it is too. There is a barrage of effects, like wipes and checkers and stuff. All very nice, and with a big selection of special high resolution smooth fonts which have all been specially anti-aliased for the purpose. There is also another program which will take fonts, even ones you have created yourself, and anti-alias them for you.

Big Alternative Scroller (Alternative Image)

A new program from a firm usually known for its video work rather than software. A very simple program designed to do one particular job really well, and that is scroll text horizontally and vertically. You tap your text into the editor and out it comes as a title or caption. Brilliant when used with a genlock over your home videos. Version 2.0 will probably be out by the time you read this, featuring the ability to read in text files, with extended font control and more exotic effects.

The Director 2 (Right Answers Group)

The bee's knees, animation wise. A lot of the most famous demos you see in the Public Domain are done with The Director 2. Its basically a programming language (like BASIC) with which you shift around graphics. Totally brilliant.

All you do is write your program in a sort of BASIC language, and then run it through the Director 2 program which compiles it into a little chunk of code. Then you run it using the player, and the graphics and transitions are set in motion. You can make very sophisticated movies with the Director 2, and in spite of the fact it is a programming language more than an easy to use program like Deluxe Video, I'd still rate it higher and more powerful than any other program, with the exception perhaps of CanDo.

Scala 2

Scala 2 is a presentation package, and a very excellent one. Combine the ease of use of Deluxe Video and the fonts and graphics quality of Broadcast Titler 2, and you've got a pretty good idea what Scala 2 is like. It's a very friendly package, doing everything from easy to understand menus. You have a huge range of fonts to play with, and some five disks full of artworks to get you going! This is a quality product with some very professional results to be had for very little effort.

Real 3D (Activa)

This is a primo ray-tracing package, brand new and very good. Renders so fast you scarcely have time to make a cup of tea, whereas previous packages require that you leave them overnight. The program also does animation, which very few rendering programs actually do very well.

The program is much faster than most of the traditional ray tracing programs, Sculpt 3D for example, and there is even a faster version made for use with turbo processors. These are faster versions of the standard 68000 chip like the 68020 and 68030, which for various reasons either just run faster or are more elegant designs which turn in better performance. You can either add to your system as a card or buy installed in your Amiga if you get yourself a 3000.

Imagine

Although not as easy to use as Real 3D, Turbo Silver is one of the best ray tracers I've ever used, and certainly one of the fastest. The texture mapping is excellent, and there are several effects in Turbo which I've not seen anywhere else.

Professional Page v3.0 (Gold Disk)

The best DTP package around, still favourite with most professionals. This is a very stable new version of this quality package. You can create documents and output them to disk in PostScript format, then take them to a bureau for laser or Linotronic printing!

The strength of Pro Page is that you can print on anything from a dot matrix printer to a laser or imagesetter, which means you have a chance to do DTP whatever your circumstances. Some of the best output I've got from it has been on my old HP DeskJet 500, which turns out page after page of beautiful text using ProPage's Compugraphic fonts. These are scalable fonts made by Agfa, which draw smooth lines around each letter and then fill it in, meaning you can draw the fonts at any size and they will still look good. The range of fonts for the program is expanding with at least five disks worth to be going on with and a possible 70 different fonts to choose from at the time of going to press.

Professional Draw v3.0 (Gold Disk)

The best structured drawing package on the Amiga. Ideal for producing line drawings for DTP packages like ProPage. ProDraw has got some stunning special effects, like the Blend function which in-betweens two curves, creating smooth transitions of shape and colour, and giving you a choice of steps between them. Output from ProDraw on its own is as jaggie-free as ProPage, and prints to the best of your printer's ability.

Art Department Professional (ASDG)

This is a very sophisticated image-processing program which enables you to take in pictures from virtually any format, like TIFF, GIF, Amiga IFF 24 Bit, HAM-E, and various other image types and output as a similar barrage of image types. You can turn an IFF file into PostScript, or TIFF, or you can turn a HAM-E image into 24 bit IFF. You can also mix images from different formats. So, all sorts of things are possible with this versatile program, and if you are in the DTP or graphics game, then this is one hell of a professional tool.

CanDo (Inovatronics)

CanDo is an excellent multimedia program, which lets you create programs of any kind which can use all the resources that the Amiga has to offer. Using buttons and script files, sets of simple yet powerful commands, you can build up applications and even games using the easy menus and loading your own pictures and sounds.

AmigaVision (Commodore)

AV is Commodore's own multimedia program, and it is one of the most powerful authoring systems around. Some like it better than CanDo for some things, but I reckon it's horses for courses.

The system uses icons and a simple tabular format which enables you to simply place an Icon on the table where you want something to happen. The program allows you to access CD ROM, MIDI, CD music disks, Amiga IFF files and sound samples to create lively presentations and programs for your business or pleasure.

Elan Performer 2.0

This is a great program for doing presentations or speeches. You can tie a picture or animation to a key on the Amiga keyboard and just press the key when you want the picture to flip up on screen.

AMOS (Europress Software)

The BASIC programming language is one of the easiest to learn, and one of the most powerful for the beginner to use. AMOS is an extended BASIC language that enables you to harness the full power of the Amiga without learning any machine code or C, which is what you'd have to do if you really wanted to do this without AMOS. The program was written originally to let you write games programs with the minimum of fuss, but in the end the system became able to write almost any Amiga program you want. You can use all the graphics modes, the copper, make demos, utilities, anything you like, and the program costs just under £50! The system has recently been updated to include a 3D module and an assembler, plus the new compiler program which lets you compile your AMOS programs into super fast machine code.

If you like to program then you can do a lot worse than buy AMOS, and to be honest for under £50 you can't really go wrong.

CrossDOS (Consultron)

This is a simple program which enables you to access MS DOS format disks from a PC computer. This means you can just poke a PC disk into your drive and read the disks, copy files from them and to them. You can't run programs, as this is just a disk reader, but it does enable you to use text and graphics files from your PC at work. For more on the interesting subjects of emulation and disk readers, see Chapter 21.

A Word about Games

There are so many games for the Amiga it's hard to think how I'd even begin to categorise them. I can mention a few of my particular favourites and we'll let you go on from there.

Space Quest IV is by Sierra On Line and is a superb graphic adventure game where you move your little man around using the joystick or keyboard. The graphics are great and the sense of humour is superb. In fact you might like to try the entire Sierra range as its games are always very playable and last for months before you have to move on or finish them.

Shoot'em ups are even more numerous, with Xenon 2 by Imageworks and Escape From The Planet Of The Robot Monsters by Domark standing out in my mind. A good compilation to look out for is The Winning Team, also by Domark, which features a great many arcade machine conversions which really show off your machine. Oh yes and they're good to play too.

I would also draw you to the great many adventure games available, especially any game by Magnetic Scrolls, like Fish!, Corruption, Guild Of Thieves and The Pawn.

For strategy freaks there is a lot going on as well, with the likes of UMS II from Rainbird, Sim Earth from Ocean and Warlord from SSG.

Games for all tastes, and although many people disagree with children playing computer games, I actually think they improve the mind. But that's speaking as a veteran computer game player of about 20 years standing. Kids absorb information like a sponge, and when they tinker around with computers they pick up information about how they work. And in this modern age nothing is more valuable than a working knowledge of computers. So don't be fooled into thinking that in order for a kid to get anything out of a computer he or she has to use so-called *educational software.*

15: Good Hardware Guide

Amigas come in eight basic flavours, A500, A500 Plus, A600, A1000, A1500, B2000 and A3000. The 600 is the more leisure oriented, smallest member, with 1Mb RAM and one internal disk drive. The A1000 is no longer made, but can be obtained reconditioned. It only has 256K on board, and needs 256K upgrade to be useful. A2000s are big, and come in a PC-like case. They contain one internal drive, and come with 1 Meg of memory. They are internally expandable to 9Mb. What I'd call a base level system to allow you to do most things you might like to do to some degree, is:

- an Amiga
- 1Mb memory
- two drives
- a colour monitor

Using the Amiga through the TV is fine for games, but try word processing or drawing and you're probably looking at some eyestrain on the way! Memory is of crucial importance, and lots of it, so it's my advice to get as much as you can afford. An optimum system would be:

- an Amiga
- 3Mb memory
- one floppy and one hard drive
- a colour monitor

which would allow you to do things like DTP and video graphics.

All the Amigas come with roughly the same operating system and all use the same chips give or take a digit, being based on the Motorola 68000, with a trio of custom graphics and sound chips. The Amiga is a wonderful thing, being a creative person's daydream in the sound and graphics departments. You can hear the almost CD quality sampled sound in stereo through the speakers in your monitor or through your home hi-fi. The high resolution graphics can be rendered in any of four or five different resolutions, and in anything from 2 to 4096 colours. All the computers come with an internal disk drive, mouse, keyboard and two disks containing the graphically-oriented interface called Workbench.

The operating system, called AmigaDOS, is a multitasking OS, meaning that, given you have the right amount of memory, the machine can run many programs at once in complete safety.

And most important of all, the Amiga now has a software base in both the commercial and public domain sectors unequalled by any machine save the PC. If it continues on this upward slant, it could be the most successful and popular computer of the decade.

A500 Plus

There is the new version of the A500 called the A500 Plus, which comes with Workbench 2 and 1Mb of RAM as standard. The unit is an all-in-one affair, having the keyboard stuck on the front of the case, and the internal disk drive on the right-hand side. There are ports on the back for RGB out (to the monitor), parallel, serial, external disk drive, and audio left and right.

Although the A500 is often pitched as the games machine of the family, it has as much graphics and sound power as the 3000. Although its memory capacity and processor speed is limited to start with, it can be expanded to very high spec computer. As far as emulation goes it can handle as many formats as the larger machines, and accepts MIDI interfaces and any kind of printer from a dot matrix to a professional imagesetter. Desktop publishing is possible on a small scale, although expanding the memory is essential for larger documents.

What you have in the A500 is an excellent starter machine, and the base of operations for a range of creative and business applications, almost as many as you can think of.

A600

A tiny new version of the Amiga with Workbench 2 and 1Mb of RAM. The new machine does not accept any of the third-party peripherals designed for the A500 or Plus, as the motherboard is a different shape. The new machine also has a card slot for a RAM card like the CDTV, although at the time of writing there is no software which uses this facility. A 600HD features an internal IDE hard drive.

A2000

The 2000 is a big box with a separate keyboard, containing essentially the same guts as a 500. The major difference is that the big metal box can be opened like a PC to reveal the card slots for adding circuit boards to expand the capabilities of the machine. Although the ports at the back of the machine when you take it out of the packing are much the same as the 500, there are openings at the back of the unit, allowing other ports to be added using the card slots. The processor is the same as the 500, as are most aspects of the motherboard inside the machine, but the 2000 can accept and upgrade to the faster 68020 and 68030 chips when you need them. This costs a small fortune, but improves the performance beyond recognition. But the 2000 has the added benefit of being able to run all software, as most accelerator cards with faster processors also allow a *fall-back mode*, letting you use the 68000 if you want to.

The 2000 comes with just one disk drive, but you can add hard disks and other bits and bobs.

I would say that the 2000 is the optimum Amiga, allowing maximum expansion and possibilities for the least outlay.

A3000

The 3000 is a new breed of Amiga, containing a new chip set which heightens the available resolutions, at the cost of the need for a multisync monitor. The 3000 also comes equipped with a faster processor, the 68030. The upside of this is tremendous speed, with many programs, especially DTP and graphics applications, clocking in at over 3-5 times the speed. The downside of this is that the 3000 isn't 100% compatible with all software, due to to differences between the 68000 and 68030 chips.

The 3000 is the professional's dream machine, and is the top end of the spectrum. If you never play a game, then this one's for you.

A1500

Part way through 1990 the 1500 was released. (Not to be confused with the Checkmate Digital 1500 which is an expansion/replacement case for a 500!) The unit is basically a 2000 with two drives and a monitor, a complete computer kit, as it were, ready to go. The unit is just a 2000 with a sticker saying 1500 stuck on it, and even the manuals are 2000 manuals with a *and 1500* sticker on the front. A lot of stickers but nothing else new inside.

This machine is a very good starter pack, but if you intend to buy a hard drive at the same time then look very closely at the price of a component kit including a 2000!

CDTV

Although Commodore are trying to disassociate the CDTV from the Amiga line, the heart of the unit is in fact a plain vanilla A500. The one major change is that the unit has a built-in CD ROM drive, allowing you to run CD ROM software (of which there is now a lot), CD + G audio disk with coded graphics, and of course ordinary CD audio disks. The unit is designed to sit on top of your hi-fi, and has no keyboard. But you can add an infra-red keyboard, mouse and external drive to turn it into a normal 1Mb Amiga.

Monitors

There are only really three standard monitors for use with Amigas, the Philips 8833 (or 8833 II), the Commodore 1084S or any old multisync. The multisyncs are only of use if you have a 3000 or a 500/2000/1500 with a *flicker fixer* device to curb interlace mode flicker.

Expanding Your Amiga

Many people buy an Amiga with the idea that it will be an all in one workstation, and in many ways it is. Used properly your Amiga can be the creative and productive centre of your universe. But limitations soon arise in your day to day work with the Amiga, and sooner or later you will have to expand in some direction or other.

The problem is that like most computers the Amiga starts with a base memory of 512K or 1Mb, but unlike most computers this is not nearly enough for the vast majority of Amiga applications. DTP on the Amiga is nearly impossible, for instance, without a large memory and a faster processor. It's possible, but I challenge anyone to produce DTP on the unexpanded Amiga for a longish time without ending up in the funny farm.

Graphics are another area where the Amiga shines, but most brightly when expanded. The Amiga's version of DOS, AmigaDOS, chops out detail when the memory isn't full enough, and this is most annoying when using the structured graphics as used in packages like Gold Disk's Professional Draw 2.0. The thing is, that if you are handling graphics with hi-resolution, you need more headroom in the Chip RAM department.

Chip RAM is the base memory you get with the Amiga, and until a short while ago this used to be 512K. All the graphics operations take place in Chip memory, and so when you run out of Chip RAM, things start to go awry. If you have more headroom for the other stuff in memory, by having say 1Mb or 3Mb of Fast or Expansion memory, then the problem eases as the Chip RAM has less space taken up by non-graphics oriented tasks. But since the introduction of DTP and 24 bit graphics on the Amiga, to bring it in line with the Mac solutions, this 512K Chip RAM base level became untenable. So the base level was raised, in the newer machines, to 1Mb of Chip RAM, meaning that provided you have a pile of Fast RAM, you never run out of space. At least for the time being. 32 bit is on the horizon, and it won't be long I predict before this 1Mb design constraint will have to be lifted to 2Mb or even 3Mb! So specifically what are the problems of a base level Amiga, and why would you choose to upgrade?

Problems

As I said, the first area where you really notice the difference between a normal base-level Amiga and an expanded one is in the area of DTP. The Amiga is a very powerful computer, but it has design problems ushered in by its high specification. Whereas the PC or Mac rely on their fast processors to speed matters along, the Amiga has a slow 7-8MHz processor and support chips: Agnes, Paula, and Denise, which co-process all the graphics, sound and display information. In order to facilitate the Amiga's high performance graphics and sound, the chip set had to place limits on what could be done, and this led to the 512K limit on graphics memory. When the machine was designed, 512K was a lot, and this wasn't even the base level. When the machines were designed, they were sold with 256K as standard, which seems laughable today with our multi-megabyte machines, but this was seen as a safe base-level then. What the original designers couldn't have foreseen, was the amount of graphics data we'd need to shift in the nineties. DTP was in its infancy, and the amount of real life magazines that were done using DTP could be counted on the fingers of one hand.

So the Amiga found itself on the market and within about six months it became clear that the thing had remarkable potential, it had very little in the way of muscle. So plots were hatched by third parties in the absence of Commodore doing anything about it, and so the Amiga expansion market was born.

DTP wasn't the only problem. Graphics per se was a problem, falling foul of the old Chip RAM shortage almost right away, and the display options for hi-res mode were interlace, interlace or perhaps even interlace. Interlace mode comes in for a lot of scorn from users of other computers, as its flickery quality was far from even 640x350 EGA mode on even the most basic PC. And as for the kind of 24 bit colour you could expect from the Mac, well I for one have had Mac types actually laughing in my face.

Then the flicker fixers arrived. These use a standard similar to VGA, and give you HAM and interlace modes free of the annoying flicker. Interlace was a necessary mode for Desktop Video though, and this is one area in which the Amiga is untouched by all the fancy display modes and memory constraint free PCs and Macs. But where the Amiga really lacked the essential balls, if you'll forgive the expression, is in presentations and as a CAD or graphics engine. So after display enhancement and flicker fixers, 24 bit graphics was the next step.

Many packages on the Amiga already support 24 bit graphics modes, but until recently nobody really had any way of displaying them. But in the next few months we will see this situation changing very rapidly indeed, as at the recent Amiga show in Cologne there were at least 12 24 bit cards on display or being announced. Even Commodore are getting in on the act, and four years after the fact are producing not only a 24 bit card for 2000s and 3000s, but also the display enhancer which brings the Amiga up to the standards we have come to expect from computers in the 90s.

Solutions

Obviously the first consideration you will have is whether or not to buy more memory. RAM prices have fallen recently, so you are looking at about £60 per Mb or RAM for almost any purpose. Anyone can benefit from more memory, and you will find that your machine runs much more sweetly with 3Mb than with 1Mb or even 512K.

The Chip RAM problem can be solved simply by fitting the new (or rather not so new now) fatter Agnes chip, which will allow you to boost your Chip RAM to 1Mb, which will prevent any annoying dropping of colours in the two interlace modes.

The Enhanced Chip Set, or ECS, is now on line for the 3000, and both this and the Commodore display enhancer will be available as an upgrade for 2000 computers using any multisync monitors.

Faster processors are also available for all machines, although 3000 users won't need one as the 3000 already has a 68030 as standard. 68040 versions of the 3000 should be available next year, and an upgrade to poke into the processor slot on a 3000 should be out before the end of the year.

One slightly offbeat way of upgrading your machine is emulation, expanding the functionality of your machine by simply emulating another one. I cover this amply in Chapter 21, so if you want to know all about that I'd check there.

And finally for the 500 there are now a varied array of *expansion boxes*, which give your 500 the facilities of a 2000 for a fraction of the cost.

500 Horizons

Chief among the options for the 500 is the A590 expansion kit, containing a 20Mb hard disk, 2Mb of spaces to fit expansion memory and a SCSI interface. This is still very good value for what you get, and brings your Amiga 500 up to what I would consider to be the very basic minimum for modern use. You have 3Mb of memory and a hard disk, and the SCSI (Small Computer System Interface) port allows you to match up with laser printers, hard disks and other SCSI devices with ease. If you are serious about your Amiga, then you must be serious to the tune of about 275 quid.

On the accelerator card front, there isn't a lot of choice, with the only simple solution being Solid State Leisure's B5000 card. This features a 68030 chip with space for a co-processor and about 4Mb of fast 32 bit memory. As you can probably imagine from that slightly over brief spec, this increases the performance of your machine way beyond reasonable limits, and in combination with 1Mb of Chip RAM makes the need for upgrading to a 2000-3000 virtually unthinkable. The card has gone through many revisions, and the latest version is tested bug free and ready to ship at around £349 with 1Mb of RAM. This is a phenomenal price for what you get, and should upset a few people. Everyone except the people who buy one, I suspect. The card is fitted by pulling your 68000 chip out of its socket and replacing it with the card. The 68000 goes back into the card once fitted, to allow you to have a fall back mode. This means that you can run software that falls over on a 68030 card, making the B5000 a better prospect than even a 3000, as the 3000 has no fall back mode!

Another option is to expand the boundaries of your Amiga physically using something like the Bodega Bay. This device is distributed in this country by Amiga Centre Scotland, and it is a box which connects to your A500 via the huge 200 way port at the side. Once installed your computer has bays at the front for 5.25" and 3.5" drives, one of each, and four internal slots. Three of these slots are PC compatible, meaning you can insert a Bridgeboard and PC cards into your machine to make it fully PC compatible. The other nice feature is the sturdiness of the case which means that you can mount your monitor on the top of the unit, making it into a very smart looking piece of kit.

Yet another option in the expansion box stakes, and this is a more radical move, are the Checkmate Digital solutions the Checkmate 1500 Plus (not to be confused with the Commodore 2000 with a sticker on the front) or the new IQLR 500 tower system. The 1500 is fitted by pulling the whole motherboard out of your Amiga (ouch) and slotting it into the 1500. It makes your Amiga look like a 1000 or a SUN machine, with the internal drive turned around to the front and space inside to mount a 590 hard disk and memory etc. The 1500 is soon to be upgraded to take Amiga cards, but this is real soon now rather than right now. As well as the upgrade to the 1500, the IQLR is a new product which gives you slots galore, loads of drive bays and the ability to leave your machine on the floor and just have the keyboard and monitor on the desktop. You need to stick your disks under the table, but then that's the price you pay for a bigger machine and more space on your desk! Checkmate are adding new products all the time, so it's advisable to call them up for the latest news

There are a variety of what I'd call *trapdoor solutions*, because these are bits that slide into your memory expansion trapdoor. There are units that take 4-8Mb of memory to go in there, and obviously these are not to be sneezed at. There is also a way of mounting a tiny 20Mb hard disk (presumably the same as the type used in portable machines) inside your Amiga onto the motherboard. A great many solutions like this exist, but most are US products and are imported to the UK sporadically and not usually via the same firms. Proper Amiga peripheral dealers should have something to offer, and I would strongly recommend Bytes'N'Pieces and The Amiga Centre Scotland as good starting points.

A600 Add-ons

As yet the A600 has few add-ons, but many are in the offing, like internal hard drives, external hard and CD drives and software which uses the card slot.

2000 and One

One of the most important developments in Amiga technology in the last year is the emerging trade in 24 bit frame buffers or graphics cards. These are big chunks of fast memory on a card, which store Amiga pictures at high resolutions in up to 16 million colours. There are so many to choose from at the moment, but for the purposes of this article I'll talk about four devices for the time being.

Amiga Centre Scotland has recently brought out its Harlequin card, described as a 32 bit card. The images rendered with this board are certainly very high resolution, and if the image is made with a ray tracing package then it is nearly indistinguishable from the real thing. Glossy surfaces are like smooth mirrors, and curved are, well, curved, and not broken up with the inevitable jaggies. The Harlequin is expensive, but the results are highly professional. And it's a British product too.

Solid State Leisure are another British firm who specialise in high quality Amiga peripherals. As well as it's new B5000 fast processor, the SSL team have come up with a new 24 bit graphics engine that is not only good but also inexpensive. It is more of a home use machine though, so one would expect a lower price point.

One of the curiosity pieces in this graphics market is DCTV by Digital Creations. DCTV, apart from being an anagram of CDTV, is a device which cleverly uses the RAM in your machine as a frame buffer. You might have thought that if you don't have much RAM you wouldn't be looking at much in the way of a graphics engine, but in actual fact Digital Creations say that the unit can be used with 1Mb of memory. Sounds crazy, but apparently this is the case. It is NTSC only but does work on standard monitors. The DCTV is priced at $499, and no UK unit is available yet, but keep 'em peeled.

Knowing the ingenuity of the modern third-party developer, I'd say we have a lot more to look forward to in off the wall standards boosters like this.

3000 and Up

If you have an Amiga 3000, then it's unlikely you'll be in the market for much in the way of expansion. The key thing you'll be needing is memory, as you have a 68030, 1Mb of Chip RAM and a big hard drive anyway. Memory cards are cheap and you can pick them up just about anywhere. One thing you may like to consider for the future is an upgrade to a 68040 chip, something which has been made very easy by the inclusion of a processor buss socket in the 3000 itself. All you do is plug in the new processor on a card, and it overrides the internal processor. 68040 chips have several advantages over the straight 68030, not least of which are speed and a built-in maths co-processor. The downside is that there are even fewer programs written to take advantage of a 68040 than there are for an 030!

Best Of The Rest

There is a wealth of possibilities, as you can see, and the key is to see what you can do with the machine you have before you even consider trading up for a bigger model. With the available technology, a 500 can be made to perform like a top of the range machine at very little cost.

The strength of the Amiga is its expandability. What you can do with your system is not limited by what you have, but what you can get to bolt on to your system to make it bigger and better. With this in mind, here are some additional add-ons which are essential, neat or just plain interesting:

A-Max II (Readysoft) Macintosh Emulator

An Emulator cartridge for the Macintosh. Needs a Mac drive to read Mac disks, but contains file transfer programs for people who want to use Amiga disk drives. The A-Max II Plus is a Zorro card version which features Apple serial ports, and the ability to read Mac disks in Amiga drives.

Flicker Fixer (Microway) Hi res Display Device

Stops the display flickering in Interlace or Hi Res mode. A trifle expensive, but works like a dream! Needs a multisync monitor, so you'll have to dump your old monitor.

Datel MIDI Interface (Datel) MIDI Box

Allows you to use MIDI devices like synths and drum machines etc. Nice and cheap and does the trick.

Perfect Sound (Sunrize Industries)

High quality sound sampling for your Amiga. And cheap, too. Sunrize also do 12 bit and 16 bit samplers too, which are very high quality samplers indeed.

Disk Drive (various)

It's essential to get another drive to add to your Amiga, and there are loads to choose from. Cost about 50 or 60 quid. Disk swap for a couple of months and see how expensive it sounds then!

A501 Memory Expansion (Commodore)

Graphics take up memory. If you want better graphics and some of the better games, you must have 1 meg in your Amiga.

A590 Hard Disk (Commodore)

Memory expander, hard disk and SCSI interface all in one for the A500.

Stereo Lead (any one will do)

A lead with two RCA phonos on each end to attach your Ami's sound ports to the plugs in your stereo or ghetto blaster.

Mouse Mat

Essential for not picking up fluff and grot in your mouse ball.

Roland MT-32 and CM-32L (Roland)

Two versions of the same amazing multitimbral MIDI synth containing eight voices and a drumbox. Lovely LA synthesis sounds, and a built-in stereo reverb unit. Also works with Sierra games, for even lovelier scores.

Printers (take your pick)

Colour or black and white, doesn't matter. But you ought to have one for word processing, and even printing out graphics. You'd be surprised at the quality of even the meanest 9 pin. Of course, having a HP PaintJet wouldn't hurt! Try a Citizen Swift 9, if you want a 9 pin, and a Citizen Swift 24 if you want a 24 pin. For better quality, try the Hewlett Packard inkjets; the PaintJet for colour or the DeskJet Plus for black and white. At the top end you're basically looking at a PostScript printer.

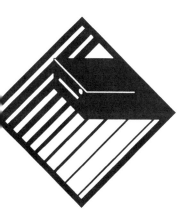

16: Using Printers

The subject of printers is a tricky one and possibly one of the most confusing for beginners. One of the reasons for this is the almost limitless range on offer, and the lack of any clear distinction between them. There are now several basic types of printer, and new printing methods are being developed and released as I speak.

If you already have a printer then you have your choice ready made for you, if you are looking to purchase then check out the second half of this chapter as I'll be talking about the different types of printer and suggesting what might be right for your needs.

Install a Driver

Because of the large number of printers on the market and the vast range of differing features many have to offer, the writing of a single printer control program is virtually impossible. By the time it was finished it would be out of date. For this reason Commodore supply a wide range of printer control programs called Printer Drivers. Each of the popular printers has a printer driver associated with it and before you can use the printer of your choice you need to install the appropriate printer driver.

The purpose of the printer driver program is to act as a simple interface between your Amiga and your printer. When information is sent from the Amiga to the printer it does so via the printer driver which supplies the necessary printer instructions. For instance the instructions required by a printer to produce italic text will vary from one printer to another. By having the correct printer driver for your printer you can be sure that the correct printer instructions will be issued to the printer.

The beauty of the printer driver system is that new printer drivers can be written for printers as they are released. And, if you have the expertise, there is no reason why you couldn't develop you own printer driver should you want to. But describing how you do that is not a beginner's pursuit and so has its place in a more advanced book.

Before you use your printer for the first time you must install the correct printer driver. To do this you will need your copy of the Workbench disk and the Extras disk.

Open the Utilities Drawer on the Workbench Disk and double click on the Install Printer icon. The InstallPrinter window will be displayed and you will be asked for the Extras disk. When this is available, a list of printer drivers available will be displayed.

Locate the name of your printer in the list and then type its name at the prompt. Press Return to install the printer. The relevant printer driver program will be copied across into the DEVS:printers directory of your Workbench disk. The printer driver is now installed. You can press Return without entering the name of a printer driver should you wish to abort the installation process.

Of course, it is possible that you have a printer that is not supported by a printer driver. In such instances copy across the printer driver that matches your printer nearest. For example, there is no specific printer driver for the Epson FX80 but the driver *EpsonXOld* will do the job. If you printer is not listed but is sold as being *Epson-compatible* then copy this printer driver as well. If you are in any doubt, you can contact your local dealer for help or take a trial and error approach. Try a few drivers to see which one best suits your printer.

It is also possible to *install* more than one printer driver. For example, you may have a variety of Epson printers available for use. In which case you could *install* them all by using wildcards, ie

```
epson?#
```

Printer drivers can be copied into the DEVS:printers drawer by use of the COPY command from the CLI. For example:

```
copy from "extras 1.4:devs:printers/epsonxold" to
devs:printers
```

Printer Preferences

The next stage after installation is to open the Printer Preferences window. This can be done using the icon in the Prefs Draw or by issuing the command Preferences Printer from the CLI. When the window is opened, any printer drivers you have copied will be listed at the top right-hand corner of the window. Use the up and down arrow buttons to highlight the printer driver of your choice. You can now use the rest of the options the Printer Preferences provide to fine-tune your installation, and this is outlined below. Once you have completed your selections, select the OK gadget to take you to the main Preferences window where you should select Save. This saves your Prefs to disk, and this means that every time you boot the disk, these Prefs will still be there, ready to go.

Printer Gadgets

The Printer Preferences window gives you the means to further configure your printer installation and these offer a degree of personal choice. Each of the gadgets are outlined below.

Parallel or Serial

The vast majority of printers are of the parallel or Centronics type. If you have anything other than a laser printer it will almost certainly be of the parallel type. Most laser printers offer both means of attachment and once again the parallel method is generally the best.

Paper Size

Narrow tractor is the default and most common type supported. Use this option for normal fanfold paper or A4 sheets. Wide tractor will only be of interest if you are using a wide tractor printer (132 columns) and software which supports this. Table 16.1 lists the paper name types and their approximate physical dimensions in inches. Custom allows you to define your own paper sizes by using the length and other gadgets.

Type	Width	Length
US Letter	8.5	11
US Legal	8.5	14
Narrow Tractor	9.5	11
Wide Tractor	147/8	11

Table 16.1. Paper types and sizes in inches.

Length

This sets the number of lines printed on each sheet of paper – 66 is the normal setting.

Paper Type

Fanfold is the standard continuous printer paper. Single should be selected should you wish to use single sheet paper.

Quality

Dot-matrix printers generally offer two types of print quality, namely Draft and Letter. Draft is fast and ideal for proofing. Letter provides a *typewriter* : like quality and is slower in operation. Use Draft for general use and Letter for final output. Note that Letter can only be used if your printer supports either Near Letter Quality (NLQ) or Letter Quality (LQ) printing.

Left Margin/Right Margin

These two gadgets allow you to define where on the paper the left and right margins begin. The default values are 1 and 80 characters respectively. For example if you wished to ensure a wide margin on the left hand side of the paper you could do so by resetting the left margin to a suitable value eg 20 characters. To change either of these settings simply click on the gadget to display the editing cursor. Use the Del and numeric keys as appropriate.

Pitch

Text can be printed in three different styles namely Pica, Elite and Fine. Pica is the default setting and prints at 10 characters per inch. Elite prints at 12 characters per inch and Fine at 15 characters per inch.

Spacing

These two gadgets allow you to select how closely lines are printed. There two settings are six lines per inch and eight lines per inch.

Graphic 1 and Graphic 2

These two gadgets allow two extra windows to be opened which allow you to define the way in which printer graphics are handled. These are both discussed below.

Graphic 1: This gadget provides the means to allow you to adjust the way in which graphics are printed in terms of orientation and density. There are four gadgets which can be used. Two Image gadgets are provided which allow you to select the type of graphics dump produced. Positive, ie black on white, or Negative (reversed) white on black.

The Threshold slider gadget is useful when you wish to dump a colour screen image to a black and white printer. You select the printer threshold by dragging the arrow slider gadget left and right. As you do so the threshold number highlighted will change. If you slide it to lighter then the contrast of the resultant image will be lighter, and less dense. For instance with a setting of 1 only black will be printed as black. With a threshold setting of 15 all colours will be printed as black and only white will be printed as such, with even light colours such as yellow also printed as black. The default value of 8 is a good compromise, although for dense printers like inkjets and dot matrix, a lighter tone is needed, like 4 or 5. The action taken by the threshold setting is itself determined by the Image gadget. The default setting for Aspect is Horizontal and this ensures that screen dumps are printed across the page. They can be rotated through 90 degrees and printed down the page by selecting Vertical.

Shade determines how graphic dumps are printed on the paper with respect to the colours which they contain. Colours contained within a graphic dump can be reproduced on a black and white printer in grey scales. This works in much the same way as a black and white TV displays a colour picture. The Grey Scale option implements this. The Grey Scale 2 option is to enable the printing of images designed using the A2024 Monitor which only supports a maximum of four grey scales. The Black and White option does not allow the use of grey scales and colours may only be printed as either black or white. In both these instances the threshold setting is used to determine the printer dump image. The Color option should be selected when a colour printer is available for use.

Graphic 2: This gadget provides access to a second window of printer graphics features, nine in all, which are detailed below.

Diagonal lines can sometimes look very ugly when printed as they are reproduced using stepped blocks, or *aliased*, rather than a smooth line. This can be particularly annoying in text applications such as Notepad which print pages as graphic dumps. Text therefore looks ragged and distract the reader. The Smoothing On gadget, if selected, will attempt to smooth and therefore iron out any raggedness on diagonal lines as they are printed. The default for this option is Off as there is about a 2:1 speed reduction overhead when it is enabled. As such it is best left Off for draft purposes and enabled for final output.

The Left Offset option works in much the same fashion as the Left Margin option described earlier. It offsets the printer dump specified measurement from the left-hand side of the paper. The offset is given in inches and increments of tenths of an inch.

The Center (sic) option centres any printer dump on the page. When ON it overrides any setting in the Left Offset gadget.

Some printers support varying degrees of print density, ie very dark to very light. The advantage here is that lighter print densities take less time to print than darker ones and also create less wear and tear on the printer head and ribbon. The default density setting is 1, but just click on the numbered gadget to change the printer density. On a colour dot matrix printer, don't use any density higher than 2, as the quality of your ribbon deteriorates within a few strokes of the head.

The Colour Correct option is for use with colour printers and provides three simple on/off gadgets - R, G, B which relate to to the colours Red, Green and Blue. By selecting any or all of these options the printer driver will endeavour to more closely match the respective screen colours with the printer dump. The effect of this is best seen and understood by printing screen dumps with and without the various options enabled.

Without colour correction enabled, the Amiga printer drivers can print all 4096 colours displayed by the screen, however with colour correction applied, there is a loss in the number of colours that can be printed. A catalogue of this loss is shown in Table 16.2.

Option	Colours available
None	4096
1	3788
2	3480
3	3172

Table 16.2. Colour loss table.

Dithering

Once again this is an option for colour printers only. Dithering is a technique by which colour printers produce shades of colours while using only four main colours. The dots on the paper are printed in such a way that they are very close together, and the colour of the dots combines to produce the desired shade. There are three options that can be selected:

Ordered: The colour intensities are produced using an ordered pattern of dots.

Halftone: The colour intensities are produced using a halftone dither method. This works best on high density printers, eg printers with a resolution greater than 150 dots per inch.

F-S: The colour intensities are produced using the Floyd-Steinberg error distribution method. There is a 2:1 speed reduction overhead when this method of dithering is in operation and best results are obtained on high density printers, eg printers with a resolution greater than 150 dots per inch. Note that Smoothing cannot be used with this dithering method and will be disabled automatically if F-S is selected.

Scaling

There are two button gadgets here which allow you to select either fractional or integer scaling. With the former, normal scaling is performed but, integer scaling is more involved.

With integer scaling selected every dot on the screen is guaranteed to appear as an even number of dots on the screen dump in both the horizontal and vertical axis. For example, if the screen image is 320 by 200 bits then the image dumped to the printer and printed will be either 320, 640 or 920 dots wide by 200, 400 or 600 dots high and so forth. The actual size of the dumped image will in fact be the size requested, scaled to the nearest multiple of the picture width and height. This scaling may be either up or down. This option can be useful when it comes to dump a screen image that contains thin lines running across the image in either axis. Similarly it can be used with applications such as Notepad which use graphics dumps to produce print-out to ensure that any fonts used do not get distorted due to fractional scaling. Try them out for yourselves to see the results.

Width and Height Limits

These two gadgets are ghosted (cannot be selected) while the Ignore option of <-Limits is selected (see below). They are used to select the limits of the width and height of a picture. The unit of measurement will vary depending on the Limit option selected.

<-Limits2

This option provides five button gadgets which will be used to determine how your screen dumps are printed, if you use GraphicDump for example. The default option is *Ignore* and no action is taken by the printer driver. In other words the printed image is unaltered and will just dump out onto the printer. The screen dump is constrained only by the physical limits of the paper. The other four options are:

Bounded: This option allows you to set the maximum size of the output so that you do not have to change text settings such as margins when you wish to include a screen dump within text. When the Bounded gadget is selected the Width Limit and Height Limit gadgets can be used. For example, if you wished to ensure that any screen dump was no bigger than 4.5 by 6 inches you would set Width Limit to 4.5 and height Limit to 6.0. (Note: this does not fix the size of the picture, just its maximum size.) Therefore, dumps smaller than this maximum size will be printed normally.

Absolute: This option allows you to fix the size of the printed image regardless of its true size and aspect ratio. If you like you can use this method to produce some very distorted images! For example, if you wish the printed image to be 4.5 inches wide by 6 inches high, select Absolute and then set the Width Limit and Height Limit accordingly.

This option also allows you to maintain distortion free images while printing to a specific width or height. For instance if you wish to print an image exactly 5.3 inches high while printing to the correct width for this height, to produce a distortion free image, set height Limit to 5.3 and Width Limit to 0.0. This technique also works in reverse for printing to a specific width, in which case the Height Limit should be set to 0.0.

Pixels: This option works in an identical fashion to that for Absolute, however the Width and Height Limits are specified in pixels.

Multiply: This option allows you to increase the size of an image. When selected, the Width and Height Limits can be specified in multiplication increments. For instance, if you required an image that was twice the size normally produced, set both Width Limit and Height Limit to 2.

Initialising the Printer

There will be times when you wish to initialise or reset the printer to its standard defaults as specified in the Printer Preferences. This can be done with the InitPrinter command which can be used from the command line or by double clicking on the InitPrinter icon which can be found in the System Drawer.

Printing Hints and Tips

There are a few points to bear in mind when you come to printing pictures either from within applications or utilities like GraphicDump.

1.   When quality is important use a new ribbon to print the master copy.

2. Friction fed paper normally achieves better results than tractor fed.

3. Only use multiple pass printing for black and white dumps.

4. For a fast proofing/dump, use a Low Density print setting.

5. Horizontal dumps are faster than vertical ones.

6. Printing is slowed by setting Smoothing On.

7. Printing is also slowed by using F-S dithering.

8. er...

9. That's it.

Choosing a Printer

While there are quite literally hundreds of makes of printers to choose from and although this is important, it is also important to remember that there are also different types of printers. This should be your first consideration. Following that, consider the price and the make, as these are secondary to what the printer actually does. The distinction between types is important because the type of printer determines the way in which the printer produces its final printed output. At the time of writing the following are the most common types of printer technology:

Daisywheel

Dot-matrix 9-pin and 24-pin

Inkjet

Laser

Thermal

Of these the dot-matrix technology is certainly the most popular, not least because of its versatility but also because of its cost effectiveness, in other words it is a very cheap method of getting running with a reasonable printer. However, it does have some limitations and may not be suitable for your requirements. Anyway, let's look at each of the technologies in turn and see what each has to offer.

Daisywheel

The daisywheel printer is popular in business. It is rather like an electronic typewriter in that it uses a wheel of characters which is rotated to the selected character and then printed.

For producing high-quality text to a professional standard, the daisy-wheel printer is very good, but it is often slow, and can only produce a very small range of printing effects like bold, italics, and underline, and no graphics at all. Different type faces can be produced however by changing the daisy-wheel.

Dot Matrix

Without a doubt, the dot-matrix printer is more versatile and the latest models allow you to select a near letter quality (or NLQ) effect, which is acceptable for letters and documents. Some dot-matrix printers even support letter quality (or LQ) print, which can at its best be almost indistinguishable from daisywheel output.

The most popular type of printer is the dot-matrix machine, of which Epson, Citizen and Star all make good examples. (Hang on, I'm getting to the Daisywheel in a moment.) The DM printer constructs each character by pushing out a grid of small pins formed into the character shape. The pins strike the paper through an ink ribbon, thus producing the character.

Dot matrix printers print using a ribbon, not unlike a typewriter, but instead of metal letters banging through the ribbon to make an impression on the paper, you have a row of pins which form the letters by tapping dots through the ribbon which scan across the paper to produce letters.

If you are going to buy a dot-matrix printer, there is one golden rule: it is a good idea if it's Epson-compatible. The Epson printer, and in particular the Epson FX80, has been adopted as an unofficial world standard and the codes that control the special effects have been carried across to most (but not all) printers.

An Epson-compatible printer is thus one that supports, and will recognise, all of the Epson effect codes (referred to as control codes). This does not mean that you should rush out and buy an Epson printer; on the contrary, you should buy one that has the facilities that you want, but supports the Epson standard set. It should also have NLQ capability, and colour is an option but not a necessity.

Nine pin printers deliver good quality print, but the 24 pin variety are much cleaner in their output and provide a greater range of clarity in the formation of the characters on the paper. All dot matrix printers are good at graphics.

Inkjet

The inkjet printer is a variant of the dot matrix, although instead of the little pins or hammers, the inkjet uses a tiny matrix of holes, through which ink is squirted onto the paper. This is a highly precise process and the output from Inkjets is very high resolution, almost as good as a laser printer.

Colour inkjets are also available, which allow you to print out the amazing colour graphics that the Amiga can generate.

Thermal

This type of printer is another variation on the dot matrix theme, except this type uses a heated matrix and a waxy ribbon. The saturation of colour is usually very good indeed, and the thermal printer comes up very high on the list of best printers for graphics. Some are quite cheap too, being under £200, although the better quality PostScript ones are obviously a few thousand pounds.

Laser Printers

The laser printer is based on the same kind of technology as photocopiers, using an electrostatic toner to make marks on normal A4 sheets. They are much higher quality than any other kind of printer, but whereas you can get a dot matrix or an inkjet for a couple of hundred pounds, a good laser printer will cost you over £1000. And if the printer is PostScript compatible, you can expect to double that.

Which One to Choose?

The type of printer you choose in the end is governed by two things, what you want and how much you can pay. If you're on a tight budget, then a cheap daisywheel will suffice. If you want to get graphics then a cheap dot matrix. The optimum printers in this class are the Citizen Swift 9 and Swift 24 printers. They are cheap to buy and the output quality is very high. Colour can be added to the printer at very little cost, and this makes it a bargain at under £250 or thereabouts.

If you want to do DTP and can't afford to stump up for a laser printer, then the inkjets are the thing. My favourite is the DeskJet 500 by Hewlett Packard. This delivers a fine quality of print, and all for under £500 if you shop around. For colour, try the Hewlett Packard PaintJet, which turns out beautiful renditions of your colour pictures onto fine art paper.

Finally, if money is no object then you have to go for a laser printer, and I would again recommend either Citizen or Hewlett Packard. The HP LaserJet series also have PostScript emulation cartridges, which enable you to get the very highest quality from your output, especially from Professional Page 2.0.

Workbench 2

Under Workbench 2 Printer Preferences have been somewhat re-arranged in line with the new 3D Preferences presentation outlined elsewhere in this book. However, the options outlined in this chapter are all applicable and present in their various guises. That said, graphics are far better supported under WB2 that WB1.3 as one might expect.

Being such a vast topic – and often quite a contentious one at times – if you have a printer or are looking to buy one you may be interested in a sister publication by Robin Burton called *Mastering Amiga Printers*, full details of which can be found in Appendix E.

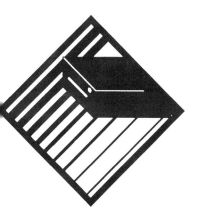

17:
Comms
and
Modems

What with the recent controversy over hacking and the laws passed against it, you may wonder what a chapter about using a modem and logging on to other computers is doing in this book. Surely comms is dreadfully complex and only real computer experts can partake of this pastime? I only discovered comms as a sort of *side hobby* to computing fairly recently, as I'd always thought prior to that it would be a complete pain to do, expensive to feed and a drain on my computer time. I've since found that this couldn't be further from the truth.

I'm a subscriber to a number of online services, and all of them are great fun, and actually very useful. The amount of public domain software and shareware I've downloaded (from the host computer to mine then onto my disk drive) is huge. Also if you think about it, computer clubs are okay for a beer and a chat and a play with each other's computers, but Bulletin Boards are by far the best way to meet other computer users. You can share ideas, software and news, and use your computer at the same time. I didn't think it was actually possible to enjoy my computer more than I already do but with comms it's a fact. Simply put, it's like a cross between one of those 0898 chat line numbers, a game show, a shop, a library, an information service and a computer club all rolled into one, with all the pros and cons that implies.

So what do you need to do comms on your Amiga, and what are the boards which offer the best services? Here's a quick guide to comms, so you can make up your own mind.

What is Comms?

Comms is short for *communications*, the art and science of connecting your computer to a telephone line using a device called a modem. Once connected to the phone line you can load a piece of software called a terminal program, and using this you can automatically dial a computer bulletin board service and log on. Once you are online, connected to the computer at the other end of the phone, you can read all the messages on the BB and leave some of your own. You can also get programs and text files to run and read.

What is a Modem?

A modem is a box with a lead coming out of it with a BT phone plug on the end. In the modem itself is a BT socket, so obviously you plug the modem into the BT socket in the wall and plug your phone into the modem. Your phone will work as normal even if the power isn't plugged into the modem.

The modem takes text and files from the computer, turns the data into audible tones (or *modulates*), and sends these high-pitched screeching sounds down the phone line. At the other end of the phone line, another modem decodes (or *demodulates*) these sounds and turns them into the code and text again. It's the same principle as a fax machine, except that when you fax something it is scanned at one end and printed out at the other. That's why it's called a MODulator/DEModulator or *modem*.

What is a BBS?

Bulletin boards are computers set up by companies or individuals which have a single or multiple line modem attached. Users with computers and modems dial the number and log on to the system, to exchange idle chit-chat (the electronic equivalent of Citizens' Band I suppose), post messages to each other, send faxes (you can do this if the system you dial has a fax machine), send telexes and send (or *upload*) or receive (or *download*) files from the computer. These files can be programs to run on your Amiga, text files to read, bug fixes for various commercial and PD programs, or just fun demos to show off the power of the machine when properly programmed.

Getting Set Up

You already have the most expensive bit of hardware you need, an Amiga computer complete with a serial port to plug a modem into. Then after that you need a modem, a lead to connect your modem to the computer, and a piece of terminal software.

There are a lot of different types of modem, and a good rule of thumb is to buy the fastest one you can afford. The fastest kind you can buy is the HST type, which runs at speeds like 19200 baud. Next stage down are the 4800 baud type, and down a stage from that are the 2400 baud type, and these are the best choice for a beginner, as they are reasonably priced and quite fast. At a push you can get by with a 1200 baud modem, but I wouldn't recommend this for extensive use, as the lower speed incurs extra costs due to you having to spend longer online. My favourite modem is the Supra 2400 MNP, and this is what I would call the perfect Amiga modem. It's small, fast and error free, and as efficient a piece of kit as I've ever come across. You can just plug it in and go. You may have to buy a special lead from your local Tandy or phone shop, as the Supra modems have American phone plugs on them. This isn't a problem, and the leads are cheap. You want one with a US fitting on one end and a BT one on the other. So having got the modem, all you need now is software.

There are two types of modem software, those that cater for scrolling or text-based BBs and those that are for Viewdata or videotex systems. The reason for this is that there are two distinct types of online service; viewdata and scrolling.

The viewdata boards are colour graphics based which looks like the teletext you get on your TV set. The services use *pages* of information, filled with coloured text and ultra low-res graphics. They are a lively source of information and although the system is popular in Europe, especially in France, and in Australia, in America the format never took off. So there is no American viewdata software for Amiga! The best bit of software for viewdata is SuperTex 2.

Terminal or scrolling boards are more popular, and far more numerous due to being easier to set up, and are your first guess if you don't know what kind of board it is you are logging onto. CIX, Usenet, JANET, CompuServe, PeopleLink, BIX and Delphi all use scrolling format. (If you've got lots of money to spare, then using an American service is great. But it is expensive, about $5.00 to $11.00 per hour online charge, and that's without the astronomical international phone bills.) One of the best scrolling terminal programs is NComm (reviewed in Chapter 20), and this is the program which is currently used by about 90% of all the comms people I talk to, so it must be good. I use it myself every day, to log on to bulletin boards and send my copy to the magazines I work for. It's never let me down, and copes with all the standard protocols and speeds.

Both type of BB support uploading and downloading of files, and all of them have a mailbox service, where you can leave closed message for other users, and open message services, sometimes called conferences.

Obviously to log on to a BBS you have to have the right settings on your terminal software. Most BBs are what we call 8N1 boards, meaning that if you set the data length to 8, parity to none and stop bits to 1, you will match up with about 95% of all UK BBSs.

Another obvious point is that, in using the phone line, you have to watch how much time you spend online, with an eye to keeping costs down. You can use BBs responsibly and not get huge bills, but a little lapse of attention when you are online and you could realise that you've been calling a BB in London for an hour and a half. This is easily done as a lot of BB work is very absorbing, especially on some of the larger BBs.

As well as the cost of the phone calls, you stand to cop a bill from the BB too if it charges for connect time, so it's as well to look out for ways to trim this cost down. One of the best ways is to limit your call time. Another way is to only use BBs which are local to you. Some major nationwide BBs allow you to call a local number to connect to the central computer, so obviously this is one way of allowing you to be more generous with your call time. Dialling the BBs at night is another good way, as calling during the day can be very pricey indeed. My phone bills have been as much as £400 when I've been unable to call in the evening, for example.

If you can't call a local BBS to get the sort of service you want, then look into getting a Mercury phone account, as this gives you clearer phone lines (less garbage on the screen) and cheaper long distance and international calls.

(Note: On the support disk for this book I've included a phone call calculator program to help you figure out how much your modem is costing you, plus a good terminal program.)

Do It Yourself

There is a another way you can go. You can set up your own BB, using the wealth of software available. You can buy a package from Y2 Computing which allows you to make your own viewdata BB, or from about 3 million other outlets you can buy or get scrolling BB software in the PD.

BBS is a BBS program written in AmigaBASIC, and TagBBS is another BB program, both of which are freely available on the Fred Fish PD disks you can get from your local PD library. (You could also download these from a BBS if you can find a copy on one, but watch out because both are very large files and you'll have to sell the car to pay your phone bill. Better to get them on disk.)

The nice thing about running your own BBS is that you can call it what you like, and you can call the shots. Also you can contact a lot of people without having to dial them up! They all call you, that's the beauty of it.And if you have a well run BBS, it's like a well run pub, word gets around. If you end up having to buy bigger equipment and running it full time, then you can run it like a business and charge people money to log on. Have a free area for first time people, but tell them if they send you a subscription, you will send them a password which will enable them to get more access to your system.

Bad Habits

Although comms may seem like a bit of a free for all, like most public communication hobbies it has its etiquette. For example a netter who is downloading all the time, or troughing, but never uploading is a very unsociable person. The whole point of BBs is to contribute something to them as you go. If everyone contributes then the BB scene stays alive.

Some BBs crack down on troughing by giving you what they call a download ratio. If you upload two files, you can download three, that sort of thing. So every time you use a BB, contribute something. A file for upload, a message commenting on something someone else has said. Don't worry about seeming foolish, as everyone takes a little time to get used to communicating in text. And sometimes typing can be a bit tiring if you're not used to it. But never be afraid to comment. Unless it is very poorly run BB you won't get shouted down, and most users will be very helpful and tell you everything you need to know.

Another problem on BBs is sarcasm, which as you are aware looks the same as real anger if you see it in print, unless of course you see some clue that the writer is joking. If you are making a joke, append it with a *smiley* symbol made from a colon, dash and right bracket characters, like so:

     :-)

If you turn your head sideways to the left this looks like a little eyes, nose and mouth. This tells other netters that you are joking without you having to say so. It's a textual equivalent of a wry grin. There are other emotions you can express like this, like being cross:

>:-|

with the less than symbol looking like your eyebrows furrowed in anger. Or you can even make a little o mouth to show surprise:

:-o

And so on. My own smiley face has a bigger nose made out of a question mark, like this:

:?)

which is mine, so don't you go using it. And what about if you wear glasses? Try this:

8?)

Oh, the possibilities are endless, but it's as well to know about this, as you may mistake smiley symbols for line noise and not notice sarcasm.

Uploading and Downloading

As long as you are responsible and contribute to BBs, they can be a tremendous (and instant) source of PD software. In order to contribute PD or get it from the BB, you have to download or upload it. You can just push a button and it happens, at least not without setting some kind of common protocol that both the computer you are using and the host computer down the phone line can understand. And with the quality of the phone lines not quite up to scratch, you will get a very degraded image of the file down the phone unless you find some means of checking that what you are sending is what's being received at the other end. And so there are different up/download protocols.

Protocols in common use are XModem, YModem and ZModem. XModem is the oldest and not a very good one. As long as the lines are fairly noise free, like in the dead of night, you stand a reasonable chance of getting a file down from a BBS intact. But during the day forget it. A better bet is YModem or ZModem, both supported by NComm incidentally.

These are error correcting protocols, and there are all kinds of smart features built into them, like the ability to re-send a corrupted part of a file if it doesn't reach the other end of the phone in the same state it left. Use these whenever possible. Most major BBs support them, but a few smaller BBs may not have ZModem.

Another thing when you start up and downloading files is the amount of files that are *archived*. The files for download are usually compressed (to save time when you download them) and you use a program to de-compress them at your end. The files on the BB might look like this:

```
game.lzh
```

The example archive contains a number of files, which are all archived together, so rather than download one file after another you can get the whole bunch in one go. The reason you would archive files together is if all the files in the archive are needed to make the program run.

The programs that do this to files are called *archive programs*. When they compress a file and create an archive, they add a postfix or file extension to the filename, like the *.lzh* in the above example. Table 17.1 shows the popular archive programs and their file extensions.

Program	Extension
arc	.arc
lharc	.lzh
warp	.wrp
zoo	.zoo
zip	.zip

Table 17.1. Archive programs.

Arc was the original archive program, and although you still find files that are arc'ed, the more common methods are lzh and zip. Zoo is another format that isn't used very much any more, although it's handy to have copies of both in case you come across an old program that you need to unarc. Warp is the odd man out here as it compresses a whole disk into a file. Then when you download it from the BBS, the file can be unwarped to make the disk again at your end. This is a clever way of shrinking and reforming a whole disk with all its directories intact.

My Favourite BBS

Here is a list of the BBs that I use, or have used at some time, which I've liked enough to stay on for an hour or so a week. This should give you a flavour of the kind of things that are available, and give you some numbers to type into your terminal program phonebook. You can mailbox me on CIX with *snouty* or on the Direct Connection/Usenet on uad1135@dircon.co.uk.

01-For-Amiga (free) scrolling, all speeds

London Amiga based BBS run by Tony Miller, and very good it is too. As I recall it's based in Whitechapel, across the road from where Jack the Ripper used to murder people. Strange. A large downloads directory of all sorts of interesting stuff. BBS: 071-377-1358.

MAX-BBS (free) scrolling, all speeds

A mainly PC-based board, but with a large Amiga section. Very lively, not to say slightly barmy. Ran into problems a little while ago, but now back up and running. BBS: (0905) 754127.

CIX (subs only) scrolling, all speeds

Good for meeting technical types and sharing info. Lots of different groups to join covering all sorts of pursuits, computing or otherwise. Software to download. Brilliant closed user group of Amiga gurus and software developers. BBS: 081-390-1244. Tel: 081-390-8446.

Cheam Amiga (free) scrolling, up to 1200 baud

Excellent Amiga-based board with very good downloads and a lively bulletin board for messages etc. BBS: 081-644-8714.

The Direct Connection (subs only) scrolling, all speeds

Newish serious BB system, with conferencing service and access to USENET, the biggest computer network in the world, covering all the universities and companies in the US, Canada, UK and Europe, even Australia. Inexpensive service, with a standing monthly charge. BBS: 081-853-3965.

Gnome At Home, viewdata type, 1200/75

Lively viewdata board with quite a bit of CBM and Amiga action, but doesn't change very rapidly. Mailbox facility for subscribers. Lots of bulletin boards. BBS: 081-888-8894. Tel: 081-888-8815.

Scottish Opus (free) scrolling, all speeds

PC based BBS north of the border, with a large Amiga section. BBS: 041-880-7863.

Academics (free) scrolling, all speeds

Solihull and Midlands based, run by John Kelly. Lively Amiga section on this board for OU Students. BBS: 021-705 2906.

Belfast Amiga (free) scrolling, all speeds

Serving Belfast and Northern Ireland and run by Kieran Sullivan. BBS: (0232) 852407.

Quasar (free) scrolling, all speeds

Based in Dromore, County Down, Northern Ireland and run by Dave Byrne, it caters mainly for Amiga users. Formally known as DABBS. BBS: (0846) 693067.

Empyrion (free) scrolling, all speeds

Amiga orientated and run from Swansea by David Westron. BBS: (0792) 580781.

061-For-Amiga (free) scrolling, all speeds

Worsley based BBS run by Andy Grifo, mainly Amiga orientated. BBS: 061-799 4922.

18:
Doing
Business

When you bought your Amiga you probably had some idea of doing some kind of serious computing on it. The Amiga is capable of running business programs, but as a computer with good sound and graphics, it usually finds uses in the music, graphics and leisure fields before the usually considered *drier* areas like spreadsheets, databases and wordprocessing.

But packages do exist and some of them are very good at their job. Here is a selection of thoughts on the current state of the Amiga business software range.

What is Business Software?

Business software is a way of using your computer to make your work more productive. Obviously most of the tasks performed by computers in offices are easy to do by hand, but not as quickly.

Some tasks you might like to use your Amiga computer for are very suitable, like word-processing. But others you might dream up when someone says "what use is it?" are not. Keeping databases of all your friends' telephone numbers is a job best done on paper. So is keeping a database of all your LPs or CDs. Unless you have a warehouse full of LPs this isn't really necessary, and the work you put into the database would be more than the benefits you'd get out of it. Balancing your chequebook is not really worth doing on computer, unless there are hundreds or thousands of transactions.

"I want to be able to press a button and find out my balance", a friend said to me once. But you can do this at a hole in the wall machine any day of the week, and what you don't realise when you first enter into computing is that, in order to get data in, you have to type it in yourself. Computers aren't mind readers, and they don't run on magic either. In order for a computer to take in data like lists of your records, CDs or bank details, and sort them and spit out useful information, you have to either write a program or buy one which has already been written to make the computer do these things. The only way to make this worthwhile is if you have too much information to remember or write down. Then, and only then, is it worth putting your data onto computer.

So what are all these business programs?

Spreadsheets

A spreadsheet is like a sheet of paper with columns and rows down it, like an accounts sheet. Each is numbered or lettered to give you a way of specifying a point on the sheet. So the top left space on the sheet will be A1, the next one to the right will be B1 and the one below it will be A2. Numbers are put on the sheet, and they can tally up at the right-hand side and along the bottom, just like a page in an accounts book.

Unlike a normal sheet of paper though, the computer spreadsheet can recalculate the totals at the bottom of the page if you change any of the figures, meaning you can have templates of the kind of accounts you want to do, and the computer will add up the figures for you as you type in the numbers.

There are many spreadsheets in the Public Domain, and some you can buy, and the reliability is usually proportional to how much you paid for it, like most things in life. Visicalc is a good commercial one, and many clones of this style of spreadsheet can be found in most PD houses.

Databases

A database is a program which allows you to store information in your computer, and lots of it. Databases are usually used for storing names and addresses of clients, keeping records of products for the purposes of stock control, or making lists, say of movies and who starred in them. The difference between a database and a sheet of paper is that you can electronically search for information and get the record you search for in seconds.

For example, say you have set up a database of films in your video collection, and this is only any good if you have a few hundred cassettes, as I said earlier. If you wanted to get a list of all the films by Ken Russell, you would type his name into the space reserved for the director's name, and you would get a list of all the films by him. If you also typed the name of one of the stars, say Glenda Jackson, you would get a list of the films directed by Ken Russell which star Glenda Jackson, and no others. This is called cross-referencing, and this is one thing that databases are really very good at.

A Word about Data Protection

Note that under the law, if you intend to create a huge database of names and addresses, your database should be registered with the Data Protection Bureau. Get a copy of the:

> Data Protection Act 1984
>
> ISBN 0105435848
>
> £4.80 from your local HMSO

and read Chapter 35 of the Act for clauses that apply to you. The Act is specific to individuals who own databases, and if the act applies you have to declare where you got all the data from in the first place (ie a bought mailing list, electoral roll etc) and the address where the people on your database can get access to their entry, should they wish to exercise that right under the act. You must also declare to whom you will disclose the data, such as a direct mail company who might like to buy data. Data is described as "information, recorded in a form in which it can be processed, by equipment operating automatically, in response to instructions given for that purpose." A pretty loose description that, but that's law for you. If you are in any doubt if your database is liable for registration, get a copy of the act and read it, or consult your legal adviser if you have one.

Wordprocessors

A wordprocessor is an electronic version of a typewriter, which rather than typing each letter onto the page as you type, allows you to type the whole of your text into the computer and store it on disk, only printing it to paper when you've told it to. The trick is that you can edit the whole document before it hits the paper, thereby reducing the amount of errors which make it to the page. Word processors also have spelling checkers, sometimes even grammar checkers, and thesauruses to help you choose exactly the right word.

Once you've written something using your wordprocessor, you can edit it to your heart's content, changing all the words around if necessary to get it just exactly the way you want it. Then you have to print it out, or paste the text into a DTP program for more complex layouts for printing professionally. If you want to print out yourself, you must get a printer of some kind, and you can find out about all of those in Chapter 16.

Other Types of Productivity

There are some programs on the Amiga which, although not directly related to business, do help your productivity. Desk Top Publishing is a prime example, enabling you to produce documents, newsletters and reports on your computer, and end up with impressive results. Printers further enhance your productivity as they can give you *hard copy* as it called, a printout of a picture or text file. If you have a laser printer or an inkjet, you can also print out DTP. This book is typeset on a DTP program as it happens.

Fax Machines are becoming a necessity in business these days, and if you haven't got one, you'll not only not be able to send and receive faxes (which is not only good business, it's good fun), but you will be behind in the information race. There are two ways to become fax compatible with your Amiga, and these are Fax Modems and On Line Services. Computers like the Amiga can send faxes, if you have a suitable modem with the Sierra Fax Modem Chip Set and the right software. You just plug the modem into your Amiga's serial port, plug the modem into the phone socket, run the appropriate software, and off you go.

Modems are a good idea too, as they enable you to get onto useful on-line services like Telecom Gold, CIX and The Direct Connection. These services not only give you access to company information and up to the minute shares/business news, but they also enable you to send and receive Telex, and send (although not receive) faxes.

Emulators are another way in which the Amiga can help you be more productive. Running an emulator on the Amiga can allow you to run software which would normally be incompatible, and also (especially in the case of the IBM PC or other MS DOS machine) allow you access to software which is good for business. There are a lot of very good business/productivity programs on the PC, and these can be run on the Amiga with the addition of a PC emulator board.

Business Software

Works Platinum (MSS)

This is an integrated package which is composed of many smaller packages, all of which are pretty good, but not the top of the range. The word processor was called Scribble, and it is the forerunner of the Excellence! 2.0 program.

Excellence! 2.0 (MSS)

Excellent is right, as this is one of the biggest and most fully-featured wordprocessors on the Amiga. American grammar and spelling checker, but otherwise very good indeed.

Wordworth (Digita)

Another fully-featured wordprocessor, but this is an English product and so has full English spelling checker as well as a built in online Thesaurus.

Gold Disk Office (Gold Disk)

Another integrated package from the makers of Professional Page and Transcript.

Superbase Professional 4 (Precision Software)

The biggest and best database program on the Amiga, now in revision 4.

Procalc (Gold Disk)

A fully-featured business spreadsheet from Gold Disk, which includes several graphics modes.

Protext 5 (Arnor)

The current best and most powerful wordprocessor on the Amiga, although no graphics. Big dictionary and thesaurus, plus mail merge and massive macro language for many tricks and shortcuts.

Kspread 4 (Kuma)

Excellent and most powerful spreadsheet on the Amiga. Many emulations of top spreads like Lotus 1-2-3. Now handled by HiSoft.

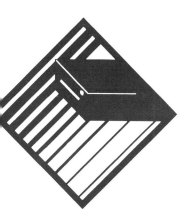

19:
Virus
Attack

Some of you may have heard about computer viruses and thought they were either a joke or a speculative piece of science fiction. Well they are real, and a very real threat to your computer. In this chapter I will be asking what are these things? Where do they come from? And how do you make sure that you don't pass them on to anyone else? Here is the beginners guide to bugs that go squeak in the night.

This is a cautionary tale, although I wouldn't like you to get all paranoid and start seeing a virus every time your computer goes a bit peculiar. Most crashes are down to lack of memory, software bugs or pilot error, so let's not lose our heads here. Viruses are a threat, but they are not going to destroy the world. If you're sensible and follow the tips and tricks mentioned in this chapter, you'll be alright.

What is a Virus?

Computer viruses are like human viruses, in the sense that they infest the host and pass themselves on through a point of contact. On the computer the point of contact is disks, so when a disk comes through the post from a PD house (although most are very conscientious, I assure you) or from a friend, there is a risk that there will be a virus on that disk.

Once you put the infected disk into your computer, the virus spreads into the system, and infects any other disk you put into the computer. If you pass any disks onto your friends then they put the virus on their machine, and so it goes on. The trick with viruses is that they alter the *reset vectors* in the machine, so that the virus can survive a warm boot, the reset you do by pressing CTRL-A-A. Virus killers can detect the change in the reset vectors, but some store themselves on disk and rarely alter the memory.

Its no good saying "I only get disks from reputable PD houses and off the covers of magazines". Mistakes happen, and more than one computer magazine to my certain knowledge has put out a virus on their cover disk, and the same goes for PD houses. There are some silly smaller ones which don't check their disks properly, and sometimes a strain of virus which has never been seen before slips through the net.

So you need to be vigilant. Every time you get a disk, check it.

Where Are They From?

Believe it or not, viruses are written by someone, in the mistaken belief that it is a lot of fun to have your disks ruined. The same kind of people write viruses who buy stink bombs and balance buckets of toxic waste on door frames waiting for unsuspecting people to walk in and get surprised. These people aren't interested in the harm they might cause, just the challenge of writing a virus that can beat the virus killer programs, and the *kudos* that this might bring them, albeit anonymously.

Programming viruses is a really skilled task, as you have to know a lot about a computer before you can find loopholes in the operating system that are big enough for a virus to get in. So it makes you wonder what on earth makes these obviously talented (but stupid) people waste all this expertise on making a virus. In a sense it's a variation on the cracking of copy protection on disks or hacking into computers and altering data. The people who do it can't see past the challenge to the kind of damage they cause. (They are so deeply involved in what they are doing that they are blinkered to it.) Although that is not to say that certain coding crews, young men mostly, actually get a kick out of the thought of damaging other people's data without them knowing. They grow out of it, eventually.

Killing Viruses

The only sure way to be virus free in this day of over 100 known viruses is to use a virus killer program. If you don't have a virus killer (and I strongly urge you to get one) then there is something you can do, although it is a little fiddly and doesn't help with all types of virus.

For the most part a virus will die if you switch the machine off. Obviously it still lives on the disks you have infected, but it won't linger in your machine if you switch off. And if you write protect a disk (put the little tab up so you can see a hole through the corner of the disk) the virus can't get onto the it. Once you have switched off for about 30 seconds, turn back on and boot with your Master Workbench disk (with its write protect tab on). Open a Shell, and insert the virus infected disk. Then install the bootblock by typing:

```
Install dfn:
```

where n is the drive you want to install. This prints a healthy bootblock over the infected one, so curing the problem. But when you inserted the infected disk to install it, the virus has infected your system again. But don't panic. Switch off the machine again, wait 30 seconds, and then reboot. You will now be virus free. Unless what you have is more sophisticated.

This method of killing viruses is only any good for viruses which live in the bootblock. Certain viruses, a type called the 'link virus', attach themselves to a healthy file and lie in wait, immune from being Installed. So, as I said at the start, the only certain way to catch these little beggars is to use a reputable virus killer. And choosing the right killer can be as important as having one at all.

For example there is a new kind of virus now, one called a *Disk-Validator* virus. There is only one type of this new virus at the moment, although there will probably be more by the time you read this, as it doesn't take long for people to re-write these things. The thing is there is only one virus killer that detects and rubs out this particular new strain! So you have to choose wisely, if you want to be safe.

(**Warning:** Some of your commercial software will have slightly out of the ordinary bootblocks on them. This is for copy protection, and if you kill them off with your virus killer, the program will not load. This is obviously undesirable as the program could be quite valuable, and although most software houses will replace a damaged disk with no questions, the fault is yours so they might not. Some virus killers recognise benign bootblocks, like those on a game disk, but some don't. Use a killer that knows about some of the more common benign bootblocks like the Electronic Arts variety for example. If in doubt, don't kill a block, especially on software you've bought.)

Virus Killers

There are a great many virus killers on the market, and all of them are freely distributable. PD houses stock them, and usually you can guarantee that a virus killer disk at least will be free of viruses. (Obviously the guy who programmed the killer would take the trouble to kill the viruses on his own system!) There are many different types, and all of them are pretty good by now, having undergone many different revisions since the virus problem became apparent on the Amiga in around 1987. To help you choose your virus killer, here is a list of the killers I've tested on your behalf.

CheckVectors

Written by Mike Hansell, and the current version of CV at time of writing is 1.2. This killer is a command you can add to your startup-sequence. It checks for any system vectors that may have been changed to conceal a virus. CV is very clever, and very small too. When you run the program it says:

```
Check Vectors rev 1.2 All Rights Reserved more
TUPperware © by Mike Hansell

Reset vectors ok, Nothing resident, Trackdisk.device
not intercepted, DoIO ok

System appears to be free of viruses and trojans!
```

What all this means is that the program has checked the reset vectors, looked to see if there are any resident programs hiding in the computer, and verified that the disk and input/output routines haven't been tampered with.

Master Virus Killer

Massive program written by Belgian coder Leclerq Xavier, with a range of around 105 different virus known to it. It clobbers all known types and is very friendly to use. Current version of MVK at time of going to press was v2.1.

MVK boots up with a control screen, and a sound sample booms "Welcome!", a sound effect from a Frankie Goes To Hollywood record, if memory serves. Anyway, after that all the currently mounted disks are checked to see if they have any viruses. If all is well you are given prompted to insert disks you want to check. At the time of writing MVK is the only killer to seek and destroy the Disk-Validator type of virus.

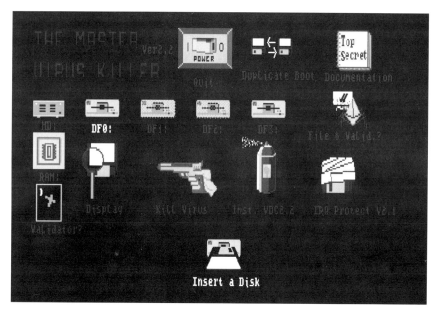

Figure 19.1 Master Virus Killer.

VirusX

One of the original virus killers on the Amiga, now in its fourth version. As with the other three versions, version four was written by Steve Tibbett and detects and kills most types of virus (although it has to be said not as many as MVK). Virus X remains resident in a little window above your Workbench and is activated by clicking on it and then pressing the right mouse button. The program will check any disk that is inserted in your drives, and will report any non-standard bootblocks it finds. After reporting the finding of a strange bit of code it will either analyse the block and identify it, or simply say that it has found something, doesn't know what it is, but asks you if you want it destroyed. This gives you a chance to rescue any proprietory bootblocks like the kind used on some commercial programs.

VectaCheck

Written by Tony Wichett (Or Dave of Warriors depending on the version you get), VC is sometimes found on PD disks, and is not unlike CheckVectors in that it is a Shell-activated program, and as such is available to be run as part of your startup-sequence. It is slightly more advanced in the kinds of things that it looks at, for example it tells you if you have a Fatter Agnes installed, if you have any add-ons connected and if you have any fast memory. A little bit redundant, as you will know most of this already, but fun I suppose.

Type Vectacheck and you get something like the following:

```
VectaCheck V2.0. Written By Tony Wichett. ´ see
docs for info. '

´ SYSTEM VECTORS ARE INCORRECT - POSSIBLE VIRUS
STILL IN MEMORY '

CURRENT CONFIGURATION IS AS FOLLOWS:

YOU HAVE A 68000 PROCESSOR ON BOARD.

ORIGINAL FAT AGNUS INSTALLED - (NO ECS).

RAM EXPANSION MEMORY IS ON.

DRIVES AVAILABLE ARE : DF0:
                            DF2:
```

If there is a virus in your machine, you get a big scary red flashing box, like a Guru message, which tells you a virus is present, and do you want to kill it? Very cute, but not as smart as it could be.

ZeroVirus

An Australian program, written by Jonathon Potter, and a very good one at that. It covers a lot of virus types, and is very easy to use. The screen is divided into four big buttons enabling you to look at bootblocks or check files for link viruses etc. The program uses what are called *brainfiles*, files against which to compare any viruses it finds, to give the program an idea what it has found. A lot of benign bootblocks are listed in the brainfiles, and so this is one of the more intelligent killers.

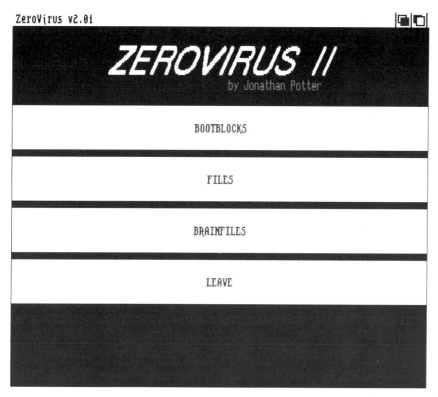

Figure 19.2. Zero Virus.

Pseudo Ops VK

Sneaky and very hackish. A lot of very dangerous viruses are covered by VK, and the program is resident too. Very cleverly, the program wedges itself in memory, and reboots. Instead of a blue disk prompting you to insert your Workbench, you have a red disk, the Pseudo-Ops logo and a piece of music. This means you can trap a bootblock virus before it even boots! The program also searches for link viruses too, by allowing the disk to boot and reading the most likely files.

NoVirus

Written by another Australian, Nik Wilson, and this time a more graphic interface. You click on the disk drive you want to check, or simply insert a disk in any drive, and the program will look at it. The program knows all the usual viruses, and any newer ones can be learned.

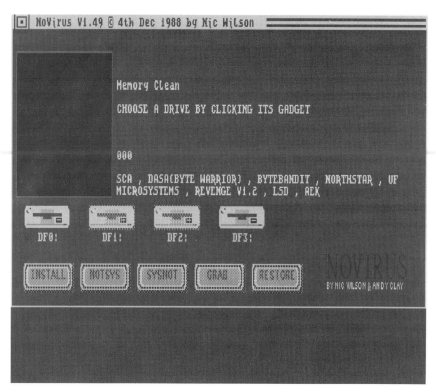

Figure 19.3. NoVirus.

Seek and Destroy

An exotic and versatile killer, which on this particular utilities disk has a flying starfield pattern behind it. Admittedly you could always lift it from the disk to lose this effect, but why bother? Link viruses are killable, as are the usual bootblocks, just by punching the appropriate buttons.

Kill Da Virus

A new program from Mike Hansell, writer of CheckVectors. Another program which hides behind a little window on the menu bar most of the time. It will speak up if it finds anything, but the rest of the time will keep silent. You can access the KDV menu if you click on the mini-window and then use the right mouse button on the menu bar.

Viruscope

A curious killer this one, written by Maxon Computer of Germany, better known as Jan Anton and Peter Lass. The disk loads with a nice graphic of a desert and a pyramid, and the pyramid and desert and camel motifs are with you till the end. To select the three different tools that the Viruscope has, you click the mouse on a portcullis inside the pyramid, which rises up. This is quite a powerful virus killer, despite all the flash graphics and sound. It's nice to see things embellished, but really was all this stuff necessary? No is the short answer, and if you are irritated by tunes and graphics on your utilities then this is not the one for you.

Amiga Body Scan

Written by M Lazenby, Amiga body scan is a CV and VC type CLI killer, which gives you similar information about your system. Type *body*, and you get three windows of information, while the program checks all the vectors are intact, looks your memory over and congratulates itself for being such a good program.

IRQ Killer

This simple program from *Malone* and *Master Coder KTP* asks you which directory you want it to search. It then looks through the directory looking for the tell-tale file size which indicates the presence of an IRQ or link-type virus.

Interferon

This is a bootblock itself, written by Rob *SS20* Hill, and on booting it you automatically destroy any virus in the computer, making it hard for any viruses to propagate from memory. I couldn't find any program which installs this bootblock, but quite a few virus killers allow you to load and save boots from one disk to another, and you can find Interferon on the 17 Bit disk 949 with all the other killers.

ViewBoot

A colourful and very versatile program written by *Late Night Hacks*. It allows you to view the bootblocks of any disk drives you have fitted, install any disk in any drive and also checks or displays memory to look for any resident virus.

Which Killer?

The best killers in my opinion are ZeroVirus and Master Virus Killer, as they both cover over 100 viruses and seem to be the most intelligent about which bootblocks and files they kill. As well as these programs to detect and kill a virus if you think you have a problem, I'd recommend having a small killer in the C directory on your bootdisk, with a command to run it in your startup-sequence. I'd suggest CV, because it seems small enough to fit on a floppy as well as a hard drive.

(Note: Most of the above killers are available on 17 Bit Software PD disk number 949. Master Virus Killer v2.1 is on 17 Bit disk 894. VectaCheck is on 17 Bit disk 950. Seek And Destroy is on 17 Bit disk 947. Viruscope is on Sector 16 disk number 309.)

List Of Known Viruses

I don't want to worry you unduly, but the list of known viruses is growing daily. For your information as of the time of going to press, here is the list of viruses that the Master Virus Killer program can detect and destroy. Some of the viruses are of the virus-link type which is noted afterwards in brackets. Some are just simple bootblock types and these are easily eradicated. MVK is good because it also detects a nasty new variant called the Disk-Validator virus, which can be the hardest to detect, especially if your killer doesn't recognise this type! Anyway, here is the list, just so you know what you're up against.

CrackRight by Diskdoctors

16 Bit Crew

2001

Abraham (aka Class Abraham or MCA)

Aids

AmigaFreak

ASS Virus

Australian Parasite

BamigaSectorOne

BandVirusSlayer

BGS9 I (link)

BGS9 Mutant (link)

BlackFlash

BlackStar (aka North StarI)

Blade Runner

Butonic's (aka Bahan)

ByteBandit I

ByteBandit II

ByteBanditClone

ByteBanditNoHead (aka ByteBandit v3, ByteBandit+ or The Mutation)

CancerSmily by Centurions (link)

CCCP Virus

CCCP Virus (link)

Clist (or UK Style)

Clonk

Coder

Dag

Dasa (aka Byte Warrior, DasaI or DasaII)

Destructor

DigitalEmotion

Disaster Master (link)

Diskguard

DiskHerpes (aka Phantastograph, Phantasmumble and Herpes)

Extreme

F.A.S.T.

F.I.C.A.

FastLoadByteWarrior

Forpib

Gadaffi

Graffiti

Gremlins (The True)

GXteam

Gyros

HCS 4220 I

HCS II

Hilly

Hoden

Ice

Incognito

IRQ typeI (link)

IRQ typeII (link)

Jeff Butonic V1.31 (link)

Jeff Butonic V3.00 (link)

Jitr

Joshua I

Joshua II (Switch OFF Virus)

Julie (or Tick)

Kauki

LamerExterminator I (LamerStrap, LamerSpecial)

LamerExterminator II (Gremlins The False)

LamerExterminator III

LamerExterminator IV (SelwriterLamer)

LamerExterminator V

LamerExterminator VI (Rene Lamer6)

LamerExterminator VII

LamerExterminator VIII

LSD!

MAD II

MegaMaster (or MGM)

MicroMaster&AEK

MicroSystem

Morbid Angel

Newbeat (Alien Newbeat)

NoName

NorthStarII (starfire)

NorthStarIII

Obelisk 1

OPapa

Paramount

Paratax I

Paratax II

Pentagon Circle Virus Slayer I

Pentagon Circle Virus Slayer II

Pentagon Circle Virus Slayer III

Return Of Lamer Exterminator (aka R.o.l.e, a Disk-Validator Virus)

Revenge

Revenge of the Lamer Exterminator I (link)

Revenge of the Lamer Exterminator II (link)

RevengeLoader

SCA1 (Uses move.l to copy itself in memory)

SCA2 (Uses DoIO to copy itself in memory)

SCA-AIDS

ScarFace

Sendarian

SinisterSyndicate

Sinmut

Suntronic

SuperBoy

SupplyTeam

System Z PVL v3.0

System Z PVL v4.0

System Z PVL v5.0

System Z PVL v5.1

System Z PVL v5.3

System Z PVL v5.4

System Z PVL v6.1
System Z PVL v6.3
System Z PVL v6.4
System Z PVL v6.5
Target
Telstar (System Z v6 variant)
Termigator
Terrorists (link)
The Ripper
The Time Bomber (Troyan)
The Traveling Jack I (link)
The Traveling Jack II (link)
TimeBomb
Tomates-Gentechnic-Service
Turk
UltraFox
UltraKill
Virus II by Obelisk (very like Obelisk1!)
Virus-killer-Virus
Vkill I
Vkill II
Warhawk
Warsaw
XENO (link)

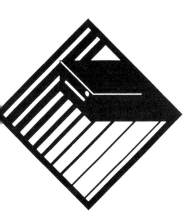

20:
The Public
Domain

Some of the very best software for the Amiga is in the Public Domain, usually referred to as PD. This is software which can be freely distributed to anyone, and it is therefore described legally as being in the public domain, or free to anyone who wants it. Free software? Yes, Public Domain is software and is free to anyone? There must be a catch though surely? No there isn't, unless of course you count the fact that there is so much PD software to choose from that it's hard to say what you're going to have first.

What Is PD?

PD is a concept borrowed from early mainframe systems, where hackers, as the original computer freaks were called, produced programs and distributed them to their friends and fellow hackers, asking for no payment but only recognition as a true hacker. The copyright to the program was waived by the author, and so the program was said to be in the Public Domain, ie anyone in the public had a right to copy and use the program however they wished, provided that the author's credit and documentation was distributed with the program. Since the rise of computers in the home since the late 70s, PD has been nurtured by the use of Bulletin Board Systems (BBS) where anyone can log on, download a lot of demos and utilities, leave a few messages, and log off. PD is good currency, and you've only got to log on to a BBS to find out how much fun the swapping and collecting of PD can be.

And what can you get? Here are just some of the things available from the many PD houses:

Utilities

These are programs to help you use your computer. Some are just simple commands to use from the CLI, but others are complete menu-driven programs to compress files, convert them from one form to another or even rescue broken disks. The best disks to look for are the collections of utilities with a selection of the best utils all squeezed onto one disk. Virus killers are one of the most useful PD utils, and the best thing about them being PD is they are freely updated and distributed all the time.

Applications

Some of the best programs are PD. SID for example is one of the best graphic interfaces for AmigaDOS, and it's PD, or to be more precise, *shareware.* This is a branch of PD that you pay for, but the author lets you use the program to see if you like it first. Shareware isn't expensive, as the author usually only asks for between £5 and £25 for his efforts. In most cases it's worth paying in the end, as you get free upgrades and documentation.

Demos

This is the field of Amiga art, where a team of hackers, usually called a crew or team, get together and have a late night hack attack and create a dazzling demo of their programming abilities. Demo teams usually go on to be pro programmers, so their demo days are usually numbered. Scoopex and Silents are two of the best teams, and also the likes of Kefrens are not to be missed. Imagine a cross between a dance record, video and lightshow and you're getting the idea.

Game Demos

In recent years the various major software houses have watched the PD area growing and noticed that people buy demo disks. So they release demos, sometimes playable demos, of their new releases, allowing the punters to try their game before they buy. Demos of this kind usually turn up first on the covers of magazines like Amiga Format, and then later the demos appear on their own out of a PD library. A successful and popular demo often translates into a very popular game, as has been the case with Lemmings from Psygnosis.

Slide Shows

Graphic artists spend a lot of time creating screens of graphics and making them into slide shows for your enjoyment. Some are scanned pictures, but most are drawn and accompanied by a nice bit of music. If you're clever you can grab the art and examine it to see how it was done, and with the permission of the author you can, in most cases, use it as clip art for your DTP packages. Some of the most stunning stuff comes from Tobias Richter of Germany. He uses a ray tracer called Reflections and turns out some amazing stills and animations.

Music Demos

Some authors are music nuts, and they spend their life churning out disks of tunes for you to play on your Amiga. Some are Soundtracker or Noisetracker sampled tunes from the charts. Others are synthesised tunes from the classics. Most are pretty good.

Licenseware

These are programs which are licensed to specific PD houses to prevent the free distribution of the program, although the price to the consumer is somewhat the same. The only difference is that the PD house pays the author a percentage of the take each time the program is sold.

Disk magazines

Magazines on disk are not new, but there are more now than ever before. Newsflash, 17 Bit Update, Computer Lynx, and Jumpdisk are prime examples of the type of thing I'm talking about, and they are all very good, usually containing PD software, demos and music, plus a lot of graphics and text as well. The text is usually reviews of software, or perhaps a bit of hardware, and usually quite short to keep the amount of different text files up and leave space for programs too.

Buying PD

If you haven't got a modem and access to a good BBS, then the only way to get your PD is to spend money and buy some. But you thought I said PD was for free? Well PD is free, but disks, postage and the wages of the men who sit all day at the copying machine aren't, so be prepared to pay between 99p up to about £2.50 per disk. The price you pay for your PD is up to you, although some people get a bit cross paying £2.50 when other houses do disks for 99p. I suppose it depends on where they buy their disks, and from whom. Plus it depends how they dupe their disks. If they have an office and a duping machine, then it costs money to run. But if they've built the PD house into an existing business or are a one man outfit anyway, then obviously they have no overheads to speak of. Either way, it's up to you. Some 99p houses are good, others are terrible. The only way to find out for sure is to spend 99p.

Top PD

Here is a selection of some of the most interesting PD I've come across lately. The Fish Disks are compiled by Fred Fish in the USA, and they are available from most PD houses. Any files marked *download* were downloaded from CIX using a modem, but they should be available on a PD disk somewhere.

SID (Fish disk 338)

This is a very useful program for all sorts of filing tasks, being a sort of graphic interface to AmigaDOS commands. Using it you can rename files, copy them, set all kinds of flags on them, and if they are picture files or sounds you can see or hear them. Worth much more than the asking price.

MSH (Fish disk 327)

Allows you to read MS DOS disks from an IBM PC and copy the files over to the Amiga side. All you do is pop the disk in your external drive and it gets read like any other Amiga disk. A bit tricky to install for the beginner, but there is a very detailed manual to help you.

VirusX (Fish disk 287)

Checks for all known virus types, and is one of the more powerful virus killers, apart from MVK.

NetHack (Fish disk 189 and 190)

An addictive game based in a dungeon. I can't stop playing this one and it has found itself a permanent place on my Hard Disk.

MacView (Fish disk 35)

Allows you to view MacPaint screens from an Apple Macintosh. You can save them off as IFF files to load into a graphics program like DPaint.

ScreenX (Fish disk 158)

Screen grabber, which enables you to save an Amiga screen to an IFF file for treatment with DPaint and other paint programs, or for inclusion in a DTP package, not unlike all the screens in this book, for example.

Spectrapaint (17 Bit disk 961)

Excellent fully-featured paint program, looking and working a bit like DPaint. Provides a lot of very advanced features, and represents some of the finest value for money I've seen in PD for a long time.

Master Virus Killer (Amiganuts disk 971)

This is a virus killing machine, written by Belgian coder Leclercq Xavier. This is version 2.0 of the MVK and features the particulars of 105 different viri, including some I've never even heard of. It also recognises 47 different kinds of benign bootblocks, which means you don't get an alert from a non violent block like one which prints up a scrolling message!

The MVK detects and erases virtually any virus, including IRQ type file viruses which attach themselves to a file rather than the obvious bootblock hiding place. If it cannot detect and identify a virus, it will log it for future reference. An IRQ protector program can be put onto your most sensitive disks, just to make sure they don't catch these particularly nasty little bugs. A lot of the docs are in French (presumably with a Belgian accent) although all the most important stuff is in English too.

MED v3.0 (Amiganuts disk 973)

If you are in the market for a music-making program, then this could be the moment you've been waiting for, because MED v3.0 is here! This is one of the best value PD programs on the market. As well as being a fine Soundtracker type music program, it also allows you to sample, construct synth sounds, and read and write Soundtracker files and modules!

This is version 3.0 of this popular program by Finnish coder Teijo Kinunnen. The program works using a series of pages of CD or video type transport controls, and the program uses two different methods of editing, the traditional tracker type upward scrolling lists of numbers and a new sideways scrolling score. Although this isn't a traditional blobs and bars type interface, it is easier to learn for musically talented but classically untrained beginners.

For music fans there is much to get your teeth into, and you should be able to crack in right away and do some wicked music. There are demo tunes to run, plus a module from Soundtracker to help you along the way. When you play a tune the four channels have hopping bar meters to show the notes, plus an oscilloscope display too. As well as that you can see a sort of fake spectrum analyser too, so there's a lot to look at while the tunes are happening.

The sample editing is nicely done, with facilities in common with some of the top end sample editor programs like Audiomaster. It is very easy to use, and comes with a directory of ready made sounds for you to re-edit and make your own. All the ranging and mixing options are there for you to take the noise out of the sample, and even add effects like echo.

The synth editor is a similar affair to the sound editor you get in Sonix. The sounds seem to be naturally slanted to some of those funky old C64 type sounds. Not that there is anything basically wrong with C64 sounds, the SID chip was the best computer synth of all time in my view, and I've heard some startling stuff on that. The best thing about synth sounds is that they are generally more expressive than samples, as they have an ADSR envelope and are more musical for that. Some of the bass sounds you can get through synthesis have a more *gutsy* quality than you'd have thought possible from chip music. The synth voices also take up a hell of a lot less room too, being based not on a chunk of memory but a tiny waveform and an ADSR envelope! So thumbs up for the synth section there.

Unlike Soundtracker, you are not limited to the numbered ST-xx sample disks and so you can load any old samples you've got around and use them to create beautiful music. And also, unlike the very unfriendly Soundtrackers, it is easy to install on your hard disk. Just copy all the files from the disk onto DH0: or whatever and you're off. No stupid assigns to make, no nothing.

Another really classy thing about MED is its use of MIDI, allowing you to send or receive MIDI information on any MIDI channel, and even a load at once. One of the sample tunes on the disk outputs a sequence to a Roland U20 if you have one. If you haven't I'm sure you can re-route it to some samples or to appropriate sounds on your own synth perhaps.

The really astonishing thing about MED 3.0 is the sheer amount of stuff you can do with it, and as a music tracker it is second to none. Although MED is not shareware, I urge you to send a donation to the author if you buy and use it, just in recognition of the sheer *work* that's gone into writing and testing this program. Well done, Teijo, and more of the same please while you're at it.

Metallion's Utils (Amiganuts disk 848)

Metallion is one of the famous Kefrens demo team, and here he is turning his attention to a bunch of hot utilities for any Amiga *power user*.

New Topaz alters the system font by changing the look of Topaz 8. Also included on the disk is a selection of fonts for you to choose from, plus an editor to make your own. The fonts are saved in a generic RAW format, and the program can be added to your startup-sequence to alter the font before anything is printed. This turns your system into the most totally customised thing around, as the topaz font is everywhere on programs and windows alike.

Alter the shape of the system font and your computer starts to look really cool. This is something that you can do on the A3000 and other newer Workbench 2.0 machines, but up until now it's been a fairly laborious and flaky process. Metallion fonts are stored in a tiny RAW data format, which only takes up a single file of just 768 bytes, as opposed to between 3000 to 7000 bytes for your average normal Amiga font.

If that one program wasn't brilliant enough for you, and it was for me, there are a couple of very groovy programs for creating automatic menus for your demo disks. The first one is Powermenu, which is demonstrated on the disk itself as the method by which you select the utils. The menu is a starfield from which you select your programs using the mouse. A strange floating copper bar follows the mouse, leaving a purple ghost image. The effect is stunning, and very easy to use with your own programs too. The second program of this type is Powerboot, which does a similar job, but more simply and installs the menu on the bootblock, good for large programs.

There are two font editor programs, one for 16x16 and one for 8x8. The fonts can be for the NewTopaz program or for general use, as you can save the files in a variety of useful formats suitable for programmers and ordinary users alike. Also on the disk are two other programs Window and QuickRAM.

A-Gene (Amiganuts disk 933)

This is a genealogy program, which is basically a highly specialised database to plot your family tree. Into the program you put all your family data, like who married who, when people were born etc. You cross reference everyone and you are then able to produce reports based on the data.

The kind of reports I'm talking about are like flowcharts, with you at one end and your oldest known relative at the other. We're talking ancestors here, so get talking to your granny, and see if she knows anything more than she's saying. Perhaps you're related to a famous historical figure?

Be warned, this is just a limited version of the program. To get a full two disk version you have to mail off £15 to the author in Australia. The full version is very comprehensive, coping with 2000 people and 500 marriages, and not only that you can have a separate disk full of digitised pictures too, so you end up with a huge multimedia family tree. But don't forget, you will spend most of the next two years of your life typing in information or down at Somerset House (or wherever the dickens that place is where they keep the records), looking stuff up.

Although you need the full program to get really professional, the limited version is enough to get a tree going on a fairly casual basis, and the program works fast too. Personally I'd rather give the fifteen nicker to some bod to look up the births 'n' marriages for me. But then I'm the kind of bloke who uses a remote control on his car stereo, so take no notice.

Juggler 2 (Amiganuts disk 913)

This animation is a joke on one of the earliest demos for the Amiga. In the beginning there was Boing!, which was a huge red and white checkered ball bouncing around in a grey room. (Trivia point: Boing! can be found on the Mastering Amiga Beginners Disk. T'was rumoured that one of the Amiga system programmers banged his garage door to get the boing noise.) Then after Boing! came the Juggler. Now old Juggles was the very first ray-traced image on an Amiga, and the first animated ray-traced demo too. The juggler stood in the by now familiar checkered landscape, juggling a trio of mirrored balls. It was stunning at the time, and sold more Amigas than Boing! did, I can tell you.

Now it's the 90s, and Juggler 2 arrives. It's a cartoon made with the Moviesetter program from Gold Disk, starring our old friend from the Juggler, plus a new friend of his. I won't spoil it by telling you what happens, but it's very funny.

Antiflik.lzh (download)

This file is readily available on a great many bulletin board services in the UK, although I downloaded it from CIX in London. (The .LZH on the end of the file indicates that it is a compressed file or *archive* containing a number of other files, and the file compression program used is the one called LHARC.) Upon uncompressing the file we're presented with a number of other files, all called Antiflicker.<something or other>. The meaning of this program is clear: what it intends to do is prevent interlace flicker found in the Amiga's hi-res 640 x 512 mode. It does this using a software trick to de-interlace the display, making the boundaries around letters and edges on the screen appear slightly fuzzy, thereby reducing the effect of interlace flicker.

The one minor drawback to using Antiflicker on your Workbench, is that the Topaz 8 font is unreadable. In most cases you must use bigger fonts like Topaz 10 or 11 for the best results. The reason you use the -c parameter after using Antiflicker, is to produce a four colour Workbench as normal. Antiflicker is one solution to interlace flicker. Unfortunately, it is not the *final* solution. The only way to get rid of interlace flicker on your application programs is to invest in some kind of display enhancer (like the one from Commodore if it's ever freely available!) or some kind of Flicker Fixer and a VGA/Multisync monitor. But for certain applications, especially where a lot of text is needed on the screen then antiflicker is a not bad solution to the problem. But don't get your hopes up too much.

Phone.lzh (download)

This program was also downloaded from a bulletin board system, namely CIX in London, and is similarly compressed using lharc. It is a simple command which is typed from the CLI prompt to run, that is to say you type:

        phone

at the CLI prompt. After the word phone you then type in a telephone number as the parameter like this:

        phone 443322

and after you press return the two speakers of your Amiga will produce touch tone telephone sounds. Although not a very comprehensive auto-dialler program, phone is a very simple and effective way of getting phone tones out of your computer. If you need these for any reason this could be a very useful addition to your C directory.

Where Can I Get It?

For those of you who want to know where to go to get your PD, here is a short list of some of the best known PD houses for you to call and write to:

Amiganuts United: 169 Dale Valley Road, Hollybrook, Southampton, SQ1 6QX.

AMOS PD Library: 25 Park Road, Wigan, WN6 7AA. Tel: (0942) 495261

Comp-U-Save: PO BOX 157, Hayes, Middlesex, UB3 4SR.

Crazy Joe's: 145 Effingham Street, Rotherham, South Yorks, S65 1BL. Tel: (0709) 829286

Digital Applications: 118 Middle Crockerford, Basildon, Essex, SS16 4JA. Tel: (0268) 553963

EMPDL: 54 Watnall Road, Hucknall, Nottingham, NG15 7LE. Tel: (0602) 630071

ICPUG: PO BOX 1309, London, N3 2UT. Tel: 081-346 0050

KAD-Soft UK: 2 Ebor Paddock, Calne, Wilts, SN11 0JY. Tel: (0249) 817174

NBS: 132 Gunville Road, Newport, Isle Of Wight, PO30 5LH. Tel: (0983) 529594

Kernow Software PD Library: 51 Ennors Road, Newquay, Cornwall.

PAS Amiga PD Club: 3 St John's Walk, St Ives, Cornwall, TR26 2JJ.

PD Soft: 1 Bryant Avenue, Southend-On-Sea, Essex, SS1 2YD. Tel: (0702) 612259

Public Dominator: PO BOX 801, Bishop's Stortford, Herts, CM23 3TZ. Tel: (0279) 757692

Riverdene PDL: 30a School Road, Tilehurst, Reading, Berkshire, RG3 5AN. Tel: (0734) 452416

Sector 16: 160 Hollow Way, Cowley, Oxford. Tel: (0865) 774472

Seventeen Bit Software: PO BOX 97, Wakefield, West Yorks, WF1 1XX. Tel: (0924) 366982

Softville: Unit 5, Stratfield Park, Elettra Avenue, Waterlooville, Hants, PO7 7XN. Tel: (0705) 266509

Start Computer Systems: Barbican House, Bonnersfield, Sunderland, SR6 0AA. Tel: 091-564 1400

Vally PD: PO BOX 15, Peterlee, Co Durham, SR8 1NZ. Tel: 091-587 1195

Virus Free PD: 23 Elborough Road, Moredon, Swindon, Wilts, SN2 2LS. Tel: (0793) 512321

Workbench PD: 1 Buccluech Street, Barrow-In-Furness, Cumbria, LA14 1SR. Tel: (0229) 870000

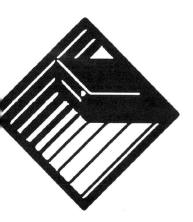

21:
Emulation

Many of you will have heard that the Amiga can emulate other computers, and this is the case. The Amiga can readily emulate the Apple Macintosh, the IBM PC, CP/M machines, the Atari ST, the BBC B, the Commodore 64, the Sinclair Spectrum 48K and the Sinclair QL. Most of the emulators are public domain, and most are flaky and unreliable to say the very least. But most work well enough to run some kind of software. It all depends why you want to use an emulator.

Why Emulate?

A common start point for most of the mail I get on a daily basis, apart from "Now then, I know nothing about computers...", is the letter that begins with "I've got this PC at work...". It seems that a lot of people have gotten wind of the fact that you can use a file at work all day on your PC and then use the file in your Amiga at home. It just seems like a convenient excuse to own a flashy and very exciting computer, to me. But then I'm a bit of a cynic.

Scenario 2: Someone wanders up to me at a computer show and says: "Can I get this disk into my computer?". After a few seconds' careful questioning I understand three things:

1.   The man is holding a PC format 5.25" disk in his hands.

2.   The computer he has at home is an Amiga machine, and...

3.   The man is clearly an idiot. (Just kidding.)

I patiently explain that computers come in different flavours, and no program from one computer will run in another. I go on to say that it's always been like that and in many ways it's getting worse. He looks at me sideways with that look of innocent confusion and says, "Well, what's the point of that?".

Thinking about it, the guy at the show isn't as stupid as he looks, because accidentally he's stumbled across a major truth of modern computing: There really *is* no point to all computers being different, as anyone knows who's tried to get graphics or text from one system to another.

But rest assured, wherever there are computers there are people trying to bridge the gaps between them, all types and models. In the battle against computer incompatibility there are two prongs of attack, emulation and file exchange.

Basically what file exchange is all about is converting files from one form into another. Then the file is usable in different machines, or even the same machine but a different program. What are we left with? Why, emulation of course! Emulation, on the other hand, is a method of programming one computer in such a way that it imitates another computer's ROM and disk operations. So after the programming you can do what our beginner wanted to do in the first place, just put the disk from one computer into another. The host computer emulates all the system calls and disk drive operations just like a normal model of the target computer, so the disk thinks it's running in a native machine. But there is a downside with emulators that you don't get using an actual machine, and that is speed. Most emulators run very slowly, but we'll go into that in a second.

At the centre of the emulation world is the PC, the one computer which you can emulate on anything from a slide rule upwards. (Even sometimes a PC!) But seriously, if you want to run programs in a business environment, apart from the enlightened businesses who already run Amiga environments like those in the audio visual and music markets, you have to be PC compatible. In order to be a serious contender (in these days of rising PC popularity) you have to be able to get to a PC format disk somehow. And emulators, and their near cousins the disk readers, are the way you do it.

Your Emulation Station

The Amiga is one of the most versatile computers on the market, but quite apart from its obvious charms in the graphics and sound departments it also has possibilities beyond mere gamesware. The stability of its multitasking operating system makes it a perfect alternative to the PC, and its custom chip set boosts the power of its rather slow 68000 processor beyond normal limits for its clock speed. The Amiga emulates more computers than almost any other machine, taking on the PC, ST, Mac, BBC, and C64 sides of things with great ease.

The Kolff Computer Supplies Power PC board (usually known as the KCS) emulates a CGA PC XT, and fits into the memory expansion trapdoor underneath your Amiga. This is a no-solder procedure and takes no more than a couple of minutes to do. The software which drives the emulator takes the form of a boot disk which activates the board, and takes over your Amiga. The software doesn't allow multitasking, so you can't run any other Amiga software at the same time. The reason for the shut down of the Amiga side is purely and simply speed. Unlike most emulators, the KCS runs at the speed of a native machine of the same spec. The chip at the centre of the KCS is the NEC V30, and the BIOS is Phoenix, just like a regular PC. The reason the machine runs all software is that it isn't pretending to be a PC, it *IS* one.

Some may object to the KCS taking up the space normally reserved for battery-backed clock and half meg of RAM. Not to worry, as not only does the KCS contain a battery-backed clock, it also has 1.5 megs of RAM on it; half meg for the Amiga, 640K for the PC side, and a large Ram Disk for the PC takes up any slack. The board comes with a program called PC-Clock, an Amiga command to replace SETCLOCK to load the time off the KCS for the Amiga side and PC side alike. There is also a setup program, which you start by holding down the mouse button when you boot the disk. Then a simple point and click menu system allows you to set all the preferences for your PC emulation.

By contrast the Vortex ATOnce board is an internal circuit board which fits into the 68000 slot, allowing you to fit both the 68000 and a 80286 chip in the same socket. Although specifically aimed at the A500 market, the unit should soon be available in a form more suitable for an Amiga 2000/3000, ie on a card. The ATOnce's biggest bonuses over the KCS are that it is a genuine 286, and it can multitask with the Amiga. But I have to say that in use they perform about equal. I prefer the KCS, but that's my business. It all depends what you need from a PC emulator. Obviously if you have a craving for Windows, then the 286 is your man, but what the flip is wrong with Workbench, eh?

The best (and indeed only) Macintosh emulator on the Amiga is the A-Max II by Readysoft. The first A-Max had a few bugs in it, and no support for the Mac's sound. These things have been fixed, although it still has problems which may or may not be fixed in a new version by the time you read this. There are two versions of the A-Max II, the regular II and the II Plus. The II is a version of the original A-Max cartridge (containing two 128K Mac ROMs) with a software upgrade, while the II Plus is a new card for the Amiga 2000/1500/3000.

The A-Max II cartridge fits into the external disk drive port of the Amiga, and you can connect a Macintosh 800K drive and an Amiga drive to the two ports on it. Using the Mac drive you can read and write Mac disks, but like the old Magic Sac Emulator on the Atari ST, you can't stick Mac disks into the Amiga itself. The reason for this is that the Amiga drives move at a constant speed, and the Mac drives change speed depending on which track they are reading on the disk. This is called GCR, and the Mac drives can handle it, because they are built to do it from the start. It's a bit harder to do this on an Amiga drive, and at the time of writing nobody has cracked reading and writing Mac disks in Amiga drives yet.

So the format of the disks for the Amiga drives is a special A-Max format, although this becomes invisible in use if you have a Mac drive attached to the system; you can copy the disks across as if both the Mac and Amiga were both native drives on native machines. The operating system treats all the drives as if they were Mac drives.

As well as the internal, external and Mac drive (that's three in case you weren't keeping score) you have, if you press F1, a Ram Disk, which the system also treats like a normal Mac disk. You can format it, name it, fill it with programs, eject it, load it again, and all the info stays intact on it until you power down the computer. This is a boon for that extra hand when all your disks are full, and for those users without external drives.

The only down side to the A-Max is that, to give the computer a similar high resolution, it has to use the unpopular flicker or interlaced mode. It's okay when you're doing TV graphics (what it was designed for) but flickering away on a black and white Mac screen...well, I'm afraid even proprietary migraine medicines aren't man enough for the job. Eyestrain is the only plausible result of watching that thing for very long.

You can use a flicker fixer, but that means more outlay, for both the flicker fixer and the Multisync monitor unless you're already made that investment. The best way to minimise flicker if you haven't got a flicker fixer is to use a filter over your screen or turn the contrast way down. This reduces the difference between the colours and filters out most of the annoying wobbling. Unfortunately, the Mac operating system uses a lot of closely spaced horizontal lines, which is the worst thing for flicker. But if you take the steps I told you about just now the system is usable for most things. And although copy protected software can't be run (due to needing to have a key disk inserted in the boot drive, which in this case is an Amiga drive!) non copy protected stuff works like a dream. All of the text for this book was ported over to a Mac disk using the A-Max II installed on my mutant Amiga 1500 machine.

If you have slots on your Amiga, which you do on a 1500, 2000 and 3000, very soon you will be able to use the A-Max II Plus. This is a card to plug into your Zorro format slots, which holds not only a Mac emulator but also gives you the GCR capability. This lets you put your Mac disks right into an Amiga drive to read and write them. When this comes out this will be the Amiga to Mac solution of choice, as it enables you to run copy protected software, which as I say the previous versions of A-Max didn't.

A new emulator is also on the market now, called EMPLANT (Utilities Unlimited). This is a universal emulator, which to begin with is said to emulate a Mac II and even a Mac Quadra, although versions for Atari ST and IBM 486 are said to be in the pipeline! This is impressive stuff, although I suspect emulating a Quadra could be hazardous to your wallet! Contact the UK supplier Blitsoft, 6 Dorney Place, Bradwell Common, Milton Keynes, Bucks MK13 8EL, telephone 0908 666265 for more details.

For Amiga users who moved up to the Amiga from the Commodore 64, the new A64 Emulator should open a few eyes. Not only does it load from a C64 1541 disk drive via a serial cable and a special piece of hardware, but also it reads C64 programs to and from Amiga disks once you've got them there (either floppy disks or hard disk partitions) as well. And the program multitasks with the Amiga too, so all the usual perks of the multi-screen environment are not lost. It also runs at a reasonable speed, which is more than you can say for most of the previous efforts at C64 emulation. I say reasonable, because you can't generally expect a software emulation to run at the same speed as the target machine. The C64 Emulator runs slower than a normal 64, but for most things the program runs well enough and any C64 programs you load will run. And by far the nicest thing about the program is that it's PD. The one drawback is that the hardware cannot be copied and you have to send off to get it from the author.

On the BBC side, you may have noticed the BBC Emulator in the Class Of The Nineties pack. The Emulator, as it was called, allows you to run software from the BBC/Acorn computers. Not only does the Amiga run the programs, it runs them up to seven times faster. Unfortunately a lot of graphics modes aren't supported, but it will run some things. This was a Commodore product originally, but now comes out through Genisoft, so check with them for availability.

One thing the ST can't do is emulate the Amiga. One might say the closest it gets is the STE, but that would be just bitchy. (I never stoop to that kind of thing. Gosh no.) However, the Amiga can emulate the ST! Medusa ST and Chameleon ST are two products from Germany which turn your Amiga into a fully-functioning Atari ST. Medusa is a hardware-based solution from Macro System, which consists of a tiny Zorro card which plugs into one of the 2000's internal slots. A 500 version will be available soon. You need access to an ST, in order to run a ST program called GetTOS. The program downloads the operating system (TOS) from the ST and allows you to load it onto the Amiga. (The OS only takes up about 200K.) The main advantage of emulating a ST in an Amiga is for things like music, for which the Atari is so much better served by software. Using the emulator, you can use your Amiga to drive any MIDI interfaces, as the emulator drives the serial port from calls to the ST's MIDI ports. And all this for about £150.

As well as the Medusa there is the Chameleon (their spelling not mine), which is almost exactly the same, except for the fact that it is all software. No hardware widgets to fit, just boot the disk and go. Oh yes, you have to grab the TOS again, but that's an easy thing. The price is about £30 in Germany, but when and if it comes over here it's likely to creep up to around £80. The other thing is that it does seem to be a tad illegal too, unless of course the ST you are copying from is your own. If you've borrowed the ST to copy the TOS code, then you are doing the same thing as if you were copying a software program.

This is a bit of a grey area, and one which plagues emulators right down the line. Is it piracy to copy another system's ROM code. Well yes it is. So how do you get an emulator to work without doing this? The A-Max solves this by using actual Mac ROMs in its cartridge. These are made by Apple, so no copying is needed. But the ST emulations are done using a digital image (or copy) of the TOS, so they are a copied version and therefore illegal. Although it is legal to sell the programs which do it, when you use them you break the law. Obviously it is impossible to police the use of such items, so they will continue to spread and indeed flourish. But why is not some provision made for emulations, as they are so useful in allowing you to use and convert to/from another computer? Why don't manufacturers sell their OS chips to emulator manufacturers? Well the answer is greed, basically. If they sold to emulator makers, what with emulations being so cheap, they would lose money, and that hurts.

In the PC emulator business, it has been made easier with the creation of chips which give you the same ROM codes as a PC but from another maker. When hardware clones become available, then making emulators which are free from illegal code becomes easy. This should soon be the case for the Macintosh, as Apple are about to sanction clones of their machines, which means more Mac emulators, with full hardware compatibility, should be available very soon.

Disk Readers

Finally, there's a wealth of disk readers including number in the public domain, of which the Fish Disks hold the best range. On the commercial front, there are two important products Dos2Dos By Coast To Coast, and CrossDOS by Consultron.

Dos2Dos temporarily turns one of your disk drives into a PC drive, allowing you to read and write PC and Amiga disks, and copy between them. CrossDos is a kind of resident version of this idea, but is transparent in use. Basically if you want your startup drive to be an Amiga drive, you refer to it as df0: as normal. But if you refer to it in a CLI command as A: or whatever you call it for PC use, then it becomes a PC drive. Wickedly simple, but very solid and reliable too.

Summary

Connectivity and interchange mean more than just fooling about with files for the sake of it. If you can use another computer's software, you double the amount of programs available to your machine. Not only that you have access to programs not yet available on your machine, which can only be a big bonus when you're talking about the PC software base being available to your Amiga machine. The PC has been around longer and has enough software to choke a cow the size of Suffolk. But soon it's going to get more serious than that.

With the inception of the CD ROM, all computers will able to read, if not run, a CD disk from any other computer. So the file formats native to any one computer will soon become a far more interesting issue for the rest of us. Generic graphics formats will be available for every computer, in the world of clip art especially where it'll be a case of "one file fits all".

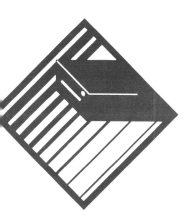

22: Introducing C

After you've been programming in BASIC for a while, and even after a long time using the fabulous extended BASIC programs like HiSoft BASIC and AMOS, you will want to move on. One of the best options is to try to learn the C language, as this is one of the languages used originally to program the Amiga for all sorts programs. C is a very popular language, mainly because it combines the ease of use and keywords structure of a high level language like BASIC, and the power and small code size of machine language.

You can do almost everything in C that you can do in machine code, except that you will have to learn less. It depends entirely on you how much you need to learn to become C literate. There are books on C which you can buy, and there are a lot of C compilers in the public domain now, plus tutorial disks for you to load and study. But what is C and how can you get started in using it?

What Is C?

I'll give you a brief history of what C is all about. The language was originally written by two programmers called Brian Kernighan and Dennis Ritchie when they were working at AT&T in the USA. They developed the language to write operating systems, and the first system they wrote using C was UNIX, a very popular operating system on all manner of mini and micro-sized computers. (Recently also the Amiga 3000UX was released, an Amiga using UNIX as its operating system.)

C was developed from a language called BCPL, along the lines of a subset called simply B. It was natural that the language after B should be called C. After the language was written, it became very popular in systems programming, to the extent that today you can pretty much get a job in systems programming if you know C! Of course you need a bit of experience as well, but that's market forces for you, eh?

The C language was made very simple, so that people who knew just about any high-level language like BASIC or Pascal could switch to C with very little pain. The real beauty of C is that, like Pascal, it's a compiled language, so after you've written your source code, it's compiled into machine code for running.

Another nice thing about C is that it's very simple to port it across to different machines, as apart from certain machine-specific graphics type routines, the code for C on any computer is just about the same. So a program like NetHack, a popular PD game which is text and character graphics based, can be ported across to many different computers without much in the way of re-writing. Another benefit of C is that it is very good at writing programs for a multi-tasking environment, like UNIX and of course the Amiga.

Obviously the scope of this book is limited to just a preliminary skip through the basics of C, but this should give you a taste of what you can expect if you decide to embark on learning this elegant and very popular computer language.

C for Yourself

An obvious subheading that, but I got a kick out of it even if you didn't. Obviously the first step is to get yourself a C compiler, and which one you go for depends on how really serious you are about this. Are you £2.00 serious or £150 serious? The PD options are Matt Dillon's DICE (standing for Dillon's Integrated C Environment) or North C by Steve Hawtin. Both are widely available and being updated all the time, so the benefits of other people using the program and testing for bugs are passed on to new users. The programs are both complete C programming environments for the Amiga, so go right ahead and get one for your first forays into C.

The £150 serious option is the SAS Lattice C compiler, and this is something of an industry standard in Amiga circles. If you pay the dosh for something like this you expect it to be really good, right? Well it is, and so if you anticipate being hooked by the C bug, you must start saving for this program right now.

Starting Off

The first thing is to write your programs. You need a text editor to create your programs, source code as it is called. This can be any editor you like, in fact pick one from Chapter 12, to save time.

Once you have your text editor, you can tap in your programs and compile them with your favourite compiler. Once compiled the programs are ready to run from the Shell, by typing their name, or from the Workbench, when you create icons for them. In most cases you simply type:

```
cc amigaprogram.c
```

and the compiler will whizz through your code, compile it, link it and spit out a perfectly-formed executable program. So that's the process, how's it done?

Writing C Programs

To start with, the only programs you'll be putting into your C compiler are examples from the book you're learning from. But sooner or later you will need to know how to structure a C program.

The format of a C program consists of a series of functions which you define before the program starts. Then you call these functions in the main program. Each function is marked by a label, or name, and followed by a pair of parentheses or brackets, like this:

```
main()
```

The beginnings and ends of a function are marked by braces or curly brackets:

```
{}
```

like those. Information is passed to the functions by putting it into the parentheses, like so:

```
printf("Hello world");
```

and each line of the program has a terminator on the end, which looks more like a semi colon (;) than Arnold Schwarzenegger.

So a simple program would look like this:

```
void main()
{
 printf("This is my first C program.\n");
 printf("Isn't it nice?\n");
}
```

Type this into your C compiler and save it as *first.c*, then compile it. You will find a program on your disk called *first*, and you run it by typing:

```
first
```

just like any other AmigaDOS command or program. Notice the \n embedded in the text lines. This is what C calls an escape sequence, and these are used to format the text. The printf function is exactly like the PRINT statement in BASIC, except you must enclose the text in brackets to feed it to the function. But unlike PRINT, unless you tell it to do a Return at the end of the line, it will just stay there at the end. So if you do more than one printf in a program they will all be joined together. Take out the \n and the program will produce:

```
This is my first C program.Isn't it nice?
```

rather than what it should do which is:

```
This is my first C program.

Isn't it nice?
```

You can use variables, just like you can in BASIC, although being C of course the usage is much more specific and faddy. For example to take a keystroke into a variable called B, you would type:

```
void main()

{

  int press;

   printf("Tap a number key\n");

   scanf("%d", &press);

   printf("\n\nYou typed a %d\n", press);

}
```

This program uses the scanf function, which takes input from the keyboard and feeds it to a variable. In this case the variable is *press*, and the data type is asked for by the %d, meaning the program wants to see an integer value. The variable *press* was defined as an integer variable at the top of the program, and the data was fed to it in the scanf line.

Format specifications are always preceded by a % sign, and they tell the compiler what a variable should be, and also indicate to the program where a variable should be in a line of text. Very clever stuff.

Control structures are nice, just like BASIC in essence. For example:

```
if(error = 1)

   printf("%c is the wrong letter!\n", letter);
```

is one way of testing a variable. There are other ways too, like while loops.

```
void main()
{
    int count;

    count = 10;
    while(count > 0)
       {
       printf("Count is %d\n", count);
       count = count - 1;
       }
}
```

which decrements (lowers by one each time it goes around the loop) the *count* variable by one each time. While the count variable is greater than zero, the program continues.

The *for* loops are similar to BASIC, except that they don't require a NEXT at the end. Here are two loops in BASIC and C to show the difference:

```
FOR N=0 TO 500 STEP 2: NEXT N
for(n = 0; n <=500; n = n + 2)
```

Both of these *for* loops have the same effect, to count up from 0 to 500 in steps of two, and you can see how they both do it.

Finally, comments are the C equivalent of REM statements. In C any comments are bounded by the /* and */ symbols. Like so:

```
/* This is a comment! */
```

When you are programming in C you have to be careful not to get them the wrong way round, or you'll get an error. And remembering to close comments is important too, or the rest of the program to the end will be considered a comment and will not be compiled!

That's it, You're on Your Own

So there you have it, a quick flip through the basics of C language, and although not really enough to get you going properly, it does give you a flavour of C. It's not a very hard thing to learn, and if the book you get to learn from is good you'll be up and running in a few days. Of course getting to the degree of being able to create your very own code may take a little longer, but that's the problem with all languages, computer or otherwise.

Helping Hands

There are many books and things to help you along your way on your journey to C heaven. The C manual disks, all four of them, are an excellent guide to the major uses of C on the Amiga. As well as bags of examples of good C source code, the disks also contain executable programs made from the source, to prove they work and show you what they look like. The disks are written by Anders Bjerin, the popular PD program author, and are distributed to most good PD houses.

DICE is the Dillon Integrated C Environment, and is written by veteran Amiga programmer Matt Dillon. Matt is well-known for his exciting Amiga hacks and programs, and this is one of his most major contributions to the Amiga PD world. A tad tricky to get set up, it is an excellent workhorse, but not a really good starter. Unlike North C.

North C is another PD C compiler, this time written by Steve Hawtin. If you're going to get a version of this program, get the one with a special front end by Mark Meany, as this is the easiest and best C compiler going. It even has a built in text editor!

For those of you interested in the PD side of programming, all of the above are available from Amiganuts United PD library. For the address see Chapter 20.

Further Reading in C

Here is a brief bibliography of books on C which you may find useful:

Inside The Amiga With C

by John Thomas Berry (Howard Sams & Co)

A guide for C programmers who can already code in C, instructing them in the use of the language on the Amiga. The Amiga's variant of the C language is rich in graphics commands, and it's a good idea to know all about these before you get too deeply involved in the system side of things.

Amiga C For Beginners

by Dirk Shaun (Abacus)

Translated from the German, and it shows. Although it is an excellent book on C, the lack of a really conversational writing style means it's all a bit uphill. Heavy going but all the stuff is there if you keep at it.

The C Programming Language

by Kernighan and Ritchie (Prentice Hall)

This really is the book about C, and whatever book you use to learn, you really ought to have a copy of this one to fall back on. Lucidly written, packed with information and background, and recently updated to meet with the full ANSI specification for C. Costs about £25, but worth every penny.

Mastering Amiga C

by Paul Overaa (Bruce Smith Books)

This is an excellent book from the same publisher as this one you are reading. It's an easy to read and use guide to the C language, and to my mind is much more readable than the other two I mention here. Nice examples for you to type in, and the support disk to accompany the book has the North C compiler on it so you can get going in C straightaway. You'll find full details in Appendix E.

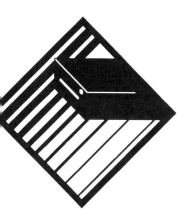

23:
Where to
from Here?

Now you've read the whole of this book from start to finish, you may be wondering what else you can read? Well, you could always read this book again. No, I'm serious. No, not from cover to cover, like you just did, I mean use it as a reference guide. The book has been carefully written to act as a reference book, so you can dip into it at any point using the index and find anything you want. So that's enough from me, what about further reading?

This is what this chapter is about, just a quick list of books to read on various important subjects. I get quite a few letters every month asking about what books are best for the Amiga, on all kinds of subjects from C language, BASIC, Intuition, which side of the disk do I spread the butter...all that kind of stuff. So here is my list. Bear in mind it's difficult for me to recommend any books except the ones I've read, not being what you might call a book reviewer. That being known, I do actually have a lot of books, and read them and refer to them when I'm working all the time. So here's my roundup of the best in Amiga reading, on my bookcase at least.

The AmigaDOS Manual

(Bantam Books) by Commodore-Amiga Inc

The original guide to the Amiga's DOS, and a good few other things besides. In the second edition you can find all the basic information you need about 1.2 and 1.3 versions of AmigaDOS, but you may have to delve around a bit. If you want to be an Amiga Programmer, then you have to have this.

Mastering AmigaDOS 2 Volumes One and Two

(Bruce Smith Books) by Bruce Smith and Mark Smiddy

Latest AmigaDOS guide covering all versions of the Amiga OS, up to and including the new version 2. A full guide covering two volumes, and put together with the full backing of Commodore UK. Don't let the fact that it's published by the same company as this book make you think I'm being less than impartial here. A lot of the basic information for this volume was looked up in this book. An invaluable reference guide.

AmigaDOS: A Dabhand Guide

(Dabs Press) by Mark Burgess

Another comprehensive guide to AmigaDOS up to 1.3 for the complete idiot, with lots of sound information and interesting hints and tips. Makes any old Joe into a real Amiga expert in a very short space of time, and while not as up to the minute as the Mastering AmigaDOS 2 book, it still stands up as a good reference book.

AmigaBasic Inside And Out

(Abacus) by Rugheimer and Spanik

This book is never far away from me, as I read it all the time. I got my copy free with HiSoft BASIC and I haven't put it down since. It's readable, informative, and considering it's translated from the German, even funny on occasions. It's a very thick tome, over 530 pages, but it's got everything you need to know about the language. Although I'm learning C now, I used BASIC for 11 years before reading this book. Shame it wasn't around 11 years ago. If you really are a *complete* beginner, this is the one for you.

Hackers Handbook IV

(Century) by Hugo Cornwall

This book is unfortunately responsible for feeding the media's misunderstanding of hackers. I consider myself a hacker in the *old* sense of the word, ie one who spends his time twiddling with computers, and I wish everyone would go away and leave hackers alone. There's only about five people in the country capable of massive computer fraud, and like Hugo Cornwall and Steve Gold they are earning enough talking about computer security not to need to steal the money. If you're interested in modems and computer communications, then this is the place to read about them. One of my favourite books at bedtime. This is the fourth edition, but any of the first three are just as good if you want to get them second-hand.

68000 Reference Guide

(Melbourne House) by Woodcock and Burkitt

Totally meaningless if you don't know machine code, but if you do then it's a whole little library in itself. May be out of print, so try your local library.

The Kickstart Guide To The Amiga

(ARIADNE) by Dave Parkinson

One of the most comprehensive programmer's guides around, and very easy to read too, even if you're not so hot on technical stuff. Contains all manner of technical tables and info, including hints and tips that Commodore don't tell you. And very funnily written too. (Nice one, Dave.) Rumours are around at the time of writing of a new edition in the works, so watch out for it.

Inside The Amiga With C

(Howard Sams & Co) by John Thomas Berry

Another book to teach you the C programming language, and very readable it is, although you will have to be conversant in another language before you can really get the best from this. As with most computer languages, C isn't just a language, it's an *attitude.* Not really a part-time pursuit. Lovely book though.

Mastering Amiga C

(Bruce Smith Books) by Paul Overaa

A new and very easy to read first C book, with none of the other C books' reliance on you knowing a bit about C before you begin. Same goes for this one as for the last one. C isn't so much a hobby as a way of spending your whole time, so be prepared for a bit of studying.

Organisations

ICPUG

This is the only Amiga organisation to belong to, really. They carry a register of local user groups affiliated to ICPUG, so you can join the national club and get a line on your local branch for regular weekly or fortnightly meetings. You get a subscription to the magazines they produce, and lots of online help. You also get to meet a few Amiga owners too, which can only be to the good. Call or write to: Jack Cohen, Membership Secretary, PO Box 1309, London N3 2UT. Tel: 081-346-0050.

Magazines

Here are some magazines to try, some of which I write for and some of which I don't.

Computer Shopper

Contains my Amiga column, which at the time of writing has been going in every issue of the mag since it began nearly five years ago. The rest of the mag has a PC bias, but always plenty to read.

Amiga Computing

Used to be the least interesting Amiga mag but has perked up a lot in recent months to be one of the best. I write a regular AMOS column in here every month. Excellent reviews and news.

Amiga Format

One of the oldest, biggest and best Amiga mags around, and one of the few to have a disk on the cover every month since issue one. I've got them all stashed away somewhere. Reviews are top notch, and massive games coverage.

Amiga Shopper

From the same publisher as Amiga Format. Pulpy pages and okay if you're a bit technical but beginners should steer clear.

Amiga Action

Retina bruising games magazine, full of hints and tips and great reviews.

Amazing Computing

The best and meatiest Amiga magazine going, made in America. One of the strongest sources for bang up to date Amiga information. More European bias than other US mags and I should know because I'm the UK correspondent.

Amiga World

Arty US publication, very flashy and good for hardware roundups and software reviews. Beware that some of the items shown may not be available in the UK.

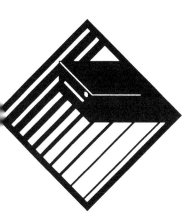

A:
A Sort Of
AmiGlossary

This glossary was partially gleaned from an old chestnut by the First Amiga User Group Newsletter, via UKAUG. I've added a few things I know, gossip, folklore and I've supplemented it with entries on the things I get asked about most. This should be the definitive Amiga dictionary. Until the next one. Anyway, here go.

Agnes

One of the *big three* custom chips inside the Amiga. (Originally called Agnus, Portia and Daphne, for reasons obvious to classical scholars.) Agnes controls RAM addressing, Direct Memory Access (DMA) and timing. Inside the A500 is a new chip called Fat Agnes, a big square 84 pin version of the original Agnus chip.

Ami or Amy

Short form of Amiga, a diminutive used by lazy writers like me.

AmigaDOS

The Amiga's Operating System (OS). Computers originally had operating systems, programs which make them go and which make all the mundane system decisions and controls. Micro computers were fitted with Disk Operating Systems (DOS) which had to be loaded from disk before the computer would go. AmigaDOS is a further extension of this idea. On one level it deals with all the system functions. On another it interfaces directly with the user via windows on the screen called Command Line

Interfaces, or Command Line Interpreters (CLI). The Amiga has the option of being operated by the user with Windows, Icons, Mouse and Pointers (WIMP) using the Workbench program, or with AmigaDOS using a CLI.

ANIM

An Amiga IFF format for animation. Designed by SpartaFilm's Gary Bonham, and used in Videoscape 3D and Deluxe Paint III. It compresses a series of screens into a smaller bundle by only noting the changes between frames.

ARC

A program, borrowed from the IBM PC, which compacts files and puts them in an ARChive. Used mostly on bulletin boards for transmitting a number of files in a smaller single bundle, rather than as large separate files. The files are crunched by scanning for spaces and identical bits, and in most cases the bundled files end up 50-70% smaller. See also Zoo.

BASIC

A high-level computer language, allowing beginners to program their computer. The word is an acronym standing for Beginners All-purpose Symbolic Instruction Code.

Batch Files

A list of AmigaDOS commands written with a text editor, which can be actioned with the EXECUTE command. Each command in the list is executed in turn, as if you were typing them and pressing Return.

Blitter

A custom graphics chip in the Amiga. Short form of BLock IMage Transfer, sometimes called a *bimmer* as in Bitmap IMage ManipulatER. Can do logic operations as well as line drawing, hardware fills, and stuff like that. This chip is mostly responsible for the fast colour graphics you know and love.

Boot

Short for Bootstrap. In the old days computers used to start themselves from disks and the programmers used to watch a huge machine grinding and flipping relays and joke that it was pulling itself up by its own bootstraps. The name stuck.

Bootable disks are the ones you can put in at the *Insert Workbench* prompt. Incidentally, you can make a disk bootable simply by typing INSTALL <drive> at a Shell prompt.

BTW

A bulletin board convention, short for By The Way. When you're typing over a modem there isn't time for some frequently used words or for retyping errors. Other examples are OTOH for On The Other Hand, and IMHO for In My Humble Opinion.

Another convention is the smiley, made from a colon, dash and right bracket,

    : -)

indicating the preceding words were meant as a joke. Like this:

    >Hey, why are you such a dork? :-)

My own smiley has got a better nose, made from a question mark,

    :?)

but the variations are endless!

Buster

A custom chip on the A2000.

C=

Commodore shorthand for the logo of the company. Internally this is known as the *chicken head* due to its remarkable resemblance to the Corn Flakes chicken.

C Directory

On every bootable disk there is a directory marked *c*. This usually contains all the AmigaDOS commands, and this is the directory in which the computer will search when you type a command. Not to be confused with the C language which is something quite different.

C Language

A computer programming language invented in the late seventies by Dennis M Ritchie. C is a compiled language, and its original use was for programming operating systems. AmigaDOS was originally written in a mixture of C and the forerunner of C called BCPL.

Chip Memory

The memory accessed by the custom chips in the Amiga, usually 512K, which funnily enough is how much you get when you buy it. Expansion memory, like the A501 or memory boards on the A2000 is called Fast Memory. Newer Amigas have 1Mb of chip memory, making it easier to use certain graphics intensive programs. Older Amigas can be fitted with 1Mb of chip RAM at your local service dealer.

CLI

The CLI is the Command Line Interface, the more traditional interface of the Amiga, which uses text commands that the user types in on the keyboard. On later versions of AmigaDOS you have a new CLI called the Shell. This is a later version of the CLI with more features. Basically the Shell uses the same commands as CLI, but there's a lot more bells and whistles on it. For example, in the normal CLI, if you mistype a line, you have to retype it. Whereas, on a Shell you can edit the line before you hit return to execute it. Not only that it has a command memory too. For example, suppose you typed this line:

```
1> dirt df0:
```

meaning to type dir not dirt. The computer has no command called dirt, so it will say so. To get the last command back, you just tap the up cursor arrow and the last command is brought back. Now all you do is use the left and right arrows to get to the *t* at the end of *dirt* and erase it with backspace or delete. Then just press Return (you don't have to go back to the end of the line) and the command is executed. Much simpler than retyping. You can step back and forth through the most recent commands you've typed by pressing the up and down arrows. Try typing ten or so commands and using this feature to step through them. And remember, you can be sure of Shell. (A joke for our older readers.)

Copper

Not, as you might think, a policeman, but a display COProcEssoR, responsible for *video display synchronisation.* A simple chip, having only three instructions, but very powerful for that. You can change the resolution on any line, modify the palette, and even pageflip without any 68000 (the main chip) involvement. Having said it's simple, you'd have problems programming it in anything other than C or Machine Language.

Delete Keys

There are two keys for deleting characters on screen, the delete key marked DEL, and the backspace key (above the big L-shaped Return key) marked with an arrow pointing to the left. DEL deletes the character to the right of the cursor, and backspace deletes the character to the left.

Denise

New name for Daphne, the custom chip which deals with video output, mouse input, etc. A sort of ritzy I/O chip.

Disk Drives

The drives on the Amiga are all called DF something, after Disk Floppy. The internal is called DF0:, the first external DF1:, DF2:, DF3: and so forth. The colons after the numbers are important, as AmigaDOS perks up and pays special attention to things ending in a :. (This is the same in MS DOS, like the A: command.) You can specify a certain drive to look at, for example:

        cd df0:

means: *I don't care what you're looking at now! Get yer ass over to DF0: and keep looking at it until I tell you what to do next.* You can also specify an actual disk which isn't yet in a drive. This is handy if you've only got the internal drive.

Say for example you have a disk called MYDISK. Just type in

        cd mydisk:

and the computer will ask for you to:

        Insert Volume MYDISK

Other drives which you can look at are DH0:, a hard disk drive, and RAM: the Ram Disk. You can also CD to other logical devices, like SYS:, C: and DEVS: as these are not only directories but general devices as far as the system is concerned.

Drawer

A subdirectory which is visible on the Workbench, the icon looks very much like a drawer.

Extra HalfBrite

Usually called EHB or just Halfbrite. A special mode which gives you 64 colours rather than the usual 32 maximum in any one palette. The computer is fooled into producing a ghost palette containing all the same colours as the main palette only half as bright. Or should that be brite? Deluxe Paint III supports this mode for drawing and animation.

Fast Memory

(See Chip Memory)

Filename

The name of a file on a disk. All files have names, and this name is how you refer to the file in the Shell when copying, deleting, or running the file.

Filenote

Attaches a short note to a file, which is only visible when you use the List command from the Shell.

Gadgets

Amigaspeak for the little buttons on windows which manipulate them on the screen. The sizing gadget on the bottom right of the window changes the size of the window. The two gadgets on the top right are send-to-back and bring-to-front. The square with the dot in it on the top left is the close gadget.

Gary

Another custom chip in the Amiga. This time a Gate ARraY. Clever, huh? In the A500, Gary replaces a lot of the chips and other components that were in the original A1000.

Genlock

A gizmo which lets you combine computer images with live TV pictures. Useful for titling and special effects. It works by replacing Colour 0 (the blue background to your Workbench for example) with the TV image. Genlocks are now as cheap as £99 for the Amiga!

Guru Meditations

When an insoluble error occurs on the Amiga, the power light is flashed and a system request appears in the top left of the screen. You click on cancel, and the machine appears to reset. But before it returns control to you, a Guru Meditation is shown in red at the top of the screen with a flashing border round it. The number indicates the type and source of the error for debugging purposes. The most common numbers before the . are 3 and 4, meaning *address error* and *wrong instruction* respectively. The error messages are called Guru Meditations for a very weird reason. When Amiga Inc started out it made joysticks for the Atari VCS console and Commodore 64. Among the input devices they invented was an item for surfing and skiing games, called the joyboard. You stood on a big board with contacts on each corner, and held a small stick in your hand. Hmm.

Predictably, nothing came of the joyboard, but the point of the story is that Amiga Inc wrote a meditation program which used it. You sat on the joyboard and the more relaxed you were, the higher you scored. I dunno. Californians! Don't you just love 'em?

HAM mode

Hold and Modify mode. A special display mode which gives you all of the Amiga's 4096 colours on screen all at once! This is an excellent mode for digitised pictures but imposes *heinous* stress on memory.

Icon

A small pictorial representation of a file which appears on the Workbench screen. Clicking on the picture with the mouse starts the program. Icons can be seen on the CLI as having the same name as the file they serve, but with a *.info* suffix. The .info file contains information about the file, like what sort of file it is and which other programs it needs in order to be used. Icons fall into four categories: disk, drawers, tools and projects. Disk icons are the icons of each disk you put into a drive. Drawers are like little electronic filing cabinets in the disk window, where you can put programs, or tools. Tool icons are for the programs you have inside the drawer windows. Projects are data files made by tools, so a file from a wordprocessor is a project.

IFF

Stands for Interchange File Format, a kind of standardised file family used on Amiga computers, covering sounds, tunes, pictures and animations. New types are being added all the time, but the basic ones you should know of are InterLeaved BitMap (ILBM), 8 Bit Digital Sound Samples (8SVX), ANIMation files (ANIM) and Simple MUsic Score (SMUS). The files are portable between programs from different manufacturers. Although sometimes you hit problems, for example HAM format ILBM files won't go into programs like Deluxe Paint III. But by and large the portability of images and sounds is pretty good.

ILBM

InterLeaved BitMap. An IFF picture file, like those made with Deluxe Paint III.

Interlace

To get a higher resolution in hi-res modes, the Amiga uses *interlacing* to get more vertical lines on the screen. This is achieved by alternating two sets of vertical lines, so instead of 200 steady lines you get 400 thinner, slightly more flickery lines. Interlace is used in many packages for higher res, but can be annoying if you have to look at it for a long time. The solutions to this are 1) take lots of breaks, 2) buy a high persistence monitor, screen filter or Flicker Fixer device, 3) turn the contrast down on your monitor.

Intuition

The name for the system behind the Amiga's WIMP interface. Intuition uses simple low-level commands and graphics libraries to form the graphics for the windows, menus, gadgets etc.

Kickstart

The old Amiga 1000 needed a Kickstart disk to load the operating system. The 500 and 2000 have Kickstart in ROM. The new 1.3 Kickstart is available as an upgrade both as disk and a chip, for those with 1.2 computers. Recent buyers of Amigas will have bought 1.3 ready installed. Kickstart 2 is only as yet available on the Amiga 3000, but soon an upgrade kit will be around for 500s and 2000s.

Lharc

An archive program like Arc. See Arc, Zip and Zoo.

Library

Certain basic Amiga system calls are grouped into libraries, like exec.library, intuition.library, dos.library, etc. These libraries are found in the LIBS directory on bootable disks.

Machine Code

Machine code is the programming language that the computer understands with no interpretation. Unfortunately most people don't speak binary, so either you have to learn machine code or you have to employ a higher level interpreted language like BASIC or a compiled language like C.

Multitasking

The Amiga is a multitasking computer. This means that you can run more than one program at once. You can run programs in different windows on screen at the same time and they act like a little computer on their own, as if they had the whole computer to themselves.

NTSC

The notoriously ropy American video standard, which has less lines than the PAL standard used in the UK. This explains why some programs cut off three-quarters of the way down the screen. Jokingly called Never Twice the Same Colour.

Operating System

The program which controls the computer. All the chips would be mute slabs of silicon without this program coursing through their little electronic veins. AmigaDOS is the operating system for the Amiga, and it deals with all the routine jobs like disk operations and memory and all the stuff that makes your head hurt. DOS stands for Disk Operating System.

Overscan

Amigaspeak for a full screen picture. Gimmick of AmigaDOS which allows you to display colour computer graphics on the entire surface of a screen, with no border cutoff. Useful for video applications, and home video titling/DeskTop Video.

PAL

The European colour video standard, consisting of 625 lines.

Paula

The custom chip responsible for audio digital to analogue conversions (DAC), serial events, and fancy disk control, allowing you to read other formats.

Phoneme

A basic syllable used in speech synthesis. In the Amiga, the phonemes are built into words either manually, or automatically using the command SAY. The SAY command translates any English sentence into phonemes and then says it. In AmigaBASIC, you can use the word SAY (TRANSLATE$), which does the same job.

Pixel

The basic building block of a video picture. One dot on the screen. The Amiga PAL format resolutions are 320 x 256 pixels up to 640 x 512 pixels.

Ram Disk

An imaginary disk drive using memory space (Random Access Memory or RAM) instead of magnetic disk space. The Ram Disk appears on the Workbench as an icon and on the CLI as a disk volume called RAM:. The benefits of Ram Disks are obvious. Transfer of data from Ram Disk to memory is almost instant, and so provides a very fast drive for all kinds of file-based programs.

ReadMe

On almost any program disk you will find somewhere a README file, sometimes called read.me, or even readme.doc. This is a text file, usually telling you things about the program that were added after the manual was printed. In the case of PD programs, they might even *be* the manual. These files can be TYPEd at a CLI prompt, or loaded into your favourite text viewer/word processor for viewing.

subdirectory

A directory within a directory. The root directory of a disk is the first one you find when typing the Dir command from a Shell. Within that directory are a number of subdirectories, which you can list using the Dir command followed by the name of the subdirectory in question. The CD command makes the computer enter that subdirectory and stay there. CD stands for Change Directory.

Vulcan Nerve Pinch

Also called the Three Fingered Salute, this is a pet name for the CTRL-A-A warm boot keystroke. Also known as Scouts Honour, but I think someone made that up just to be pervy.

WIMP

Short for Windows, Icons, Mouse and Pointers. A computer interface technique designed by Xerox at Palo Alto Research Centre, and later copyrighted by Apple Computer of Cupertino, CA.

Windows

A rectangular area on the screen which contains the input and output from programs you run on your computer. On the Amiga, each window can contain a separate, concurrently running program.

Workbench

The Intuition-based WIMP interface program for the Amiga. Using this program you can start programs and perform file functions without having to type in any commands. You merely *point-and-shoot* with the mouse.

Zip

An archive program like Arc. See Arc, Lharc and Zoo.

Zoo

An archive program like Arc. See Arc, Lharc and Zip.

Zorro

The format of the slots in the A2000. Into these slots you can fit circuit boards (sometimes called cards) containing various new circuits, expanding the capabilities of the machine in any direction you like. Hard disks, fax cards, extra memory, modems, you name it. The name Zorro is taken from the nickname of the original A1000 circuit board prototype.

B: AmigaDOS Commands

This is a short roundup of some of the most useful AmigaDOS commands. Obviously a complete guide to AmigaDOS is outside the scope of a Chapter or an Appendix in a beginners guide, although this will be a good point of reference while you're learning. If you want to know more about the Shell or AmigaDOS, why not get a good book on AmigaDOS itself like Mastering AmigaDOS 2 by Mark Smiddy and Bruce Smith.

ADDBUFFERS

`Syntax: addbuffers <drive>`

The Amiga has quite slow disk drives, by the standards now set by fast hard disk drives. Addbuffers creates a small cache in RAM which buffers ins and outs from the disk, and if a section of code has already been read from the disk before, it is held in the buffer and loaded from there if it's still hanging around there. This speeds up access a little, and explains why some things that you re-load after a few minutes seem to come from nowhere.

ALIAS

`Syntax:`
`  alias [<name>][<string>]`

A simple command for changing the names of certain expressions or commands. For example:

`    alias del delete`

allows you to use del instead of the delete command, which might be useful for users more used to MS DOS!

ASK

Syntax: ask <prompt>

A script command for use in batch files for getting input from the user. For example:

```
ask "Press Y or N"

if warn

echo "Okay"

else

echo "Why not?"

endif
```

Ask uses a simple Y or N trap for asking questions. The warn command is set if there is a Y typed in, and if not the command slips through to the else condition. Just pressing Return sends a N to the command.

ASSIGN

Syntax: assign <directory><pathname>

Assign has many uses. It is used to assign a directory or file, making it in effect a logical device. This can simplify the location of important files or directories on disks. For example, if you want the computer to know where a particular directory is at all times, then you can specify where it is on what disk, and in which directory. To assign a directory called "DTP" to the drive dh0:, you must type the following:

```
assign dtp: dh0:dtp
```

Now, on any requesters within a program, you simply have to type DTP: into a text input line and the directory will be automatically looked into. In the same way, Assign is necessary when using certain programs to tell the program where to find particular directories and files. Most installation programs will do this automatically, but if a program asks for a disk it usually means that it can't find a certain directory which the program is expecting. To fix the problem just type:

```
assign <directory>
```

into your startup-sequence file in the S directory. In Workbench/Kickstart 2.0 you can even assign multiple directories or files to the same device.

BINDDRIVERS

Syntax: binddrivers

This command is only used in the startup-sequence file in the S directory on a Workbench disk. It joins any additional hardware to the system, like RAM expansions and hard disks. Any auto-configuring hardware (it will say this on its box) doesn't need a binddrivers command.

CD

Syntax: cd <directory>

Change directory. Tells the computer to turn its attention to another directory, even if the directory is on another disk. Typing CD on its own prints up the current directory.

COLORS

Syntax: colors [0,1 2 3 or 4]

Simple program on AmigaDOS 2.0 only which allows you to change the colours on the foremost screen.

COPY

Syntax: copy [from] <filename> [to] <filename> [all] [quiet]

A complex little command, this. In its simplest form just copies a file from one directory to another or one disk to another:

copy df1:billy.doc to df0:

although you can just type the more terse:

copy df1:billy.doc df0:

Copy can be used to send text to the printer by using:

copy <file> to prt:

the prt: device being the printer. In fact you can copy to any Amiga device, like RAM:, CON:, PRT:, DF1:, RAD: etc, and indeed any device you've created with assign!

DATE

Syntax: date [<day>][<date>][<time>]

The Amiga has two clocks, one in software and one in hardware. On the A500 this is an extra, whereas on the 2000/3000 it is fitted as standard. This command sets the date on the Amiga's internal software clock, using the format described above. For example to set the date and time to half past ten on the 25th of December 1992, you would set:

```
date 25-DEC-91 10:30
```

If you are happy with the date but the time is wrong, then you can do this:

```
date 10:45
```

and the Amiga automatically knows you mean the time and not the date, because you typed a colon instead of a dash between the numbers. If the time was right but the date was wrong you could type:

```
date 12-DEC-91
```

and just the date would be altered. You can also mention a day of the week, and the clock would advance forward to the next available day with that name, like:

```
date thursday
```

As well as days of the week, the Amiga also understands *today*, *yesterday*, and *tomorrow*.

DELETE

```
Syntax: delete <name or pattern> [all] [quiet]
```

Deletes the named file or files. This can be done in a very simple way, like this:

```
delete readme.doc
```

or you can delete a series of files which match a pattern by using the #? wildcard, like so:

```
delete #?.asc
```

which will delete all the files ending in a .asc. So all files like:

```
doc.asc
```

```
PhilipSouth.asc
```

```
Antiaircraftgun.asc
```

will be deleted. If you specify all, then all files will be deleted, even the directories which those files are in. If you specify quiet, you won't be told which files are being rubbed out. All and quiet should be used with caution, as they are capable of destroying every file on your Amiga, in the wrong hands!

DIR

```
Syntax: dir <directory or pattern> [opt a]
```

There are other options, but for the time being this is the way you'll use Dir, to get a directory of a disk or directory. Type:

```
dir df0:
```

to see what is in drive df0:. Any of the directories you see can be CD'd or Dir'd. Try:

```
dir c:
```

```
dir devs:
```

to do a dir of your C or Devs directory. If you make your own bootable disk, make sure you put copies of Dir and Copy in the C directory, as it makes it easier to add commands you need to the disk.

DISKCOPY

```
Syntax: diskcopy [from] <drive> [to] <drive>
```

This command copies disks, and the usual method is to say:

```
diskcopy from df0: to df1:
```

or something similar. This program will only copy AmigaDOS format disks, and in case you were wondering why it doesn't appear in the C directory, it actually lives, for some arcane reason, in the System drawer.

DISKDOCTOR

```
Syntax: diskdoctor <drive>
```

This program checks a disk and mends it if there is something wrong with it.

ECHO

```
Syntax: echo <string>
```

This is for putting text on the screen in script files. Check your startup-sequence for a good example of this. For example:

```
echo "This is an Amiga disk"
```

will print these words up in a Shell window.

ED

```
Syntax: ed <filename>
```

ED is the text editor which comes with the Amiga system. You can see a few details about this in Chapter 12, Text Editors. If the filename exists then the file will be edited. If the file does not exist, it will be created.

EDIT

> Syntax: edit <filename>

An old fashioned editor, a sort of scaled down version of ED, and as such can be erased from your working copy of Workbench to save a bit of space.

ELSE

Syntax: else

A part of the IF...ELSE...ENDIF structure. You use the word as part of a test to see if something is so, when there are alternatives. Like so:

```
if exists df0:c/dir

  echo "Dir is on the disk..."

else

  echo "Dir is NOT on the disk..."

endif
```

Good for startup-sequences and exotic script files.

ENDCLI / ENDSHELL

> Syntax: endcli
>
>   endshell

The same command virtually, only CLIs are closed by one and shells by another. I'll let you guess which does which!

ENDIF

> Syntax: endif

(See **ELSE**)

EXECUTE

> Syntax: execute <script file>

This is the way that you run any script files you create with a text editor. The files are made from AmigaDOS commands, and Execute runs each line of the file one after the other. Imagine you saved the script file we just looked at in ELSE under the filename *LookDir*. To run this script, all you have to do is type:

```
execute lookdir
```

and the script will look for the Dir command in the C directory.

FILENOTE

Syntax: filenote [file] <filename or pattern> [comment <remarks>]

A little-used corner of AmigaDOS, this. This command attaches a short bit of text to a file, which can be seen by the List command, the Info menu on the Workbench, and certain programs. I've never used it, so I don't see why you should.

FORMAT

Syntax: format [drive <device>] [name <filename>] [ffs] [noicons] [quick]

This command initialises a disk in the specified drive, adding AmigaDOS which allows you to read files from and write files to the disk. To format a disk in drive df0: for example, you would type:

format drive df0: name Blank

This will do a format of the disk you put in df0: and name it *"Blank"*, exactly the way I typed it. Once a disk has been formatted you can use it in your Amiga as a blank disk. You can also initialise disks using the Initialise menu option from the Workbench.

ICONX

Syntax: iconx

This program allows you to run script files from the Workbench. All you have to do is create an icon for the script file, and select the Info menu from the Workbench. You put the name IconX as the default tool, and then name the icon the same as the script file. Then you should be able to click on the icon to run the script.

IF

Syntax: IF

(See *ELSE*)

INFO

Syntax: info [<device>]

This is not the same as the Info on the Workbench. This produces info about the system, and although you can specify a device, you will mostly use it on its own. The output looks like this:

```
    Mounted disks:
    Unit Size Used  Free  Full Errs Status      Name
    FH1: 18M   32065 4109  88%  0    Read/Write  Work
    FHO: 1.7M  3462  4     99%  0    Read/Write  Workbench
    DFO: 880K  1141  617   64%  0    Read/Write  MasterAmiga
    RAM: 188K  376   0     100% 0    Read/Write  RAM DISK
    DHO: 918K  1622  212   88%  0    Read/Write  Boot
    Volumes available:
    MasterAmiga [Mounted]
    RAM DISK [Mounted]
    Work [Mounted]
    Workbench [Mounted]
    Boot [Mounted]
```

and this gives you information about the disks and their sizes.

INSTALL

```
    Syntax: install <drive>
```

Installs an AmigaDOS boot block onto the specified disk, making the disk bootable. You have to put more on the disk than just a bootblock, but this makes the process start.

JOIN

```
    Syntax: join <file> [<more files>] as <newfile>
```

This is a handy command for taking two files and joining them together:

```
    join file1.asc file2.asc file3.asc as bigfile.asc
```

like that. The point of this is not really apparent, but if you've got a string of text files that you want to put together as one, this is the most painless way to do it.

LIST

```
    Syntax: list <dir>
```

On its own it will list the current directory. Instead of the usual directory which gives you only the name of the file, List gives you more of an MS DOS type directory with file lengths and dates etc, like this:

```
Tools           Dir--rwed 24-Apr-91  11:34:03
l               Dir--rwed 21-Jun-91  16:56:29
Shell           empty--rwed 18-Jun-90  13:53:30
devs            Dir--rwed 15-Jun-91  20:09:21
System.inf      894--rwed 24-Apr-91  11:52:05
s               Dir------rwed Today  13:23:26
.info            47------rwed Today  15:25:31
Disk.info       838--·--rwed24-Apr-91  11:52:05
Shell.info      405--rwed 24-Apr-91  11:52:05
Prefs.info      894--rwed 24-Apr-91  11:52:05
c               Dir--rwed Yesterday  22:33:18
Prefs           Dir--rwed 23-Apr-91  09:00:41
System          Dir--rwed 23-Apr-91  09:00:37
t               Dir--rwed 15-Jun-91  13:32:16
fonts           Dir--rwed 19-Jul-91  00:21:39
libs            Dir -rwed 23-Jul-91  00:06:20
8 files - 10 directories - 147 blocks used
```

which, as you can see, is far more comprehensive.

LOADWB

```
Syntax: loadwb [delay]
```

Loads the Workbench, usually in a boot disk startup-sequence. The delay option leaves a three second delay to allow other disk activity to die down and prevent the drives thrashing.

MAKEDIR

```
Syntax: makedir <newname>
```

This command makes a new directory on the disk. Obviously it will have no icon file and so can't be seen on the Workbench, but you can see it by doing a directory of the disk in the Shell.

MOUNT

```
Syntax: mount <device> [from <file>]
```

This adds a new device to the system, which has been previously described in the mountlist, a file in the devs directory. The filename is the name of the file in the devs dir which holds the information. For certain devices you may have a separate file for each time you use the device, but most you can add to the bottom of the current mountlist using a word processor or text editor.

NEWCLI
NEWSHELL

    Syntax: newcli

              newshell

Creates a new shell or cli on the screen.

NOFASTMEM

    Syntax: nofastmem

Turns off the extra (usually called fast) memory you may have fitted to the system. This may be because the program you are running can't handle extended memory.

PATH

    Syntax: path <dir> <dir>…

Allows you to set up a series of directories that AmigaDOS will look into when a command is typed in. Mostly its used in startups to let the system know where C and SYSTEM are. If typed on its own, it'll show you what paths are set up at present.

PROMPT

    Syntax: prompt <new string>

Using this command you can alter the Shell prompt. For example:

    prompt "What now?>"

gives the prompt:

    What now?>

instead of the usual:

    1.>

In the Shell, when you first boot it, you will see the normal Shell prompt, which consists of the Shell number and the current directory, like this:

    1.Workbench.>

Which can be simulated by the command:

    prompt "%N%S>"

which will produce the exact same result.

PROTECT

> Syntax: protect <file> [+ or - <HSPARWED>]

This command sets the protection bits or flags on an AmigaDOS file. For example:

> protect readme.doc -D

protects the file from deletion.

The switches you can use in Protect are:

> H Hidden (AmigaDOS 2.0 only)
>
> S Scripted
>
> P Pure
>
> A Archived (not used as yet)

> R Readable
>
> W Writable
>
> E Executable
>
> D Deletable

The last four are the only ones you need have anything to do with, but I would hope you'd get a good book on AmigaDOS before you start fiddling around with them.

RELABEL

> Syntax: relabel [drive] <drive> [name] <new name>

Relabels or renames disks. If you have a disk in drive df1: that is called *Empty,* and you want it to be called *Docs 1*, type the following:

> relabel drive df1: name "Docs 1"

If there is a gap in a filename in AmigaDOS, you have to put quotes around it or the second word or character will be ignored.

REMRAD

> Syntax: remrad

Removes the RAD: device, a similar thing to popping a disk out of a drive, except in this case everything in the RAD is erased.

RENAME

> Syntax: rename [from] <filename> [to] <new name>

Renames a file from one name to another, a bit like Relabel.

RESIDENT

Syntax: `resident <AmigaDOS command>`

There are some complex switches and things to know, but initially all you need to see is that if you make a Shell command resident, it will be stored in a buffer in RAM, meaning you can take the Workbench disk out and the commands will still work. As the commands are stored in a buffer, they don't have to come from the C directory on your boot disk! So:

```
resident run

resident dir

resident copy

resident cd

resident makedir
```

and you will be able to look at a disk in df0: without having to swap disks all the time.

RUN

Syntax: `run <file>`

This runs an executable file as a background task so that you get the Shell prompt back right away, rather than when the program you've run has finished. The joys of multi-tasking!

SAY

Syntax: `say <switches> <text or file>`

Say makes your Amiga speak. This command is outlined in full in Chapter 11.

SETCLOCK

Syntax: `setclock <load or save or reset>`

The software clock on your Amiga can receive input from the hardware clock, but only via the Setclock command.

```
setclock load
```

loads the time from the hardware clock to the software clock. If you want to set the hardware clock use the Date command (See DATE) to set the software clock, and save it to the hardware with:

```
setclock save
```

which sends it the time you set.

SETDATE

Syntax: `setdate <file> [<date> <time>]`

Amiga files are date and time stamped, as you can see when you type List. To alter the time/datestamp on a file if it is wrong, you can do this with Setdate, like so:

`setdate Phil.doc 10-mar-60 00:12`

thereby resetting the time the file was made.

SETMAP

Syntax: `setmap <keymap file>`

The keys on your Amiga are mapped with certain characters for your country. In the UK the gb keymap is used, and you can see it being set in the startup-sequence file in the S directory:

`setmap gb`

If you want to set the keymap to a more sensible one, as most software is American, especially PD, you can do so by setting the keymap to usa1 using the Setmap command.

TYPE

Syntax: `type <filename>`

Types a text file to the screen. You can type a file to your printer too by using:

`type <file> to prt:`

And you can even look at a binary file if you add the OPT H or HEX (the same effect) argument to the end like this:

`type dir hex`

Why would you want to do this? Well if you know a bit about machine code then this sort of thing:

```
0F80: 37423D42 41434B2F 532C4445 4C3D4445  7B=BACK/S,DEL=DE
0F90: 4C455445 2F532C51 3D515549 542F532C  LETE/S,Q=QUIT/S,
0FA0: 543D5459 50452F53 2C433D43 4F4D2F53  T=TYPE/S,C=COM/S
0FB0  2C434F4D 4D414E44 0D0A436F 6D6D616E  ,COMMAND..Comman
0FC0: 64203F20 25430000 0844656C 6574656   d ? %C...Deleted
13F0: 28646972 29000000 38423D42 41434B2F  (dir)...8B=BACK/
1400: 532C4445 4C3D4445 4C455445 2F532C45  S,DEL=DELETE/S,E
1410: 3D454E54 45522F53 2C513D51 5549542F  =ENTER/S,Q=QUIT/
1420: 532C433D 434F4D2F 532C434F 4D4D414E  S,C=COM/S,COMMAN
```

```
1430: 44000000 05203F20 25430000 21496E76  D.... ? %C..!Inv
1F00: 4ED64E71 26444952 2C4F5054 2F4B2C41  N.Nq&DIR,OPT/K,A..
```

etc sends you into raptures.

VERSION

        Syntax: version

Types up the version number of the software, like so:

Kickstart version 36.202. Workbench version 36.77

so you know which revision to talk about if you have a problem.

Wildcards

        Syntax: #   match any number of the following
                          character

                   ?   match any character

                   #?   match everything up to the next
                          character

Wildcards are characters which allow you to be fairly non-specific about the characters or filenames you are operating on. If you want to delete a lot of files all ending in .info, for example, you would type:

        delete #?.info

and bobs your uncle all the icons are destroyed. (Don't do this on an important disk, by the way, as you'll never get them all back.) Wildcards are there for you to use when you're not quite sure about something, or need to operate on a lot of files with some part of the filename in common. Copying is a good example. Like this:

        copy #?.doc to ram:

strips all the docs out of a disk, and puts them in RAM:.

?

        Syntax: <command> ?

Forces a command to show you its format templates. You'll learn about this in due course, but this does give you an idea of what the command is expecting in the way of parameters.

< and >

        Syntax: Command > device:

                  Command < device:

Book Order Form

Full details of current books can be found in Appendix E. Please rush me the following *Mastering Amiga* books:

Mastering Amiga C @ £19.95 with Examples and North C Disks £...........·......

Mastering AmigaDOS Vol. One @ £21.95 with Scripts Disk   £...........·......

Mastering AmigaDOS Vol. Two Revised Edition @ £19.95   £...........·......

Mastering Amiga Printers @ £19.95 with Utilities Disk   £...........·......

Mastering Amiga System @ £29.95 with Programs Disk   £...........·......

Mastering Amiga Workbench 2 @ £19.95   £...........·......

Mastering Amiga Assembler @ £TBA   £...........·......

Mastering Amiga AMOS @ £TBA   £...........·......

Mastering Amiga News – catalogue of all titles   — *FREE* —

Postage (International Orders Only): £...........·......

Total: £...........·......

I enclose a Cheque/Postal Order* for £   ·   p.

I wish to pay by Access/Visa/Mastercard*

Card number

Expiry Date: ..../......./..........

Name...

Address..

....

.... Post Code...........................

Contact phone number. ....

Signed ....

*Delete as appropriate. Cheques payable to Bruce Smith Books Ltd.

Send your order to:

Bruce Smith Books Ltd, FREEPOST 242, PO Box 382, St. Albans, Herts, AL2 3BR.
Telephone: (0923) 894355 – Fax: (0923) 894366

sends the output of a file to a device or sends the output from a file to a command. For example if instead of typing:

```
dir
```

you typed:

```
dir > ram:dfzero.asc
```

the text from the directory would be stored as a text file in the Ram Disk rather than appearing on the screen!

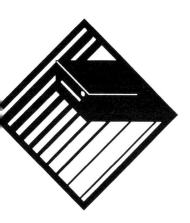

C:
AmigaBASIC
Commands

This is a short guide to AmigaBASIC keywords, and although it's not meant as a definitive guide, it does cover some of the most frequently used expressions. The variables x, y and z are used to replace any variables needed in the syntax of the keyword.

ABS (x)

Returns a positive number, even if x is negative.

ASC(x$)

Returns the numerical value of a character, the ASCII code for that character.

BEEP

Beeps the speaker and flashes the screen, to get the viewers attention.

CHDIR "directory"

Changes directory within a program. The directory name, df0: etc, appears in the quotes like so:

```
CHDIR "df0:"
```

and this can be any directory or pathname.

CHR$(x)

Prints the character whose ASCII value is x.

CIRCLE (x,y),z

Prints a circle on screen, of radius z, where the screen co-ordinates for the centre of the circle are x,y.

CLEAR

Resets everything to zero, all variables strings and arrays, and frees up any memory.

CLS

Clears the current screen window.

COLOR x,y

Set the foreground and background colours. X and y are the colour numbers set up by PALETTE.

DATA

This is where the READ statement gets its data from. Like so:

```
FOR B=0 to 5
READ A
NEXT B
DATA 23,45,56,34,37,19
```

notice the data statement is outside the loop, in fact it can be anywhere in the program.

DATE$

Returns the current date.

DIM(x)

Dimensions an array of size x to be used in the program.

END

Ends the program.

FOR
NEXT

A program loop type, begun with FOR and ending in NEXT:

```
FOR n=0 TO 2000 : PRINT "Boo" : NEXT
```

will print Boo 2000 times.

GOSUB x
RETURN

A subroutine in BASIC. GOSUB send you to a line number x, and RETURN send you back to the line after the GOSUB which sent you there! This isolates the routine from the main program, and is one of the keys to having good structure in your programs.

GOTO x

Unconditional branch to the line x, if you like it or not.

IF GOTO x / IF THEN ELSE

Conditional branches all. IF something equals this GOTO line x, and IF something equals this THEN do that, ELSE do something else.

INKEY$

Gets a key press from the keyboard.

INPUT x

Gets some input from the keyboard, can also be INPUT x$.

LEFT$ (x$,y)

Grabs the characters from the string x$, y characters from the left.

LET x=y

Assigns the value y to variable x.

LINE (x,y)-(x,y)

Draws a line from x1,y1 to x2,y2.

LIST

Lists the current program.

LLIST

Same as LIST except the output goes to the printer.

LOAD

LOADs a BASIC program into the computer.

LOCATE x,y

Puts text onto the screen at certain point, co-ordinates line x, column y.

LPRINT

Like PRINT only the output goes to the printer.

MID$ (x$,y,z)

Like LEFT$, only this time the middle characters are grabbed from the string x$, m characters long starting from yth character.

NEW

Clears the current program from memory.

PALETTE x, red, green, blue

Sets the palette of the color x, using the colours for red, green and blue. The RGB colours must be less than 1, so a nice orange colour would be:

```
PALETTE 0,1,.73,0
```

where 0 is the colour number.

PRINT

Prints a string to the screen so:

```
PRINT "Phil"
```

will print the word Phil on the screen. This can be replaced by a variable, so you could say:

```
LET x$="Phil"
PRINT x$
```

for the same effect.

RANDOMIZE

Resets the random number generator.

READ

Reads data from a DATA statement.

REM

A remark or comment can be put after a REM to comment on your program.

RESTORE

Resets the DATA statement so you can read from it again.

RIGHT$ (x$,y)

Same as MID$ and LEFT$, except that you grab y chars from the right.

RND

Produces a random number.

RUN

Runs a BASIC program.

SAVE

Saves the current program.

SAY

Makes the Amiga Speak (See Chapter 11.)

STOP

Same as END, Stops the program.

TAB (x)

Like the tab key on a typewriter, moves you over x chars.

TIME$

Returns the time.

TRANSLATE$

Used with SAY to produce speech from English input.

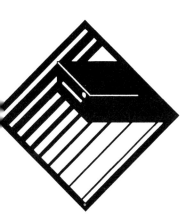

D: AmigaDOS Error Numbers

Sometimes things go wrong, but just to be on the safe side, the Amiga lets you know what went wrong. On the Workbench menu bar you will get an error number, and this will normally give you an idea of the fault. What follows is a table of the simplest and most frequent errors.

103 Insufficient free store

Not enough memory for what you are trying to do. Either you don't have enough fitted or it's too fragmented.

105 Task table full

You are running too many tasks, you multi-tasking demon you.

121 File is not an object module

The program you tried to run is not an executable AmigaDOS program.

202 Object in use

You have tried to delete a file or a directory which is Assigned or not closed for some reason.

203 Object already exists

This happens when you try to rename a file to a name which is already used by a program or file on the disk.

204 Directory not found

The computer couldn't find the dir you asked for. Perhaps you spelled it wrong? Or maybe you got the path wrong, is it on another disk?

205 Object not found

The file you asked for is not on the disk. Try doing a directory to see where it is.

212 Object is not of required type

You have attempted to do something with a file that it doesn't do.

213 Disk not validated

Oops. This possibly means the disk is corrupted, but don't panic, it may validate after a few seconds. Retry a few times. If it doesn't you'd better run Diskdoctor (or better yet, the PD program DiskSalve) to recover your files.

214 Disk write protected

Push the little tab in the corner of the disk if you want to write to the disk. Leave it on and press cancel if you don't.

216 Directory not empty

The directory you tried to delete still has something in it. Check to see if you need that file, if not delete it. Failing that, if you know what is in there and don't want it, use the ALL switch on the Delete command. (With care!)

218 Device not mounted

The device or disk you are after isn't on the system. Try pushing the disk in the drive, if you haven't. (The usual cause!) Either that or you spelled the name incorrectly.

221 Disk full

Yep, you'll have to get a new disk for this file, because you just filled the disk up.

222 File is protected from deletion

The Protect bits have been set so you'll have to set them back if you want to delete this file. (See Appendix B. AmigaDOS.)

225 Not a DOS disk

The disk you put in the drive is either a different format from AmigaDOS, or is a demo with a wacky and highly technical bootblock to prevent you reading the files. Oh yes, it could be a duff disk or even unformatted.

226 No disk in drive

Look, I said push the disk in the drive, okay? (Just kidding.) Obvious one this.

305 File not executable

You can't execute it, so it must be a text file or a graphic. Or maybe even a sound sample. Either way, you can't run it. (This is an update from error 121, it seems.)

E: Mastering Amiga Guides

Bruce Smith Books are dedicated to producing quality Amiga publications which contain both comprehensive and up to date information. Above all, we take great trouble to make them easy to read and the information easy to understand.

Our titles are written by the best known names in the marvellous world of Amiga computing. Below you will find details of our growing range of books in the *Mastering Amiga* series.

Titles Currently Available

- Mastering Amiga Beginners
- Mastering AmigaDOS Volume 1
- Mastering AmigaDOS Volume 2
- Mastering Amiga C
- Mastering Amiga Printers
- Mastering Amiga System

Titles Imminent

- Mastering Amiga Assembler
- Mastering Amiga AMOS

Brief details of these books, along with review segments, are given below. If you would like a free copy of our catalogue *Mastering Amiga News* and to be placed on our mailing list then phone or write to the address overleaf.

Our mailing list is used exclusively to inform readers of forthcoming Bruce Smith Books publications along with special introductory offers when ordering the publication direct from us.

Bruce Smith Books,
PO Box 382,
St. Albans,
Herts,
AL2 3JD

Telephone: (0923) 894355
Fax: (0923) 894366

Note that we offer a 24-hour telephone answer system so that you can place your order directly by 'phone at a time to suit yourself. When ordering by 'phone please:

- Speak clearly and slowly

- Leave your full name and full address

- Leave a day-time contact phone number

- Give your credit card number and expiry date

- Spell out any unusual names

Note that we do not charge for P&P in the UK and we endeavour to dispatch all books within 24-hours.

Overseas Orders

Please add £3 per book (Europe) or £6 per book (outside Europe) to cover postage and packing. Pay by sterling cheque or by Access, Visa or Mastercard. Post, fax or 'phone your order to us.

Dealer Enquiries

Our distributor is Computer Bookshops Ltd who keep a good stock of all our titles. Call their Customer Services Department for best terms on 021-706-1188.

Compatibility

We endeavour to ensure that all *Mastering Amiga* books are fully compatible with all Amiga models and all releases of AmigaDOS and Workbench.

FREE Software

Where books have support disks of software these are normally provided FREE of carriage when the book is purchased directly from Bruce Smith Books. All disks are available via mail order subject to a nominal charge to cover costs.

Suitability

The following notes should help you ensure that a book caters for your particular needs. Prices correct at time of going to press but subject to change without notification. E&OE.

Mastering Amiga Workbench 2

Bruce Smith, 320 pages, £19.95, ISBN: 1-873308-08-6

The Workbench holds within its bounds a wealth of facilities that largely go unused. In this 27 chapter volume Bruce Smith explores each of them and outlines how best to use them. This book assumes no prior knowledge of the Workbench but will make you into an expert. An ideal book to follow on after Mastering Amiga Beginners.

Mastering Amiga C

Paul Overaa, 320 pages, £19.95, ISBN: 1-873308-04-6

This is the book if you wish to learn C on your Amiga. It assumes no prior knowledge of C but will soon get you programming. Covers all major compilers including the PD NorthC Compiler which we can supply with programs disk for just £1.50. So for under £22 you can have the complete start to C programming on your Amiga!

Amiga User International said *"The Mastering series is turning out to provide top quality guidance for Amiga users and those starting out in the world of C will benefit greatly from this book and its accompanying disk."*

Mastering AmigaDOS 2 Volume One (Revised Edition)

Smith & Smiddy, 416 pages, £21.95, ISBN:1-873308-10-8

Perhaps the most comprehensive introductory tutorial ever written about the Amiga's operating system. This *Bible* of AmigaDOS has been enlarged and enhanced with the introduction of updates to AmigaDOS 2.04 and new chapters on If you want to learn about AmigaDOS 1.3 or 2 then this is the book to buy. It assumes you know nothing about the subject but – if your follow the exercises – will turn you into an expert! *Free* programs disk when ordered direct.

Amiga Format's technical editor Pat McDonald recently called it *"The best hands-on tutorial that I have seen for AmigaDOS."*

Mastering AmigaDOS 2 Volume Two (Revised Edition)

Smith & Smiddy, 368 pages, £19.95, ISBN: 1-873308-09-4

This title is a full reference guide to the AmigaDOS command set and has recently been completely revised to include over 25 new commands. Arranged alphabetically, it includes many worked examples. A *must* for the AmigaDOS programmer, it fully documents AmigaDOS 1.2, 1.3 and 2. Contains details on Commodities, Mountlist etc.

Amiga Format's Neil Jackson said of Volume Two: *"The definitive book to read on the subject, don't leave your Workbench without it! A recommended purchase."*

Mastering Amiga Printers

Robin Burton, 336 pages, £19.95, ISBN: 1-873308-05-1

Printers – the most misunderstood addition to any Amiga setup. Not so now, as Robin Burton tells you everything that you are ever likely to want to know. From printer control codes to Preferences, this book worth its weight in gold if you are purchasing a printer for the first time or upgrading to one of the new technologies. Covers printing from Workbench, DOS and popular applications. Free support software disk when ordered direct.

Mastering Amiga System

Paul Overaa, 400 pages, £29.95, ISBN: 1-873308-06-X

A complete tutorial to Amiga System programming with copious examples. A basic knowledge of C is required but the book begins with short examples which only later build into full-scale programs, all of which are on the accompanying disk.

In dealing with a difficult subject, the author has avoided merely duplicating standard documentation. Instead he has entered on a journey through the different aspects of the Amiga's system, finding the safest and most effective routes to practical programs. Mastering Amiga System is an invaluable purchase for the Amiga programmer who wants to master the system software. Free disk.

Mastering Amiga Assembler

Paul Overaa, 400 pages approx, £TBA, available October 1992

Although the 68000 processor series is well-documented, the use of assembly language to write efficient code within the unique environment of the Amiga is only now explained in this *hands-on* tutorial. Working with the Amiga's custom chips and system software are only two of the areas which will be appreciated by programmers wanting to generate machine code from the popular Amiga Assemblers, all of which are supported by the many code examples in this book. Free software disk.

Contents List

The following pages list the chapter headings for each of our published books. This should give you a better indication as to their full content.

Mastering Amiga Workbench 2

Take Off, The Workbench, Drawers and Directories, Disks and Drawers, Copying Files, The Menus, The Ram Disk, The Utilities Drawer, The Tools Drawer, The Shell, The System Drawer, Commodities Exchange, The Preferences Editors, The Recoverable Ram Disk, Icons and IconEdit, Information and Tool Types, Printer Installation, Graphics Printing, Fonts, Useful AmigaDOS, ED – The Text Editor, Customising Workbench Disks, MEmacs, Tool Types Revisited, The Virus Factor, Hard Disks, Goings On, Creating a Text File, Tool Type Summaries, File Location Guide.

Mastering AmigaDOS 2 Volume One Revised Edition

Introduction, AmigaDOS and Workbench, About Directories, AmigaDOS Command, Formatting and Copying, The Shell, The Ram Disk, Wildcards and Pattern Matching, File Protection and Assigning, ED – The Screen Editor, Multi-tasking Amiga, Environmental Variables, Command Bits and Pieces, The Bootable Ram Disk, Devices, More About LIST, Introduction to Scripts, Structured AmigaDOS, Evaluating and Manipulating, Startup-sequences, AmigaDOS 1.2 Startup-sequence, AmigaDOS 1.3 Startup-sequence, AmigaDOS 2.04 Startup-sequences, Customising Disks, Practical Scripts, Scripts That Write Scripts!, Recursive Scripts, Commodities Exchange, Fountain, MEMACS, Backing Up with BRU, Multi-User Machine, Pipes, Original AmigaDOS2 Startup-sequence.

Mastering AmigaDOS 2 Volume Two

AmigaDOS Command Reference Section, ADDBUFFERS, ADDMONITOR, ALIAS, ASK, ASSIGN, AUTOPOINT, AVAIL, BINDDRIVERS, BINDMONITOR, BLANKER, BREAK, BRU, CD, CHANGETASKPRI, CLICKTOFRONT, CLOCK, CMD, COLORS, CONCLIP, COPY, CPU, DATE , DELETE, DIR, DISKCHANGE, DISKCOPY, DISKDOCTOR, DISPLAY, DPAT, ECHO, ED, EDIT, ELSE, ENDCLI, ENDSHELL, ENDIF, ENDSKIP, EVAL, EXCHANGE, EXECUTE, FAILAT, FASTMEMFIRST, FAULT, FF, FILENOTE, FIXFONTS, FKEY, FONT, FORMAT, GET, GETENV,. GRAPHICDUMP, ICONTROL, ICONX, IF, IHELP, INFO, INITPRINTER, INPUT, INSTALL, JOIN, LAB, LIST, LOADWB, LOCK, MAGTAPE, MAKEDIR, MAKELINK , MEMACS, MERGEMEM , MORE, MOUNT, NEWCLI, NEWSHELL, NOCAPSLOCK, NOFASTMEM, OVERSCAN, PALETTE, PARK, PATH, PCD, POINTER, PREFERENCES, PRINTER, PRINTERGFX, PRINTFILES, PROMPT, PROTECT, QUIT, RELABEL,REMRAD, RENAME,   RESIDENT, REXXMAST, RUN, SAY, SCREENMODE, SEARCH, SERIAL, SET, SETCLOCK , SETDATE, SETENV, SETFONT, SETMAP, SETPATCH, SKIP, SORT , SPAT, STACK, STATUS, TIME, TYPE, UNALIAS, UNSET, UNSETENV, VERSION , WAIT, WBPATTERN, WHICH, WHY, Wildcards, ;,? ,<, >, >> ,*,"",*,',CTRL+\ ,ALT+' , AmigaDOS Error Codes, The Virus Menace, The Interchange File Format, The Mountlist, Telling FIBs.

Mastering Amiga Printers

Consider the Printer!, Types of Printer, Connected Matters, Initial Setting-up, Controlling Printers, Printer Commands, Graphics Commands, Printer Peculiarities, Elements of a System, Printer Installation, Printer Preferences, Printer Driver Facilities, Taking Control, Command Line Control, BASIC Control, Graphicus Horizontalis, Graphicus Verticalis, Graphics Preferences, Graphics Options, Screen Dumping, Deluxe Paint, Problems, Problems... Printer Driver Commands, Decimal-hexadecimal-binary-ASCII Conversions, Glossary.

Mastering Amiga C

Introduction, Making a Start, Types, Operators and Expressions, Functions, Program Documentation and Portability, Flow Control, The C Preprocessor, Arrays and Pointers, Input and Output, Structures and Bitfields, Character Strings, Storage Classes, Data Types Revisited, Files, Special C Features, The Real Problem, Some Amiga Specifics, Resource Allocation, Intuition and the Graphics Library, Making the Most of C's Modularity, Debugging and Testing, Last Words, Glossary, Bibliography, The Lattice/SAS C Compiler, The Manx Aztec C Compiler, The NorthC Compiler, Bits and Bytes, ANSI C Summary, ASCII Character Set, Useful Programming Tools.

Mastering Amiga System

An Overview, Preliminary Style and Programming Notes, Exec Memory Management, Tasks and Processes, Lists and Nodes, Libraries, Libraries and More Libraries, Intuition's Screens and Windows, Resource Allocation, Talking to Intuition, Exec Messages and Ports, Intuition's Text, Line Drawing and Image Facilities, Intuition's Gadgets, Intuition's Menu System, Devices: An Introduction, The Amiga's Serial Device, Interrupts: Making a Start, The Amiga's Co-Processor, Blitter First Steps, Troubleshooting Software Problems, Last Words.

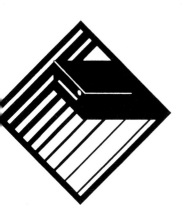

Index

Mastering Amiga series provides top quality guidance for Amiga users.

The story so far:

> **Mastering AmigaDOS 2 Volume One**
>
> **Mastering AmigaDOS 2 Volume Two**
>
> **Mastering Amiga C**
>
> **Mastering Amiga Beginners**
>
> **Mastering Amiga System**
>
> **Mastering Amiga Printers**
>
> **Mastering Amiga Workbench 2**
>
> **Mastering Amiga Assembler**
>
> **Mastering Amiga AMOS**

> **and there's more to come...**